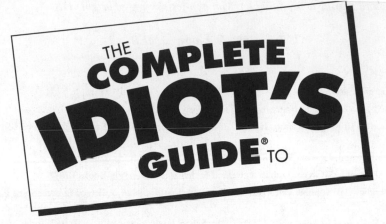

THE **COMPLETE IDIOT'S GUIDE®** TO

Success as a Mortgage Broker

by Daniel S. Kahn
and Marian Edelman Borden

ALPHA

A member of Penguin Group (USA) Inc.

To my father Hal, without whom neither this book nor the opportunity to be a mortgage broker would have been created. To Kim, Mom, Wendy, and Debby, thanks for your love and generosity, and thanks to my daughter Madison for shining so bright. DK

To John, with love always. MEB

ALPHA BOOKS

Published by the Penguin Group

Penguin Group (USA) Inc., 375 Hudson Street, New York, New York 10014, U.S.A.

Penguin Group (Canada), 10 Alcorn Avenue, Toronto, Ontario, Canada M4V 3B2 (a division of Pearson Penguin Canada Inc.)

Penguin Books Ltd, 80 Strand, London WC2R 0RL, England

Penguin Ireland, 25 St Stephen's Green, Dublin 2, Ireland (a division of Penguin Books Ltd)

Penguin Group (Australia), 250 Camberwell Road, Camberwell, Victoria 3124, Australia (a division of Pearson Australia Group Pty Ltd)

Penguin Books India Pvt Ltd, 11 Community Centre, Panchsheel Park, New Delhi—110 017, India

Penguin Group (NZ), cnr Airborne and Rosedale Roads, Albany, Auckland 1310, New Zealand (a division of Pearson New Zealand Ltd)

Penguin Books (South Africa) (Pty) Ltd, 24 Sturdee Avenue, Rosebank, Johannesburg 2196, South Africa

Penguin Books Ltd, Registered Offices: 80 Strand, London WC2R 0RL, England

International Standard Book Number: 1-59257-510-2
Library of Congress Catalog Card Number: 2005938296

09 08 07   8 7 6 5 4 3 2

Interpretation of the printing code: The rightmost number of the first series of numbers is the year of the book's printing; the rightmost number of the second series of numbers is the number of the book's printing. For example, a printing code of 06-1 shows that the first printing occurred in 2006.

Printed in the United States of America

Note: This publication contains the opinions and ideas of its authors. It is intended to provide helpful and informative material on the subject matter covered. It is sold with the understanding that the authors and publisher are not engaged in rendering professional services in the book. If the reader requires personal assistance or advice, a competent professional should be consulted.

The authors and publisher specifically disclaim any responsibility for any liability, loss, or risk, personal or otherwise, which is incurred as a consequence, directly or indirectly, of the use and application of any of the contents of this book.

Most Alpha books are available at special quantity discounts for bulk purchases for sales promotions, premiums, fund-raising, or educational use. Special books, or book excerpts, can also be created to fit specific needs.

For details, write: Special Markets, Alpha Books, 375 Hudson Street, New York, NY 10014.

Publisher: *Marie Butler-Knight*
Editorial Director/Acquiring Editor: *Mike Sanders*
Managing Editor: *Billy Fields*
Development Editor: *Nancy D. Lewis*
Production Editor: *Megan Douglass*
Copy Editor: *Ross Patty*

Cartoonist: *Richard King*
Book Designers: *Trina Wurst/Kurt Owens*
Cover Designer: *Bill Thomas*
Indexer: *Angie Bess*
Layout: *Brian Massey*
Proofreader: *John Etchison*

Contents at a Glance

Contents

Appendixes

Introduction

The New York Times heralded in a front-page story (October 8, 2005) that "a vast industry of real estate middlemen has sprouted up recently, riding the ups and downs of the mortgage market, and in many cases, accumulating great wealth in the process. Mortgage brokers, virtually nonexistent 25 years ago, now number 400,000 workers at more than 50,000 firms."

This is a career that has unlimited potential. It's based on the very basic human desire to own the place you call home. And mortgage brokers make it happen, so much so that this year they will collect $33 billion from their share of the estimated $2.8 trillion in home mortgages.

How Americans finance home purchases has changed dramatically in the last century. Once content to finance a home purchase with a 30-year fixed rate mortgage, buyers now find the range of loan options dizzying. The serial refinancer, who trades in his mortgage for a newer rate or better terms with the ease of trading in his car for the latest model has become a fixture of the home mortgage market. The Internet, which provides 24/7 information, has transformed the mortgage industry. The secondary mortgage market, which is the underpinning of home mortgages, has been reinvented with the rise of the global economy that finds American real estate a valuable investment.

These revolutionary changes signal an invitation to the smart, energetic, independent, detail-oriented entrepreneurs out there who are looking for a fast-paced career where the rewards, financial and personal, are enormous. Welcome to the world of the mortgage broker.

To meet the demand for information on this dynamic new career, the publisher sought out a successful mortgage broker who could share his own experiences with readers. Dan Kahn, as evident from his bio inside the back cover of this book, has been a top producer in the industry and is the owner of Financial Access Corporation, a mortgage broker company in Newburgh, New York. In this book, he gives you practical, step-by-step guidelines on what works and what doesn't in this career. Whether you are an entry-level mortgage broker, or an experienced old hand, there's much for you to learn from Dan's strategies and insights.

How This Book Is Organized

The Complete Idiot's Guide to Success as a Mortgage Broker is written in six parts. Each one addresses a different aspect of the business.

Part 1, "The Real Deal on Mortgage Brokers," gives you the inside scoop on whether this is the career for you. It explores why this is a business that has taken off in terms of number of brokers and profitability in the last 25 years. By spending a day in the lives of four of these professionals, you get an intimate look into their motivations, as well as the rewards and drawbacks of this career. You'll also have an opportunity to take a career assessment test designed to find out if you have the right personality and entrepreneurial spirit for this work.

Part 2, "A Seat at the Table," prepares you for the licensing requirements of this career. It then takes you to the next step and tells you how to find the right job with a firm that will encourage your growth and respect your contributions. In this book, you'll find the specifics of what's negotiable and what's not in this business.

Part 3, "Building Blocks of Success," outlines for you a plan to become a market and financing expert. You need to develop a breadth of knowledge of the economy and housing trends in order to advise your clients and manage your business in good times and bad. In a business that is at least 90 percent based on referrals, you'll learn the secrets of effective networking so you can develop the contacts that will spread the word about you, the mortgage broker professional. You'll find out what technology is essential in your office and your career. This is becoming a paperless industry, and you've got to be ready. You'll also discover how to manage your time so that you can multitask without losing control.

Part 4, "Here's the Deal," delivers the nitty-gritty of the business. You'll learn how and why you should get clients preapproved for loans. You'll learn the essential role Fannie Mae and Freddie Mac play in determining the standards for the majority of loans written in this country. You'll walk through a mortgage application, with a full explanation of each step. You'll find out the differences in the types of mortgages available on the market today and how to determine which one fits your client's needs.

Part 5, "Niche Markets Pay Off," provides you with an insider's look at these smaller markets. You'll learn about the mortgage programs designed to help low-income and minority clients realize the American dream of home ownership. You'll find out how to help senior citizens remain in their homes with a steady income stream realized from capitalizing on the equity of their homes. You'll also discover the lucrative opportunities of arranging financing for other forms of housing like co-ops, condotels, and multi-family housing. The refinancing market is booming and this section will help you jump right in.

Part 6, "Striking Out on Your Own," is a primer on how to open your own mortgage broker company. It guides you through each step of the process, from business plan to financing, from hiring the right help to retaining the rainmakers that propel your success. It teaches you how to market your brand-new business and then reminds you to keep a balance in your life in order to enjoy your success.

Extras

To make this book well organized and easy to read, there are three different types of sidebars that provide additional information.

def•i•ni•tion

These are the terms that you'll be using in your career as a mortgage broker. They're also found in the glossary.

Did You Know?

These are statistics and other information that give you extra tools and resources to succeed.

Heads Up!

These caution you about stumbling blocks and dangerous situations that others have encountered.

Acknowledgments

Special thanks to my agent, Bob Diforio, for giving me the opportunity to write this book; to Mike Sanders, my acquisition editor, who entrusted me with this task and whose insight and encouragement were so helpful; to Nancy Lewis, my development editor, for her exceptional patience and superb editing; to Megan Douglass and Ross Patty for their attention to detail; to Rhonda Dossett for her research skills; and to my father, who is my model of an extraordinary businessman and parent.

Trademarks

Part 1

The Real Deal on Mortgage Brokers

Is a mortgage broker career the right choice for you? In this part, I'll review the growing demand for mortgage brokers, no matter whether the housing market is red hot or has cooled off. You'll have an opportunity to spend a day in the life of mortgage broker professionals to see what they do, why they do it, what they like, and even what they don't like, about this exciting career. You'll even have a chance to take a career assessment test to see if this career is a good fit for you.

The Inside Track of a Fast-Moving Industry

In This Chapter

◆ Home ownership rates are soaring

◆ Buying a home is a smart investment

◆ Buyers want options

◆ The role of the mortgage broker in today's market

Today there are more than 73 million homeowners in the United States—more than ever before in our history. The demand for residential mortgages is growing exponentially as home ownership continues to be an essential part of the American dream. Commercial mortgages, which finance apartment complexes, housing developments, office buildings, manufacturing plants, shopping malls, and so on, are essential to the growth of our economy. The total outstanding mortgage debt for single-family homes is over $8 trillion. The U.S housing finance market is the largest credit market in the world.

And at the very center of all these transactions, residential and commercial, is a mortgage broker. That's the professional who arranges the financing that transforms these dreams into reality. It's a demanding, challenging, lucrative profession for smart, savvy, creative self-starters with strong people skills. Sound like you?

Exactly What Is a Mortgage Broker?

According to the National Association of Mortgage Brokers, a mortgage broker is "An independent real estate financing professional who specializes in the organization of residential and/or commercial mortgages." A mortgage broker originates loans offered by multiple wholesale lenders. It can refer to the individual or to the company. You will also see the term "loan originator" used to refer to the individual who has the responsibilities we are using to describe a mortgage broker.

Different states use different terms to describe the professional who specializes in arranging mortgages. For the purposes of this book, we will use "mortgage broker" to refer to the individual and "mortgage broker company" to refer to the organization. Mortgage brokers can be entry-level positions, with all work being supervised, or senior-level positions. Mortgage brokers can own their own companies or work for a local or national company.

A mortgage broker is like a financial matchmaker. You work with a variety of lenders to help buyers find the right loan for them. Your job is not to provide the money for the loan. Nor do you service the loan once it's given. Your job is to find the banker or lending institution with a program that meets the buyer's needs. You guide borrowers through the complex minefield of mortgage lending—and you work with lenders to match clients to their needs. It's a tough job, but incredibly rewarding.

> **Did You Know?**
>
> More than four in five Americans say a major reason to own a home is that it is a good long-term investment. Over 60 percent believe it is both a safe investment and one with a lot of potential.

A career as a mortgage broker is full of potential: financially, professionally, and personally. Given the strong long-term economic forecasts for real estate, you can be confident that there will be a need for smart mortgage brokers—like you. Let's put the housing market into perspective and see what the experts forecast about this industry.

Variations on a Theme

While in most states the mortgage broker is an individual, in Ohio, for example, mortgage broker refers to the "organization that assists a buyer in obtaining a mortgage"—in other words, the company, not an individual. Each registered mortgage broker must have an "operations manager with at least three years experience in the mortgage-lending field." The requirements for a mortgage broker operations manager are:

- Must pass a knowledge test

- Subject to a criminal background check

- Must manage day-to-day operations of the company

- Can only be the operations manager for one Ohio mortgage broker

- Must complete six hours of continuing education annually on behalf of the company

To use Ohio as an example, in that state a loan officer is an "employee of a registered mortgage broker who originates mortgage loans for a fee. Loan officer also includes an employee who solicits financial and mortgage information from the public for sale to another mortgage broker." The requirements for loan officer are:

- Must pass a knowledge test

- Subject to criminal background check

- Must be employees and may only work for one mortgage broker at any one time

- Must complete six hours of continuing education annually

- Need not be individually bonded

The Other Parts of the Equation

A *mortgage banker* is a lending institution, the one that actually funds the loan. Banks do hire their own lending officers to promote their own programs, guide clients through the application process, and close the deal. But a customer who goes to a bank for a mortgage will only hear about the rates and programs of that particular lending institution. In contrast, a mortgage broker will work with dozens of different lenders and will match the most suitable mortgage lender to a client's individual needs.

A *loan processor* works under the instructions of a mortgage broker and performs clerical functions. His responsibilities include collecting the documentation and verifications to support the loan application information, requesting information, and amending files.

Home Ownership Is a Smart Investment

No matter what the state of the American economy, in good times and bad, buying your own home is considered a smart investment. It's historically the best way most families have of creating wealth. In addition to getting a good long-term return on your money, there are significant tax benefits to home ownership. And not to be minimized, there is the personal satisfaction and pride that comes with owning your own home.

Home ownership isn't just a personal achievement. It's also good for the community. Homeowners develop deep roots, become involved in their neighborhood, and care about the future of their community. They are vested in a way that renters are not. What happens to their community impacts them directly, both financially and personally.

The Homeownership Alliance is a Washington, D.C.-based coalition of more than 15 organizations committed to ensuring support for the American housing system. In a recent study, they found that "there has not been a single year over the past half century in which the national average home value has declined in the U.S. This is a period that has included periods of both severe recession and high mortgage rates, or both (as occurred during 1981–1982 when the unemployment rate exceeded 10 percent and mortgage rates reached 18 percent). In fact, the last sustained drop in national average home values occurred during the Great Depression, when the unemployment rate hit 25 percent. With the national unemployment rate below 6 percent, mortgage rates low, and economic growth improving, the likelihood of a decline in home prices at the national level is quite remote."

Did You Know?

Eighty-seven percent of homeowners say that their homes have increased in value since they first bought them, and 76 percent report the increase in value is more than they anticipated.

Sure, in some regions there have been occasional home price declines, even some significant drops. Basically that happens when there is a sizeable imbalance between supply and demand, too many houses and too few buyers. But these conditions, says the Homeownership Alliance, "exist in very few (if any) places around the country today, and certainly not nationally." But in any case, mortgage brokers will always be needed, whether for new buyers anxious to get into the market, or for current owners looking to trade up or considering refinancing options.

As Home Ownership Grows, More Mortgages Are Needed

Less than half of Americans owned their own homes at the start of the twentieth century, and many homeowners lost their homes during the Great Depression. But after World War II, home ownership rates began to rise dramatically, topping 60 percent by 1960. The rate slowly rose during the 1960s and 1970s, but plateaued during the 1980s. But declining mortgage rates and an expanding economy pushed home ownership throughout the 1990s, reaching a record high by 2003. National home ownership surpassed 68 percent in 2003 and long-term projections suggest it will exceed 70 percent by 2013.

While non-Hispanic whites accounted for most of the increase in the number of U.S. homeowners between 1994 and 2003, minorities made marked progress in home ownership rates. According to a study by the Homownership Alliance, "During this same time period, the percentage increase in the number of homeowners among African Americans (25.1 percent), Hispanics (62.8 percent) and Asian and Pacific Islanders (103 percent) dwarfed the rise in non-Hispanic white owners (7.6 percent)." However, the home ownership rate among minorities still lags behind that of whites. In 2003, "less than half of African-American and Hispanic households owned their homes. In contrast, over 75 percent of non-Hispanic whites were homeowners."

Most of the gap is due to differences in economic circumstances and the age composition of minority populations. Income and wealth among minorities are typically lower than that of whites. The home ownership rate for households in the lowest income bracket is less than 50 percent; the rate for those in the top bracket is 90 percent. A higher income widens the choice of homes available for purchase and increases the likelihood that the household will qualify for a mortgage. Those with lower incomes find they have fewer choices in a lower price range in locations near their place of employment.

According to the Homeownership Alliance report, there is also a higher share of younger households among minorities—and this group is less likely to be homeowners. In addition, a large number of Hispanics and Asians live in less affordable urban centers on the East and West coasts. Cities usually have higher housing costs, but offer more rental alternatives.

The Homeownership Alliance forecasts "a rising home ownership rate [of] at least 10 million additional homeowners by 2013 with roughly one half of the gain accruing to minority households." Buying your own home has become a reality for even that segment of the population that had been previously shut out of the market; now mortgage programs provide financial products and services that make it possible for low-, moderate-, and middle-income families to buy homes.

The housing boom of the past decade, as well as the continued growth forecast for the future, is due to many factors. Certainly, it is, in large part, a result of record low mortgage rates. This helped drive a tremendous increase in home sales and home construction. It's also influenced by a growing number of people, "baby boomers," moving into their peak home-owning years.

Another important force behind higher home ownership rates is a growing immigrant population. More than one third of the increase in the U.S. population during the 1990s is a result of foreign-born persons entering the country. While it takes time for immigrants to move into home ownership, according to the U.S. Census Bureau, for those who arrived more than 30 years ago, their home ownership rate surpasses the national rate.

The Mortgage Industry Expands

An American Housing Survey reveals that approximately 15 percent of homes are purchased without a mortgage. More power to those buyers! But for most of us, we're going to need a mortgage when buying a house. Most people understand what a home mortgage is, even if they aren't familiar with the exact details of some of the new lending programs. Educating potential home buyers is one of the important roles mortgage brokers play. But there are many other variations of mortgages that brokers also offer.

With home prices rising, mortgage rates declining, and the tax code limiting interest deductions to mortgages and home equity lines of credit, many homeowners are refinancing. For some, it's an opportunity to lower their monthly payments. For others, it's a chance to convert an adjustable rate into a fixed rate mortgage or to simply get a lower interest rate. Others choose to cash out some of their home equity for debt consolidation, home improvements, education costs, or a combination of reasons. Over the past 10 years, 39 percent of mortgages were refinance originations.

Senior citizens who own their own homes may choose a reverse mortgage to provide them with tax-free income. It's the opposite of a traditional mortgage in which the homeowner borrows money and then repays the loan plus interest to the lender. A reverse mortgage pays a monthly income to the homeowner, and when the homeowner dies, sells, or fails to live in the house for more than 12 months, then the reverse mortgage becomes due, including accrued interest. But the homeowner is not responsible for repayment, the home is the security for the loan. The homeowner can continue to live in the residence for as long as he lives, no matter how small the equity becomes. There are no restrictions on how the money can be spent, and the homeowner's credit and income are irrelevant. According to the National Reverse Mortgage Lenders Association, reverse mortgages increased by 76 percent in 2003 as compared to 2002. (More on reverse mortgages in Chapter 20.)

There is also a non-conforming market that includes mortgages for *cooperatives (co-ops)*, multi-family dwellings, and *condotels*. This is a growing, exciting market and mortgage brokers help make these deals happen.

def•i•ni•tion

A **cooperative (co-op)** is a building that is owned by a corporation comprised of the tenants of the building. Each apartment or residence in a condominium building is individually owned and the common grounds are owned jointly by all the owners of the premises. A **condotel** is a condominium that is serviced as if it were a hotel. These kinds of units are becoming popular as vacation homes.

The number of shares a cooperative tenant holds is dependent on the apartment size, view, and location. The tenant shareholder has the right to occupy the apartment as his or her home by holding a proprietary lease to that apartment. Mortgages for these types of apartments are considered non-conforming.

Don't confuse co-ops and condos. In a condominium building, each apartment is individually owned and the unit proprietors own the common parts of the property, like the grounds and building, jointly. Condominium buyers apply for traditional home mortgages.

Did You Know?

In New York City, 85 percent of the apartments available for purchase are co-ops.

A condotel is a condominium that operates like a hotel with many of the amenities you'd find at a four- or five-star hotel. Generally, condotel units are delivered fully furnished, typically with high-end furniture, appliances, and fixtures, and the cost of the furnishings is included in the price of the unit. This is a relatively new concept in vacation home ownership and the mortgages for these types of units fall under the non-conforming umbrella.

A smaller market, but a potentially important one, is the second or vacation home. The growth in the number of buyers interested in second homes has been modest over the last decade, but that may change. It appears that baby boomers have not embraced second home ownership to the same extent as previous generations. But demand may increase if the current unpopularity of foreign travel continues and if baby boomers choose to become semi-retired, rather than fully retiring or continuing to work.

Finally, while banks handle the majority of commercial loans, a small percentage of mortgage brokers are players in this field. These types of mortgages cover bigger projects including apartment buildings and office buildings, and can range from $500,000 to more than $500,000,000.

Buyers Want Options and Mortgage Brokers Offer Them

The mortgage business is huge and with the growth predicted for the next ten years, the need for experienced mortgage brokers becomes clear. Experts predict that mortgage originations will average nearly $3 trillion per year over the next ten years. Here are some of the ten-year projections from the Homeownership Alliance:

◆ America's families will need 125 million mortgage loans for home purchase or refinance, totaling $27 million in mortgage originations.

◆ First-time buyers will remain a major component of the market, buying about 24 million homes over the next decade.

◆ Residential mortgage debt outstanding is projected to grow by 8.25 percent per year, which would lead to more than a doubling of debt outstanding over the next ten years.

According to the National Association of Mortgage Brokers (NAMB), mortgage brokers originate 65 percent of all home loans, and that number is growing. Mortgage brokers originated more mortgages than any other single loan source group in the nation.

A study by Dr. Gregory Elliehausen of the Georgetown University Credit Research Center found that consumers who use mortgage brokers pay a lower annual percentage (refer to Chapter 15) than bank customers. The report also found:

- Through competition, brokers pass on their origination savings to the consumer.
- The results of the report challenge the view that loans from brokers are more expensive because of broker steering (sending clients to lenders who pay the highest fees to the broker).
- There is an overall price benefit to using brokers.
- The benefits of using a mortgage broker appear to hold for even vulnerable market segments.

Mortgage brokers provide buyers with an expert mentor to navigate the complex mortgage origination process. By offering superior market expertise and direct access to many different loan programs, the mortgage broker provides buyers the most efficient and cost-effective method of obtaining the right mortgage that meets the consumer's financial goals and circumstances.

Whether it's purchasing a first home or refinancing an existing home, whether it's trading up to a bigger house or scaling back to smaller quarters, whether it's buying a vacation home or a commercial property, mortgage brokers make the difference. Are you ready to join this profession?

The Least You Need to Know

- Successful mortgage brokers need to be independent self-starters with strong people skills.
- Home ownership is a good financial investment; national home ownership is projected to exceed 70 percent by 2013.

◆ Mortgage brokers also arrange financing for other types of housing such as co-ops, condominiums, condotels, and second homes.

◆ Mortgage brokers provide buyers with a range of loan options tailored to the borrower's needs and financial circumstances.

Chapter 2

The Perks of the Job

In This Chapter

- ◆ You determine the financial rewards
- ◆ Challenging your entrepreneurial spirit
- ◆ It feels good to help others
- ◆ Only apply if you're a people person

A career as a mortgage broker offers financial, personal, and professional satisfaction. The earnings potential is virtually unlimited, based at least in part on your own efforts. But the personal and professional rewards are equally important if you choose this career path. In many ways, you're a small business owner, determining your own fate.

In this chapter, you will discover the financial and personal rewards of this career.

Let's Talk Money

Most mortgage brokers work on commission. Your earnings are based on how many loans you close. You earn a broker's fee for bringing the loan to the lender, you earn fees based on a percentage of the loan, for any "points" that the client pays in order to secure a lower rate, and, if applicable, a yield spread premium (a fee paid to the mortgage broker for the deliver of a loan that carries a higher interest rate). The details of each of these components is discussed in Chapter 17. But the largest chunk of the fee is based on the loan amount and the greater the loan amount, the better. An experienced broker will, on average, close at least 15 to 20 deals per month.

Many companies permit you to draw against your *commission*, that is, to take a base line of money weekly or monthly. This is not a salary. It's simply a way to level out your cash flow. As might be expected, some months you'll close a larger loan volume than others. The last few weeks in August are usually lighter. That's because it's vacation time for many people and those buyers who want to be settled in their new house before school begins closed on their homes earlier.

def•i•ni•tion

Commission is a fee or percentage paid to a mortgage broker for services rendered. **Splits** is a term that refers to how the mortgage broker company divides the fees of a transaction. **Basis points** (BPs) are one hundredth of a percent. They are used in measuring the yield differences among bonds, but in the mortgage industry, BPs describe the percentage of commission a mortgage broker receives.

The term *splits* refers to how the mortgage broker company divides the fees paid by the lender. As an entry-level mortgage broker, for example, you might split the fees with your company ⅓ to ⅔. Your company likely will take the larger share for in-house-generated business, and you will likely get paid more for personal leads.

Heads Up!

The Department of Labor stats on how much mortgage brokers on average earn reflect a broad average. In New York, for example, entry-level mortgage brokers earn between $40,000 and $60,000 the first year and can expect to double that amount every year for the next three to four years.

Sometimes the splits are referred to in *basis points*, which are one hundredth of a percent. So your BPs (pronounced "beeps") would be 33 for in-house-generated business, and you'd get more BPs for leads you generated.

As an experienced broker, you might start at a 50 percent split for in-house-generated business, and up to a 70 percent split for personal leads. Bringing in clients should always generate a higher commission. Many mortgage broker companies also pay bonuses at the end of the year, so you share in the corporate profitability.

If you own the mortgage broker company, then you will share in the fees paid for each loan, whether you close it or one of your brokers handles the deal.

According to the Department of Labor, the average mortgage broker earns between $36,000 and $45,750. The lowest 10 percent earned less than $24,200, while the top 10 percent earned more than $82,640.

Commercial mortgage brokers with 1 to 3 years of experience earn between $48,000 and $64,750. With over 3 years of experience, the earnings outlook is significantly higher—between $66,000 and $95,250.

It's Never Dull Around Here

A career as a mortgage broker is interesting and creative, and it's hard to put a dollar figure on this perk. The earnings potential of a job is just part of the equation when considering a career. The type of work you do, whether you enjoy showing up each day at the office because you find the work interesting and challenging, is equally important. It's hard to be a success if you're bored or frustrated. That's especially true in this field because your earnings are directly based on your efforts—and to succeed as a mortgage broker you've got to commit to working hard.

But one of the benefits of this job is that it encourages creative thinking. You might not think that because it seems so numbers driven. But if you're an independent self-starter who enjoys looking outside the box for answers, then a career as a mortgage broker might be the ticket.

This isn't a cookie-cutter job. Each client has his or her own unique financial and personal needs. Your job is to find a loan that will work for them. It's more than just punching in a series of numbers and waiting for a printout. For example:

- You've got to understand the client's current financial situation and be able to project down the road so that the loan they take out today works in the long-term, too.

- You've got to understand the client's plans for their purchase, because if they anticipate selling the house in three years that will affect the kinds of loans they should consider. For example, whether your client should pay points can depend on the client's current financial needs and long-term plans for the house (more on points in Chapter 17).

- You've got to understand how a client is presented on paper; for example, if they have a weak credit history or limited savings, it can make the difference between them getting the home of their dreams or being shut out of the market.

You get to think creatively within a structured environment. That can be a very rewarding work situation.

Tapping Into Your Entrepreneurial Spirit

Maybe down the road you hope to own your own business—and in Part 6 of this book, we'll tell you how to do that. But if you want a taste of that entrepreneurial spirit before you hang out your own shingle, then a career as a mortgage broker, working for an established company, is a good compromise. While you will benefit from the marketing and reputation of your parent company, the bottom line is this … to reach your earnings potential, you'll have to market yourself and establish your own network of contacts.

Since your earnings are based primarily on your own efforts, you have the satisfaction of knowing that you grew your business based on your hard work.

And if you have more than a touch of the competitive spirit in you, then this job feeds that passion. Like Donald Trump, if you get a buzz when you snag the client and close a good deal, then you'll enjoy the challenges and triumphs of being a mortgage broker.

Do Good and You Feel Good

At the end of most days as a mortgage broker, you'll feel like you earned a good living and you helped someone else. That's a powerful combination and an important part of whatever career you choose. There is something very satisfying about helping someone achieve his dream—and buying a home is certainly that.

Heads Up!

A survey by the National Federation of Independent Business showed that businesses that put heavy emphasis on customer service were more likely to survive and succeed than competitors who emphasized such advantages as lower prices or type of product.

There are some buyers who will need you to find a loan program that will accept them because at first glance, they don't qualify. Then they'll need you to walk them step-by-step through the mortgage process. For other buyers, qualifying for a mortgage won't be a problem, but finding the lender who will offer the best terms will mean sorting through dozens of deals and then carefully presenting the range of options to your client so he can make an informed decision.

Whether it's the first-time buyer or the client who's owned a half dozen homes, there is a thrill in finding a good deal and then locking it in. The satisfaction of knowing that you are part of the team that connected a buyer to the home of his dreams should certainly be considered a perk of the job.

High on the People Meter

You have to like working with people to be a successful mortgage broker. It's not a job that allows you to hide in an office and crunch numbers by yourself. You don't have to be the life of the party, but you have to enjoy meeting new people. You've got to make a connection so that you can sell your product—which is primarily you! The competition is tough and most brokers are using the same group of lenders. What else do you bring to the table?

Your ability to connect with clients, sift through the options, effectively communicate the choices, pay attention to details, and yes, remain patient and good-humored through the process is the critical difference. If you don't like working one-on-one with strangers, then this may not be the best job choice for you. But if you see each new person as a potential client—and friend—then this career offers a lot of personal satisfaction.

Flexible Hours or 24/7?

Mortgage brokerage is a service industry. Your livelihood is dependent on satisfying your clients. Otherwise they'll move on to your competition. So if you're looking for a job that's strictly 9 to 5, Monday through Friday, this may not be the profession for you. At the very least, you will probably have to resign yourself to lower earnings.

Heads Up!

Fifty-seven percent of small-business owners say they work six or more days of the week. Only 7 percent say they work fewer than five days a week. Sixty-two percent say they work 50 or more hours a week. Despite working long hours, most small-business owners were satisfied with their ability to achieve a positive work-life balance and to make time outside work to do those things that are important to them.

On the other hand, not everyone is looking to work a traditional workweek. Depending on the company—and the deal you negotiate when you join—you may be able to establish hours that work for you and your family.

But take note! You're probably going to have to work nights and weekends because you have to be available when clients need you.

A Career That Grows with You

There are different ways to measure your professional growth. One of the most obvious is whether or not you're making more money as you gain more experience. But you may also want to know that you are being given more responsibility (and getting paid for it), taking the lead on the big deals, mentoring new hires (and possibly getting paid for that), and if appropriate or desired, being offered more senior titles in the company—maybe even some kind of financial stake.

Everybody loves a winner. If you're successful in bringing in new clients and closing a high volume of loans, you should see the financial rewards.

Titles may or may not mean much to you—titles can be cheap; money talks. But there is a hierarchy in many companies and you can judge if you're moving along it at an appropriate pace. For example, you might move from mortgage consultant to senior mortgage consultant to vice president, and finally maybe even president of the company.

The Least You Need to Know

- Mortgage brokers work on commission and are paid a part of each deal they close.

- The work of a mortgage broker is varied and demands a creative, detail-oriented person.

- The personal satisfaction of helping others is an important perk of this career.

- A mortgage broker must be a person who is comfortable working with people and can easily talk to strangers.

Chapter 3

A Day in the Life

In This Chapter

- ◆ Experienced mortgage broker: Esther
- ◆ Entry-level mortgage broker: Max
- ◆ Mortgage broker company owner: Dan
- ◆ Loan processor: Melanie

This chapter puts you in the seat of various mortgage broker professionals. It gives you an insider's look at each one's day. You'll see how they spend their time, share in their successes, empathize with their disappointments, and understand what makes them choose this career.

Esther, Max, and Melanie are fictional composites of people I've worked with over the 15 years I've been in the business. The description of a day in the life of a mortgage broker company owner (Dan) is my own story.

By the time you complete this chapter, you'll have a better idea of what it takes to make it as a mortgage broker. For those of you already in the business, it's an opportunity to see how other companies work and poach some ideas to improve your own practice.

Esther, the Experienced Mortgage Professional

The day starts early and ends late for experienced mortgage brokers. They could be professional jugglers because they have to be adept at keeping lots of balls in the air. But the rewards of all this hard work are both financial and personal.

Esther's Background

Esther is our professional mortgage broker. She's been in the business for 8 years, really hitting her stride after year two. Esther started out in retail. She has a degree in marketing and worked her way up to women's wear buyer for a major national department store. She liked the work, but was frustrated with the financial rewards. By the time she left her retail job, she was earning about $75,000 a year, a combination of salary and bonus, and was working more than 60 hours a week for a boss she didn't respect.

She finally decided she wanted two things: to be her own boss and to earn an income that reflected her efforts. She toyed with the idea of opening her own store, but was hesitant about investing that much capital. She'd worked in sales before moving into management and had enjoyed the challenges. Here's Esther's story.

Why Esther Chose This Career

About 10 years ago Esther was tired of paying rent and was considering buying. She checked the Sunday papers, saw a couple of *open houses* for properties that were for sale, and headed out. At the second place she visited, she met a mortgage broker who was co-sponsoring the open house with the real estate agency. He was in the kitchen, putting out some cookies and cold drinks. They started chatting over the refreshments and he asked if Esther had been *pre-qualified* for a mortgage. Since she didn't even know what that was, he explained the process of getting all her financing set up before she found the house of her dreams. They chatted a little more, exchanged cards, and she made an appointment to see him the following day. After talking it over, she decided to get *pre-approved* for a mortgage. His help made her realize she could not only buy a house, but buy one that she hadn't realized she'd be able to afford.

Fast-forward to two years after she bought her house. Esther was ready to make a career change. She was frustrated with her job, knew she was unhappy with the hierarchy of a big corporation, and was considering opening her own store. But she was afraid of making that kind of financial commitment. Esther wanted to be her own boss, but still wanted some structure. She knew she was good at sales, and considered going into real estate. But when she remembered her own experience, she called her mortgage broker and set up a lunch to talk about the career.

def•i•ni•tion

Open house is when a real estate agent opens a house to public view. Realtors also hold open houses prior to or shortly after a house is listed so that it can get the attention of realty professionals. A mortgage broker may sponsor an open house, bringing refreshments and being onsite to answer financing questions from those inspecting the property.

Pre-qualified is the process of giving an informal estimate, based on income and debt load, of the amount of money a buyer can spend on a house. **Pre-approved** is preliminary written approval by a lender of the maximum amount a buyer can borrow for a mortgage.

Esther did some research, talked to a couple of other brokers, checked her finances, and decided to make the career switch. What's funny is that she didn't end up joining her original broker's firm. She wanted a smaller shop where she felt the mentoring would be better.

The firm Esther joined has five brokers, two loan processors, plus the owner, a man who's been in the business for 20 years. Even in just the time since she started out, the business has changed a lot. She's pretty good with math, but frankly now it's more important to be computer savvy than able to do long division. The software available today does all the calculations on a loan application.

def•i•ni•tion

Front end ratio is the total monthly housing expenses (principal, interest, taxes, and insurance) divided by the applicant's total monthly pretax income. **Back end ratio** is the applicant's total housing expense plus all other monthly debt divided by total monthly pretax income.

But she quickly learned that coming up with the right answer for the *front end ratio* or *back end ratio* (see Chapter 13) was the easiest part of the job. Having people skills, marketing savvy, and an inordinate amount of patience and organization were the key ingredients to success in this field.

A Day in the Life of Esther

Esther always has about 75 loans in the pipeline: some just in the beginning stages of the application, some waiting for document verification, some close to or at closing. She does about 25 loans a month and it takes about one to three months from application to closing. It takes a lot of organization and attention to detail to make sure that nothing gets lost or overlooked.

She doesn't get into the office until 10 most mornings. But by then, she's already read the *Wall Street Journal*, looked at the real estate section in her local paper for any "sale by owner" ads, scanned the lender rate sheets online, and checked her e-mail messages and voice mail, returning any that require immediate attention. The best "can't live without it" piece of technology she owns is her Blackberry. With it, she can surf the web, answer e-mail, make and receive phone calls, keep her calendar and address book, all in a four-ounce gadget. If it could cook dinner, it'd be perfect.

Once she gets to the office, she spends a huge amount of time on the phone and online. She's got to review pending loans and check their status with the loan processors in the office, talk to closing attorneys to set up those appointments, follow up with banks on any applications that are running into trouble, and do some hand-holding— you know, reassure current clients that their mortgages are going to go through.

A couple of times a week she goes to closings, especially for first-time buyers. Not all mortgage brokers show up, and you don't have to be there by law, but she finds it makes a difference to her clients that she's there in case there are any problems or paperwork snafus. They know her; they usually don't know the attorneys. She's the familiar face in a complicated situation. She's discovered it pays off in customer satisfaction, which translates to more referrals.

Then there is the networking and marketing component of her day. She schedules lunch at least twice a week with the various realtors and builders in her community. It's an opportunity to talk about current trends in the market, coordinate sponsoring open houses, and ensuring that her name is in the front of their Rolodex when they meet new clients. More than 90 percent of her business is based on referrals or is repeat business from satisfied clients.

Esther does get some customers from being in the office when a cold call comes in. It's a subtle dance when she's talking to a potential client on the phone. She's got to answer their questions without giving away the store. They tell her that all they want are the current rates, and she knows that any given loan has a dozen different possible rates. So she's got to interest them enough to stay on the line while she gets the information she needs to give them a realistic answer.

When she's working with a customer, she also has to avoid overwhelming them with choices. There may be 40 different loan options, but she'll go through them in her head and offer six. She can always offer more, but too much information can paralyze a customer. They trust her to understand their circumstances and suggest what makes sense.

Once a month, sometimes more, she sponsors realtor open houses, sometimes for the public, sometimes for other real estate agents. She brings refreshments and it's an opportunity to meet people who are shopping for a home—just like when she met her mortgage broker. It's a way of pre-qualifying clients so they can set up their financing before they buy. The realtor meetings are an opportunity to educate them about the new loan products available.

Esther likes being her own boss. She also likes the idea that her income is limited only by her own efforts. When she worked for a corporation, they decided how much she was worth. Being on commission, she sees the results of her hard work. She also enjoys meeting new people and figuring out what works best for each applicant.

The Appeal of Esther's Career

Here are Esther's insights into a career as a mortgage broker:

- Personality type. Friendly, detail-oriented people who don't mind juggling lots of different tasks. You have to like being a salesperson, both of yourself and your products. You also have to be ready to accept that you don't always get the client.

- Biggest rewards. She likes meeting new people and finding the right program for each one, the variety of the work, and being busy all the time. Her mind is always going 100 miles an hour so this career is a good match. She also likes the financial rewards and knowing that it was her own efforts that made the difference.

- Biggest pitfalls. When you're on commission, there's no safety net for income. If you're not working, you're potentially missing out on good deals. It's also easy to constantly be checking your messages and voicemail and not taking time off for yourself.

Max, the Entry-Level Mortgage Broker

The days are long for entry-level brokers. They have to spend a lot of time learning the business and building up a client base. The financial rewards are slow at first, but as they become more experienced, they should see a payoff.

Max's Background

Max joined a small mortgage broker firm about six months ago. He finished college with a degree in psychology. He worked his way through school in the restaurant business, starting out as a waiter, eventually serving as the night manager for a successful local restaurant. Here's his story ….

Why Max Chose This Career

Max likes people and thinks he understands them. His college degree didn't prepare him for this career exactly, but it did give him an insight into what makes people tick. And that's a big part of what makes a good salesman.

When he finally finished college, he decided that he wanted to leave the restaurant business. Unless he was going to open his own place, the income was always going to be limited. He liked the idea of being his own boss so he started looking around for a career that was based on commission. Max saw an online ad for a mortgage broker and had to look up what they did. It sounded interesting, especially since it didn't require previous experience in the field.

The owner insisted he take a weeklong course at a local community college to learn the basics of the business. It cost $600 and he had to pay for it himself. For the first month, his boss had Max work with an experienced broker. Max received advances on the commissions he was earning—actually, they were a percent of the commissions since he was just assisting the broker. Essentially, he did the paperwork for the mortgages instead of giving them to the loan processors. It actually was a good way to learn the business since he had to take an application every step of the way.

> **Heads Up!**
>
> Cash flow can be difficult to budget when working on commission. Track your income over two years and see if you see a pattern of busy versus slow seasons. When you can, pay ahead on fixed payments like a mortgage or student loans, so you can lighten up during the slower periods.

Max didn't handle any clients on his own until he'd been at the job for a month. If he hadn't had some savings and wasn't living at home, it would have been a tough time financially. During the next couple of months he made more money and finally started to get his own clients. Projecting out for the rest of the year, he should make about $35,000, but he definitely thinks that within a year or two he can at least double that.

A Day in the Life of Max

Max gets to the office early, usually before 8 A.M. That's his time, before the phones start ringing off the hook, to do his research. He reads the newspapers and trade journals. He's started preparing a memo each morning and sending it to the brokers in the office, summarizing the latest reports. It makes him focus, and they seem to like it.

He spends his afternoons doing paperwork and contacting the banks to work out any problems.

He spends about an hour a day doing cold calls, usually in the early evening. He's looked into buying lists of names of homeowners, but isn't sure it would be worth the investment. He also did a mailing to all the residents of a local apartment complex. He got a couple of calls from that and may try more.

Max has had good luck contacting homeowners who are selling their houses without a real estate agent. They like the idea of him being there for an open house. He offers to work up handouts about their home that they can give to people who are browsing. He's connected with several customers that way and gotten a few other referrals.

He works most weekends since he's more than happy to sit in realtor open houses. Again, he's picked up some customers that way.

Max has been trying to network like crazy. He did a huge mailing when he joined the firm and sent out a postcard to everyone he could think of, including his parents' entire holiday card list. He actually got a couple of customers from that mailing. And, of course, he follows up with every person he meets at the open houses.

The Appeal of Max's Career

Here are Max's insights into a career as a mortgage broker:

◆ Personality type. You have to be persistent and not be stopped by failure. This isn't a job where you can be an overnight success. It takes time to build up a client base. You also have to like people. Not only do you have to connect with potential customers, but you also have to develop good working relationships with lenders, appraisers, the credit bureau people, attorneys, realtors, and builders. You also need to be comfortable on the computer, as much of the business is done electronically. If you're afraid of working on computers—get over it.

◆ Biggest rewards. The earnings potential and the freedom to be your own boss while still part of a team (which is how the owner runs the shop). But as hokey as it sounds, he really likes helping people. His first clients were friends of his grandparents who were considering a reverse mortgage (see Chapter 20). Helping them through the paperwork and seeing how relieved they were when they were approved was one of his best days.

◆ Biggest pitfalls. You have to be very organized and detail-oriented, which is hard. Some of the experienced brokers have given him some good tips, but it's still tough to keep track of everything.

Did You Know?

"The Federal Reserve has been raising short-term rates ... to try to restrain economic growth and inflation. But those increases have had little impact on the long-term interest rates that drive the housing markets. Long-term rates have been kept low in part by demand for United States Treasury notes from Asian buyers, particularly the central banks of China, Japan and Korea." *The New York Times,* July 26, 2005

Dan, the Mortgage Broker Company Owner

The owner wears at least two hats: mortgage broker and manager of a small business. He also acts as team leader, human resources manager, educator, coach, supervisor ... how many hats is that?

Dan's Background

In one way or another, I grew up in this business. My father, who's also my best friend and racing partner (but that's another book), owned a real estate agency. He quickly discovered the convenience of one-stop shopping and added on an insurance agency, appraisal company, and mortgage broker firm.

I went to college and earned a business administration degree with a major in management and entrepreneurship, but spent every summer working in the business. I started out as an appraiser, which really gave me a feel for the housing market. But I wanted more interaction with people, so I shifted over to the mortgage broker company.

In the first couple of years, I developed a referral network of realtors, developed and promoted an advertising campaign to increase our customer base, formulated the operating budget, established new lender relationships, and eventually became responsible for the company's bookkeeping and payroll—all while becoming the top producer in the company.

Ten years ago, I bought out the company. My dad kept the real estate agency and sold the other businesses. Now, in addition to all the other responsibilities I had before, I'm also in charge of the development and monitoring of all phases of the business, as well as managing and training all employees.

Why Dan Chose This Career

I became a mortgage broker for all the reasons that others have listed: the independence, the earnings potential, the variety of the work, the people factor. But I decided to open my own company because I wanted the opportunity to run something bigger. I like the challenge of making all the various parts of the company work together seamlessly.

A Day in the Life of Dan

My day is long, but the variety of what I do keeps me interested. I continue to meet with clients, sometimes in person, but often I communicate by e-mail or the phone. I also have to keep up my relationships with realtors, builders, and lenders, but also reach out to any new professionals in the area. I read as much as I can on local, national, and international economic trends and the state of the housing market.

As the president of the company, I'm always looking at new software that will make our jobs simpler. I have to develop new advertising campaigns, find creative ways to keep in touch with former clients, as well as discover new clients.

And there is the nitty-gritty of running a business: paying the bills, hiring the right employees, finding good office space, fixing the computer system when it goes on the fritz, and so on.

I'm tired when I go home, but I love it.

The Appeal of Dan's Career

Here are my insights into a career as a mortgage broker company owner:

- ◆ Personality type. You have to be a risk-taker if you want to own your own business. While working solely on commission can be risky, if you work in someone else's company, they provide the office, the computers, the fringe benefits, etc. But when you hang out your shingle, you assume responsibility for not only your own family, but for others as well. That's a heavy responsibility.

- ◆ Biggest rewards. I like the variety of what I do. I also like that I earn a percentage of every deal made in my company, although much of my share of each commission covers the company's overhead. It's my job to pick the right brokers to join the company, make sure that I provide a collegial, supportive atmosphere, with fringe benefits that make them want to stay, and then I've earned sharing in their successes.

- ◆ Biggest pitfalls. I like the risk, but sometimes it scares me, too. On the other hand, I love to race cars. That's risky too, but like business, if you know what you're doing, you're taking calculated risks where the odds of success are much higher than failure.

I still like working with clients and making sure that they get the right loan for them. But I also enjoy the business side of the company. I like training new brokers and seeing them succeed. I like forging new relationships with realtors, builders, and lenders. I like the idea of building a company that offers quality service, good products, and has the respect of the business community.

Melanie, the Loan Processor

The loan processor is a key member of the mortgage broker company. She is responsible for gathering all the documentation and ordering any of the steps necessary to process a loan. This is a detail-intensive job.

Melanie's Background

Melanie has been with her mortgage broker company for 15 years. She was hired right out of high school, but thinks new employees would benefit from more education, especially computer training. Her boss has been good about paying for her to take whatever training programs will help to do her job better.

Why Melanie Chose This Career

When she first joined the firm, she thought the work sounded interesting, the pay was good, and the hours reasonable. Fifteen years later, she still thinks that the work is interesting, although demanding, and the pay is excellent. Of course, there's always somebody who needs something done immediately, if not sooner. But she doesn't get rattled easily and has developed a good system for knowing where everything is and what needs to be done, when. It used to be a series of color-coded files on her desk, but of course now she uses a file system on her computer that generates ticklers when something is due.

A Day in the Life of Melanie

Melanie's workday is from 9 A.M. to 5 P.M., with an hour for lunch, although that's often eaten at her desk. She's responsible for making sure that each application has all the necessary documentation for the lender. That means she's got to work with the clients to make sure they send in documentation of their income and assets, and try to anticipate if they will need to provide additional information if she can see there's going to be a question about some issue. She schedules appraisals and makes sure they get the report, pulls the credit report and attaches it to the application, forwards it all to the lender, and then fields any questions they may have.

Usually she's working on about 90 different applications at a time, but of course they're at various stages.

The Appeal of Melanie's Career

Here are Melanie's insights into a career as a loan processor.

- Personality type. It helps to have the patience of a saint in this job. On the other hand, sometimes you have to be pushy in order to get people to do what they're supposed to do. So add in diplomatic, too. It's most important that you're well organized and comfortable multitasking.

- Biggest rewards. This is interesting work. While you're office-bound, you do get to interact with lots of different people. The pay, benefits, and hours are good.

- Biggest pitfalls. Sometimes the pressure of juggling all the different applications gets intense.

The Least You Need to Know

- Working in the mortgage broker field, whether as a broker or loan processor, is very detail-oriented. You must be well organized to keep track of all the different deals.

- People skills are critical for success as a mortgage broker. You need those skills to work well with clients and to build a strong referral network.

◆ Most mortgage brokers enjoy being their own bosses and earning an income based on their efforts.

◆ Owning a mortgage broker company requires great organizational skills in order to meet the demands of your clients, as well as the demands of running a small business.

Chapter 4

Test Yourself!

In This Chapter

- ◆ Profiling the characteristics of a successful mortgage broker
- ◆ Examining your interests and styles
- ◆ Putting it all together to determine if this is the career for you

Aptitude assessment tests are a helpful way of examining your interests and strengths, and then comparing your profile to the characteristics of various career options. There's no specific mortgage broker career test. I can't offer an exam that will tell you with certainty that this is the right career for you. But in this chapter, I've asked Alan B. Bernstein, a psychotherapist who specializes in career development and career choice, and the author of *Guide to Your Career: How to Turn Your Interests into a Career You Love* (Princeton Review Series, Random House 5th Edition) and *Power Retirement* (McGraw-Hill, 2006), to provide a brief assessment test that can give you insight into whether a mortgage broker career should be considered given your interests and style.

In his practice, Bernstein uses The Birkman Method, an effective technique endowed by The National Foundation for Science, which has been in existence for over 50 years. But this personality assessment is a greatly condensed version of the full Birkman Method questionnaire. It is not intended to be specific and may not be completely accurate for everyone.

For a specific, reliable, and comprehensive measurement of interests, natural behavior styles, underlying needs, motivations, and stress behaviors, you may want to complete the 298-item questionnaire for The Birkman Method®. Contact: salesgroup@ birkman.com for more information. You can also contact Alan B. Bernstein at www.guidetoyourcareer.com.

Who Makes a Good Mortgage Broker?

After 15 years in the business, I've developed my own profile of who will be both successful and satisfied in this career. I've found you've got to enjoy what you do to do it well.

When hiring a new mortgage broker for my company, I'm looking for someone who:

- Is honest and ethical
- Has charisma
- Enjoys people
- Is vivacious
- Has great communication skills
- Is sensitive and intuitive about people
- Responds well under pressure
- Can multitask with ease
- Is comfortable with technology
- Is empathetic and enjoys helping others
- Can read and understand technical issues
- Thrives in competitive situations
- Approaches problems practically and logically
- Is detail-oriented

A significant part of your job as a mortgage broker is being a salesman. But it's not like selling a car. In this case, the product is your expertise at reading people, understanding the market, and being able to find the right loan product for each client. You have to be able to sell yourself in order to make a connection with a potential client. But you need the other characteristics I've listed in order to do your job well.

Test yourself and see if this is the right career for you.

Assessing Your Interests and Style

Bernstein has developed this version of the Birkman Profile as a simple way to visualize your overall behavior. The following questions are a condensed and self-scored version of The Birkman Method created especially for this book. The questions presented here enable you to apply this method to clarify both your interests (symbolized by "I") and your style (symbolized by "S"). This will be a major asset in defining not only what you are drawn to, but also how you like to achieve.

How the Test Is Constructed

The Birkman Interest and Style Summary plots aspects of your personality and behavior on a grid with four quadrants, each identified by a color.

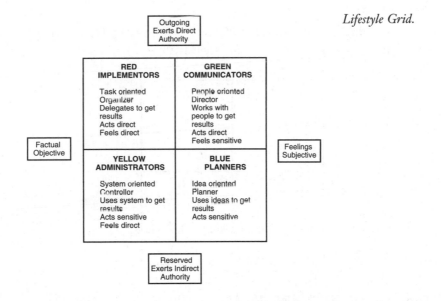

Lifestyle Grid.

The Lifestyle Grid is based on a model of how people behave in general, and this particular model has been used for thousands of years. The first person to use it was probably Hippocrates, the "father of medicine." Hippocrates claimed that he could take all the people in the world, divide them into four categories, and accurately describe how they would act or behave. Sometimes the Grid is called the "Hippocratic Model." According to Hippocrates, there are four basic temperaments. He describes people as Implementers, Communicators, Planners, and Administrators, and bases his model on this idea. Models or pictures are not perfect; they are only generalizations. This one, however, is a very good generalization of how most people behave most of the time.

There are two aspects of your personality and behavior.

An "I" indicates your interests, what you want to do, as indicated by your interest patterns. It shows the type of results you want and the kind of activities that will give you the most satisfaction. This does not measure skill or ability around those interests, only preference. The color location of your "I" suggests what you like to do.

An "S" indicates your style, how you like to do things, for pursuing your interests. This is your preferred mode of achieving your personal goals. It is how people see you acting most of the time. It is how you do things when everything is going your way. If your style color results don't match your real-life style, consider whether you are operating under stress on a day-to-day basis, and remember that when considering your score.

After you take the following Birkman Career Style Summary, use the grid below to place your interest symbol (I) and your style symbol (S).

Your Lifestyle Grid.

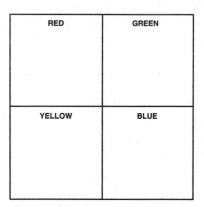

The Birkman Career Style Summary

In order to develop an estimate of your "Birkman Colors" for your interests and style, you will need to complete and self-score the following items. To do this, read each pair of phrases and decide which side of the pair is most descriptive of you, then put a check mark by that phrase.

Column A	Column B
1. ❏ I would rather be a wildlife expert.	❏ I would rather be a public relations professional.
2. ❏ I would rather be a company controller.	❏ I would rather be a TV news anchor.
3. ❏ I would rather be a tax lawyer.	❏ I would rather be a newspaper editor.
4. ❏ I would rather be an auditor.	❏ I would rather be a musician.
5. ❏ I would rather be a production manager.	❏ I would rather be an advertising manager.
6. ❏ I would rather be an accounting manager.	❏ I would rather be a history professor.
7. ❏ I would rather be a bookkeeper.	❏ I would rather be an electrician.
8. ❏ I would rather be a writer.	❏ I would rather be an elected official.
9. ❏ I would rather be a clerical worker.	❏ I would rather be a carpenter.
10. ❏ I would rather be a payroll manager.	❏ I would rather be a manager of engineering.
11. ❏ I would rather be an audit manager.	❏ I would rather be a safety manager.
12. ❏ I would rather be an artist.	❏ I would rather be a salesperson.
13. ❏ I am usually patient when I have to wait on an appointment.	❏ I get restless when I have to wait on an appointment.
14. ❏ It is easy to laugh at one's little social errors or "faux pas."	❏ It is hard to laugh at one's little social errors or "faux pas."
15. ❏ It is wise to make it known if someone is doing something that bothers you.	❏ It is wise to remain silent if someone is doing something that bothers you.
16. ❏ It's not really okay to argue with others even when you know you are right.	❏ It's okay to argue with others when you know you are right.
17. ❏ I like to bargain to get a good price.	❏ I don't like to have to bargain to get a good price.
18. ❏ It is easy to be outgoing and sociable at a party with strangers.	❏ It is hard to be outgoing and sociable at a party with strangers.
19. ❏ I would read the instructions first when putting together a new toy for a child.	❏ I would just "jump in" and start putting a new toy together for a child.
20. ❏ It is usually best to be pleasant and let others decide if your ideas are worth accepting.	❏ It is usually best to be forceful and "sell" your ideas to others.
21. ❏ I usually like to work cautiously.	❏ I usually like to work fast.

continues

continued

Column A	Column B
22.❑ Generally I prefer to work quietly with a minimum of wasted movement.	❑ Generally I prefer to move around and burn some energy while I work.
23.❑ I don't like to have to persuade others to accept my ideas when there is strong forceful opposition or argument from others.	❑ I like to sell and promote my ideas with others even when it takes some argument.
24.❑ It is better to listen carefully and be sure you understand when topics are being discussed.	❑ It is better to speak up quickly and be heard when topics are being discussed.

Now that you have made your choices, you can score them to determine the "color" of your interests and style. To accomplish this, you will need to count the number of items you marked in Column B and enter these counts in the four spaces below.

- First, count the number of items checked in Column B for the first six (1–6) items and place that count in this space: _____ (Interest H)

- Second, count the number of items checked in Column B for the second six (7–12) items and place that count in this space: _____ (Interest V)

- Third, count the number of items checked in Column B for the third six (13–18) items and place that count in this space: _____ (Style H)

- Fourth, count the number of items checked in Column B for the last six (19–24) items and place that count in this space: _____ (Style V)

Your Interest Color

Now that you have these four counts, estimate your Interest and Style Colors. To do this for Interest, simply read the following four statements and see which one describes your counts for Interest. The color associated with the statement that is correct for your counts is the best estimate of your Interest Color you can make from this exercise.

- Blue. Your Interest Color is probably Blue if your Interest H count is 4 or more (4, 5, or 6) and your Interest V count is 3 or less (1, 2, or 3). You like creative, humanistic, thoughtful, quiet types of responsibilities and professions.

- Green. Your Interest Color is probably Green if your Interest H count is 4 or more (4, 5, or 6) and your Interest V count is 4 or more (4, 5, or 6). You like persuasive, selling, promotional, and group-contact types of responsibilities and professions.

- Red. Your Interest Color is probably Red if your Interest H count is 3 or less (1, 2, or 3) and your Interest V count is 4 or more (4, 5, or 6). You like practical, technical, objective, and hands-on, problem-solving types of responsibilities and professions.

- Yellow. Your Interest Color is probably Yellow if your Interest H count is 3 or less (1, 2, or 3) and your Interest V count is 3 or less (1, 2, or 3). You like organized, detail-oriented, predictable, and objective types of responsibilities and professions.

Now place an "I," indicating your interest, in the appropriate color square of the blank grid.

Your Style Color

To estimate your Style Color, simply read the following four statements and see which one describes your counts for Style. The color associated with the statement that is correct for your counts is the best estimate of your Style Color that you can make from this exercise.

- Blue. Your Style Color is probably Blue if your Style H count is 4 or more (4, 5, or 6) and your Style V count is 3 or less (1, 2, or 3). You prefer to perform your responsibilities in a manner that is supportive and helpful to others with a minimum of confrontation. You prefer to work where you and others have time to think things through before acting.

- Green. Your Style Color is probably Green if your Style H count is 4 or more (4, 5, or 6) and your Style V count is 4 or more (4, 5, or 6). You prefer to perform your responsibilities in a manner that is outgoing and even forceful. You prefer to work where things get done with a minimum of thought and where persuasion is well received by others.

- Red. Your Style Color is probably Red if your Style H count is 3 or less (1, 2, or 3) and your Style V count is 4 or more (4, 5, or 6). You prefer to perform your responsibilities in a manner that is action-oriented and practical. You prefer to work where things happen quickly and results are seen immediately.

◆ Yellow. Your Style Color is probably Yellow if your Style H count is 3 or less (1, 2, or 3) and your Style V count is 3 or less (1, 2, or 3). You prefer to perform your responsibilities in a manner that is orderly and planned to meet a known schedule. You prefer to work where things get done with a minimum of interpretations and unexpected change.

Now place an "S," indicating your Style Color, in the appropriate quadrant of the grid.

Applying Your Symbols

Now that you have a color for Interest and a color for Style, what do they mean?

Birkman organizes the "I" symbol, occupational interests, as follows:

Occupational Interests.

RED likes to: Build Organize See a finished product Solve a practical problem Work through people	**GREEN** likes to: Sell and promote Persuade Motivate people Counsel or teach Work with people
YELLOW likes to: Schedule activities Do detailed work Keep close control Work with numbers Work with systems	**BLUE** likes to: Plan activities Deal with abstraction Think of new approaches Innovate Work with ideas

When considering which career or profession you are drawn to, you want to find one that contains aspects of the interests you are likely to use. If your occupational interest is green, you will feel comfortable in a career like a mortgage broker where you are required to promote or persuade. If your occupational interest is yellow, you will feel comfortable with the detail work, technology demands, and numbers component of being a mortgage broker. An occupational interest of red, with a strong interest in working with people, would also be compatible with being a mortgage broker.

Your Style Color: your style symbol (S) describes how others might describe you. It shows how you like to act, indicating your active behavior. Knowing the style in which you tend to pursue your interests is the first step toward describing the way in which you would like to pursue your interests. Your Style Color adds extra insight into your career choice. It's not uncommon for your Interest and Style colors to be different. A person may like the types of job responsibilities associated with their Interest, but prefer to practice these responsibilities in a manner and within an environment that is consistent with their style. For example, a Green Interest and Blue Style combination would be compatible with a career that involves persuasive interest performed in a humanistic, creative, and supportive manner. This is someone who likes selling, promoting, persuading, and group contact responsibilities, but who will be most comfortable with a product he believes in. That sounds like the description of a responsible, ethical mortgage broker who enjoys working with people to find the right loan product for their needs.

If you are someone with a Red Interest, you would likely be drawn to an active career or profession, for example a leadership role in a company. This might suggest that you'd thrive if you eventually opened your own mortgage broker company. But if coupled with a Blue Style, you're likely to need some downtime to reflect on the work you are doing, while a Red Interest and Red Style, might maintain an entirely proactive work style. A Red Interest with a Yellow Style may be drawn to a leadership role, but is likely to operate conservatively with a close eye to the bottom line. Again, a healthy combination for a mortgage broker company owner.

Birkman divides the "S" style, active behavior, as follows:

RED appears: Objective about people Commanding Competitive Practical Forceful	**GREEN** appears: Personable Directive Outspoken Independent Enthusiastic about new things
YELLOW appears: Sociable Orderly Cooperative Consistent Cautious	**BLUE** appears: Perceptive Agreeable Conscientious Reflective and creative Cautious

Active Behavior.

Remember, these are guides, intended to give you some insight into your behavior and interests, as you decide if this is the right career for you.

The Least You Need to Know

- Understanding your interests and style may help you decide if being a mortgage broker is the right career for you.

- There is no one set of interests or styles that are characteristic of being a successful mortgage broker.

- Learn to recognize your interests and style and use them to facilitate job demands.

Part 2

A Seat at the Table

Now that you've decided to become a mortgage broker, you need a guide to entering the business. In this part, you'll find information on the educational and licensing requirements. You'll learn the advantages and disadvantages of joining a large versus a small firm. There are tips on how to find the right job for you, and finally, once you have a job offer, what's negotiable and what's not in this business.

Chapter 5

Book Smarts and Street Smarts

In This Chapter

- State licensing requirements
- Testing for a new career
- Ten best test tips
- The pros and cons of out-of-state licensing

The mortgage broker industry is regulated by federal laws, federal enforcement agencies, and laws or licensing boards in over 45 states. Working as mortgage broker takes both study and experience. While a college degree in finance, economics, or business is certainly helpful, there are no college degree requirements in order to become a successful mortgage broker. On average, the earnings of mortgage professionals with graduate degrees or professional certification were approximately 10 to 15 percent higher than those without. The minimum age requirement varies from state to state.

I'd tell any job applicant that a college degree is always a plus, but to be a success, a mortgage broker needs street smarts, too. You have to be able to think on your feet, size up a situation, and read people. If you've always been intuitive, with good mental reflexes and the ability to adapt to a changing situation, then you've already got many of the skills you'll need to succeed.

In this chapter, we'll review the legal requirements to be a mortgage broker, testing strategies to ace licensing exams, and the advantages and disadvantages of a multi-state practice.

State Licensing Requirements Vary

Only two states, Alaska and Colorado, do not require mortgage brokers to be licensed. The license requirements vary from state to state (see Appendix B).

Job titles and their attendant responsibilities may differ from state to state, so be sure to check carefully which license you will need. Let's look at Ohio's licensing requirements, as they are typical of most states. As defined by Ohio statute a loan officer is "an employee of a registered mortgage broker who originates mortgage loans for a fee. Loan officer also includes an employee who solicits financial and mortgage information from the public for sale to another mortgage broker." A loan officer in Ohio must pass an exam and be licensed in order to practice. A mortgage broker operations manager is a more senior position. In Ohio, mortgage broker refers to the company "that assists a buyer in obtaining a mortgage and receives compensation for providing this assistance. Each registered mortgage broker must designate an operations manager with at least three years experience in the mortgage-lending field." A mortgage broker operations manager must pass a knowledge test and apply for a license.

Here are some of the common regulations:

◆ Mortgage brokers are required to be American citizens or lawfully admitted aliens.

◆ All licenses require fees.

◆ Many states require license applicants to be fingerprinted and subjected to a criminal background check.

◆ Many states have a knowledge exam that must be passed before a license will be granted. Others permit several years of experience working under a licensed broker to substitute for the test.

◆ Many states have a continuing education requirement for renewal of the license.

◆ Some states require a surety bond to be posted and that the broker has and maintains a minimum net worth. For example, Connecticut regulations require mortgage brokers to have and maintain a minimum tangible net worth of $25,000.

Other states, for example Delaware, don't require a physical office in the state, have no exam, no audited financials, and no fingerprint cards, but do require both a $25,000 bond and three references from businesses currently doing business with the applicant.

Meeting Professional Educational Requirements

Some states require a certain number of hours of coursework, as well as passing a licensing exam in order to work as a mortgage broker. Check your state's requirements.

The National Association of Mortgage Brokers (www.namb.org) offers online courses and self-study courses, as well as lists links to classes offered in various states. There are also commercial business schools that offer mortgage broker training. Check your state's licensing bureau to determine if a program is an "approved provider."

Sources for continuing education programs include:

◆ The State Commission or Office that regulates the mortgage broker industry

◆ Technology center schools

◆ Colleges or universities

◆ Private schools

◆ State Association of Mortgage Brokers, NAMB, or an affiliate

◆ The State Bar Association, American Bar Association, or any affiliate

◆ Education providers (organizations approved to provide courses)

What's on the Test?

The licensing exams will test your knowledge of both federal regulations and state regulations. The passing grade varies from state to state. All permit you to retake the test, but again each state makes its own rules for how often you can sit for the exam until you pass.

Here's an overview of the topics you'll need to know, using the Study Guide for the Oklahoma Mortgage Broker/Loan Officer Exam as an example:

1. The obligations between principal and agent, the applicable canons of business ethics, the provisions of the Mortgage Broker Licensure Act, and the rules adopted under the Mortgage Broker Licensure Act.

2. The arithmetical computations common to mortgage brokerage.

3. The principles of real estate lending.

4. The general purposes and legal effect of mortgages, deeds of trust, and security agreements.

To get a broader overview of testing and the subject material covered, let's look at how Ohio regulates mortgage professionals.

To get licensed, contact the Ohio Department of Commerce, Division of Financial Institutions for application forms and information (see Appendix B for contact information). The application costs $100, and the examination company (Experior Assessments in the case of Ohio) verifies your eligibility and then allows you to register for the test. After registration you're given 90 days during which you can take the test as many times as necessary to pass.

The two-hour exam consists of 75 multiple-choice questions. There are nine questions on mortgage loan programs, 18 questions on mortgage loan processes, 18 questions on Federal mortgage lending regulations, 18 questions specific to Ohio's regulations, and 12 questions on terminology. Each state has its own requirements and tests, so the best way to find out what applies to you is to contact the appropriate state regulatory agency (see Appendix B).

Top Ten Test-Taking Tips

Here are ten tips that will help you ace the exam:

1. Schedule time to study. Given all the other demands on your time, you need to make studying a priority. Carve out a block of time to concentrate on the material you need to cover.

2. Don't cram before the exam. You will be tested on a wide breadth of detailed material. It's too much to absorb in a single sitting, even if you have hours to devote to it. Research has shown that students begin to lose focus after 45 to 60

minutes of concentrated studying. Schedule time for your work, take breaks as needed—but don't use break time as a way to procrastinate.

3. Take notes, make outlines, highlight relevant material—use the study techniques that worked best for you when you were in school. You need to develop a list of key ideas so that you can review the material easily.

4. Learn the big concepts first. The mortgage broker industry is loaded with detailed regulations; learn the main ideas first and then nail down the details.

5. Consider forming a study group. Even if you study best alone, or are taking an independent online course, it's helpful to review the material with others to test your understanding and resolve any questions you may have. Make sure, however, that other group members are serious about taking the test and doing well.

6. Be rested before the exam. These tests are detail-oriented. You need to be sharp and focused. If you can't get a good night's rest before, try and grab a nap or short rest before the exam.

7. Read over the whole exam before beginning to answer, and then answer the questions that seem easiest first.

8. Don't get hung up on problem questions. If you hit a question that stumps you, consider it for a minute or two, then move on and come back to it. That's good time management and also limits getting frustrated and losing confidence.

9. For multiple-choice questions, come up with the answer in your head before looking at the answers on the test sheet. It limits the possibility of getting thrown off by trick answers. Read through all the answers and eliminate the obviously false ones.

10. Generally, your first choice is the right choice. Unless you misread the question, don't keep on changing your answers.

If you study the material, are motivated to succeed, and follow these suggestions, you should be able to ace the exam.

On-the-Job Training and Related Experience

You may decide to get your mortgage broker license after you've been working in the field or a related field. For example, starting as a loan processor is a good way to become familiar with the terms and paperwork (refer to Chapter 3 for more on jobs as a loan processor). Some companies provide training or you can enroll in a class that teaches loan processing and takes students through the workflow from origination to closing.

I worked in a variety of related fields—insurance, real estate agent, appraiser—before settling in as a mortgage broker. All those work experiences made me a more knowledgeable broker. Others make the move from work in the real estate field (and vice versa). By working in real estate, you'll have a basic familiarity with the terms and regulations.

Being a salesperson, regardless of the product, certainly gives you the experience you'll need in selling yourself and the product—although you'll clearly have to learn the details of the mortgage broker industry.

Training or experience in banking (as a loan officer, or even a teller or customer representative) is helpful.

> **Did You Know?**
>
> According to a Wells Fargo/ Gallup Small Business Index survey, "most small-business owners have a passion for their work, which leads them to work long hours many days of the week. As a result, small-business owners tend to see passion for their work as a natural part of their work-life balance."

Branching Out: Getting Additional State Licenses

As you get more experienced, you may want to get licensed in more than one state. It certainly makes sense to get licensed in the states contiguous to your primary place of business. For example, my company is in New York, so I also got licensed to practice in Connecticut. I would have gotten a New Jersey license, but that state requires that mortgage brokers maintain a physical office in the state. I had to calculate whether the cost of maintaining an office would be offset sufficiently by the profits from making deals in New Jersey. At this time, not enough of my clients were moving across the state lines that way, so I decided against it.

In contrast, I went out of my way to get a Florida mortgage broker's license. Florida requires license applicants to take a 40-hour in-state education class and pass an exam. It meant leaving my family for a week and going back to school, but it was well worth it. I wanted to be able to serve my local clients who made the decision to either retire in Florida or buy a vacation home there. Plus Florida is a booming state with tons of building activity. The investment of time and money in getting a Florida license has paid off handsomely.

Since so much of the work in this industry is done electronically, and you don't have to be at the closings (although it's often reassuring to new buyers), a physical presence in the state to conduct mortgage broker business isn't necessary.

My basic rule of thumb is that if the requirements, financially and logistically, aren't too burdensome, it's an advantage to be licensed in multiple states.

Did You Know?

The ten fastest-growing states, according to the most recent U.S. Census, are: Arizona, North Carolina, Delaware, Nevada, Idaho, Utah, New Mexico, Florida, Georgia, and Texas.

What follows is a list of the states that license mortgage brokers without requiring a physical office in the state. You can serve clients via phone, fax, and e-mail. They are as follows:

Arkansas	Minnesota
California	Mississippi
Connecticut	Nebraska
Delaware	New Hampshire
District of Columbia	New Mexico
Florida	New York
Georgia*	North Dakota
Idaho	Oregon
Illinois	Rhode Island
Indiana	South Dakota
Iowa	Tennessee
Kansas	Utah
Louisiana	Vermont
Maine	Virginia
Maryland	Washington
Massachusetts	Wisconsin
Michigan	

*If the state where you practice requires a physical office, then you must have one in Georgia as well.

The Least You Need to Know

- ◆ Each state has its own licensing requirements.

- ◆ State licensing exams cover material that is universal to the industry, but also include questions on specific state-related regulations.

- ◆ Getting experience in related industries may help you succeed as a mortgage broker.

- ◆ Acquiring a mortgage broker license in states beyond your immediate business community may permit you to better serve your local clients and increase your income.

Chapter 6

Do Your Homework

In This Chapter

- ◆ Evaluating a small firm
- ◆ Considering a large firm
- ◆ The value of a mentor
- ◆ When all things seem equal, what else is important?

Finding the right firm to begin your career as a mortgage broker is critical. Of course, the company must want to hire you, but it really is a two-way street. You want to be picky about where you work. On a very practical level, you will be giving the company almost half of whatever you earn. You want to be sure that you are getting the support and service you need in return.

Perhaps more important, you want to choose a well-regarded company that expects all its brokers to adhere to a strict code of ethics. The corporate reputation becomes your professional reputation.

When you first begin your career as a mortgage broker, hopefully you'll have some choice as to which firm you join. There are advantages to jumping into a large company, with ten or more mortgage brokers already on staff; and there are pluses to signing on with a small firm where there are only two, maybe three brokers, including you.

You should, if possible, interview at a variety of firms. Don't assume that you want one kind or the other. It's hard to know what you like until you actually go in and meet the staff, see the setup, and understand how their system works and where you would fit in.

Part of what you're looking for is a mentor. It's one thing to be supervised when you first start working. That makes sense on a practical and legal basis. But a mentor is broader than that. You'll learn more than how to process a loan application. A mentor will give you an insider's pass to the industry, guide your career, and help you move up the ladder to greater success. A good mentor helps you grow as a professional.

This chapter talks about all these things: large firms, small firms, and working with a mentor.

Trust Your Gut

We're going to come back to this concept of trusting your first instinct about companies. I can trot out the clichés to support both arguments. On the one hand, you can't judge a book by its cover, so you shouldn't jump to conclusions about a company. On the other hand, in fact, part of what will make you a good mortgage broker is that you can size up a situation, read between the lines, and judge people so well.

> **Heads Up!**
>
> Before you interview with a company, check them out with the Better Business Bureau. You want to know if there are any outstanding complaints about the corporate business practices.

But much to my surprise, when I was researching whether in fact our first instincts are almost always right, I discovered that there is a fair amount of evidence to say that our first instinct isn't always the best choice. According to researchers at the University of Illinois, Northern Arizona University, and Stanford University, people accept the myth that our first instincts are correct because it feels worse to change a correct answer to an incorrect one than to stick with an original incorrect answer. Furthermore, that feeling makes changing right answers to wrong ones more memorable than a wrong-to-right change, and seemingly more probable. You remember when you've changed from a right to a wrong answer because it feels worse to have done so.

This is a lesson to be learned in the mortgage broker business. On the one hand you need to trust your instincts; at the same time, be willing to reexamine a premise or assumption because you could be wrong.

That said, as you interview at firms, take the time immediately after you leave, while it's still fresh in your mind, to write down your reaction and impressions. You should review it later when you've had time to process the experience. That gives you the first, gut reaction, coupled with the necessary perspective to view a company clearly.

Examining Company Life

While some might decry the impersonal nature of a large firm, that's a generalization that can only be proven after you've visited the company and seen for yourself how the business works. Don't make assumptions about any company until you've done your homework and checked it out.

A large firm offers certain advantages:

- The training program may be more formalized and more extensive. You won't be the guinea pig. A large firm has trained other mortgage brokers and knows what works and what doesn't.

- A larger staff may not be stretched as thin as the employees of a smaller company. There may be more time to help you develop your career.

- There may be a larger support staff.

- There may be more resources to pay for bigger marketing programs, more outreach.

- There may be greater name recognition.

The pressure to succeed and the competition for clients, however, may be more intense at a larger firm. You're competing for your share of the business and there are more sharks in the water.

On the other hand, working for a smaller company may offer you a greater range of opportunities:

- You learn from the bottom up. There is something to be said for learning how to do every job in the company.

- You're better prepared and thoroughly understand the inner workings of the industry.

- You may have a greater input into developing and focusing the company's marketing and outreach programs.

◆ There may be direct access to the decision maker in the company. Fewer layers between you and the top guy.

◆ Small may be more efficient. You may be able to respond more quickly to a business opportunity because the staff is small, flexible, and well-coordinated.

While the competition for business is always intense, in a smaller firm, it may not be as cutthroat.

The Corporate Culture

An important part of what you're trying to assess is the environment in which you'll be working. You'll be giving a lot of your time—and money—to this business.

Drive by the company's headquarters and check it out. Then consider the following:

◆ While you will interact with clients in many places outside the office—and often via e-mail—do you feel comfortable in the area?

◆ Is it a place where you could meet clients?

◆ Just like a person, how the corporate offices are maintained tells you something about the people who work there. It doesn't have to be fancy, but the office should appear clean and professional.

Heads Up!

When you visit the offices, check out the types of computers and software they use. How current are they? While they may not be state of the art, has the company invested in technology? Does the owner use a personal digital assistant? Are the computers networked? This is becoming a paperless industry— how up to date is the company?

Inside the company offices, you want to know:

◆ Where you will be working and what equipment is provided.

◆ If your personal office space is limited or shared, is there a clean, bright conference room where you can set up your laptop and meet with clients?

◆ Do other members of the staff appear pleasant and efficient? Engaged or bored?

◆ Are their desks overflowing with papers or do they seem organized? What is your first impression of them?

◆ How does the staff dress? Is it a casual office attire or strictly business attire—even for the support staff?

Another suggestion is to study the company's website. Under the link "About Us," you can learn about the corporate history and the owner(s). If they list the staff, check out their experience and focus.

Finding a Business Mentor

Finding someone to help guide you as you start your career is invaluable. I know I'm lucky that my father was able to play that role in my life. He's been in real estate-related businesses for over 40 years. He's given me insight into what works and what doesn't when running a company, and he's also given me the room to develop my own methods and style. He's listened a lot, advised a little, and always had my best interests at heart. He is a fabulous dad, but he is also what I would define as a good business mentor. You don't have to be related to your mentor—that was just a bonus. But part of what you hope to find in your first mortgage broker job is someone who can help guide your career.

Why Do You Want a Mentor?

Not only at the beginning of your career, but even after you are well established, you will benefit from a relationship with an experienced mortgage broker and if you choose to open your own company, with other business owners. It's always helpful to have a sounding board to help you focus on the heart of an issue. It's also a relief to have emotional support as you weather business crises. Being able to talk to an experienced mortgage broker who's "been there, done that" when the housing market slows, interest rates skyrocket, clients complain, and so on is invaluable. You need someone with a long-term perspective, someone who is not being judgmental, someone who is supportive, helpful, and without a self-serving agenda. They may not be able to solve the problem, but they can help you figure out what you need to do or, just as valuable, reinforce your own self-confidence that you can figure out the solution.

The added benefit of a good mentor is that it expands your network. His years in the business means his Rolodex is significantly bigger than yours. He also probably has access to the senior decision makers in companies. Don't expect your mentor to photocopy his address book, but you can rely on him for suggestions on who to contact to resolve a problem.

How Does a Mentor Help?

The first, obvious characteristic of a good mentor is a willingness to fill that role. You can't force someone to help develop you professionally. You will undoubtedly work with another mortgage broker when you first begin, but that's not what I mean when I talk about a mentor. That person is to train you in the mechanics of the business. You want someone who will offer you more than a step-by-step guide through the loan application process. You want someone who will teach you the insider tricks to becoming successful.

Here's an easy example. Anyone can teach you which websites to check for the current interest rates available, but a good mentor will teach you how to field a phone inquiry about rates.

The initial phone call with a new client is like a blind date. Since you don't know each other, the conversation should be friendly and informative, but at the same time, you want to hold back a little. Don't give away all your secrets … yet.

Frequently, the first question, even before the caller gives you his name is: what's your best rate? While it sounds straightforward enough, it's really a trick question and you've got to be careful how you answer, otherwise you've lost before you even begin.

First of all, you know that there isn't one rate that fits all. The best mortgage rate for a young couple with limited resources is probably not the same rate that is available to a homeowner who has a big income, has built up significant equity, and is looking to trade up to a more expensive house. The best deal is tailored to meet a client's financial circumstances, short- and long-term needs, and goals.

Second, let's suppose you quote him the lowest rate currently available, without even knowing if he qualifies for it. As far as the client is concerned, you've just locked in at that number even if it's not realistic. You can't meet it and it will come back to bite you. You'll lose the client and maybe even ding your reputation.

But quite often the caller will take the number you've given and call your competition to see if he can get a bidding war started. Sounds smart, except you know that it doesn't work that way. It's in your interest to get the client the best deal available, but you can't do that unless you have basic information about his income, debt load, and available cash. Anyone who quotes a mortgage rate without that info is grabbing numbers out of the air. They're meaningless.

But let's say your competition hears your quote and decides to lowball his offer. Game over. The client hops in his car and heads straight for your competition's office. It's doubtful that the rate quoted will hold up, but once a broker gets one-on-one face time with the customer, he can get the information he needs, run the numbers, and then justify the higher mortgage rate. The customer may not be happy, but he'll probably take the deal so he doesn't have to start all over.

In that first phone call, you've got to be vague enough to cover yourself no matter what the customer's finances turn out to be, while offering enough specifics to grab the caller's attention and then get the information you need. You might say, "I've got 30 different mortgage packages. Right now fixed rates are in the 'sixes, but I've also got some lower adjustable mortgage rates that might be right for you. Or if you're willing to pay some points, we can probably get a lower fixed interest rate. Let me get some information from you and work up some possibilities."

The next important step is to make sure that the person who is the decision maker in the family will be at the meeting when you start the application process. Don't assume it will be the man. Just as frequently, it's the woman who handles the finances in the relationship. But whoever it is, that's the person who needs to be at the client meeting. Otherwise, you're just spinning your wheels.

See the difference between a mechanical repetition of how to handle a phone call—and one that will reel in a customer? You need much more than that to become successful, and if you can find someone who will help you learn the tricks of the trade, you can spend your time more efficiently.

One of the questions you want to ask when you interview for the job is who will be training you. Can you meet that person? If so, did you feel that the individual was happy to take on the responsibility of training a newcomer or burdened and resentful of the extra work? Do you think he could be your mentor as well as training supervisor?

What Makes a Good Mentor?

There are professional and personal characteristics that make an individual a good mentor. It's someone who …

- ◆ is professionally competent and experienced.
- ◆ has good interpersonal skills.
- ◆ is caring, encouraging, supportive.
- ◆ is challenging and demanding.
- ◆ is mature, wise, trustworthy, and dependable.

While you want someone who is empathic and nonjudgmental, you also want someone who motivates you, challenges you, and demands that you do your best.

So How Do You Find Your Mentor?

Talk about mentoring in your job interview. You want to judge if the company owner understands and values the role a mentor can play in developing you as a professional mortgage broker. When you meet the individual who will be training you, you'll quickly determine whether this is someone who can walk you through the mechanics of the business or give you the insight you need to succeed. If not, look around the company to see if you can develop an informal relationship with one of the other experienced brokers in the firm.

A good mentoring relationship is one of mutual respect. It's not a one-way street.

Back to Your Gut Instinct

We started this chapter talking about whether or not you should second-guess your first reaction to a company. Certainly, you can—and should—figure out the commission potential at a firm. You can add in the bonuses promised, the contributions to your 401(k) retirement fund, and any other perks offered. But a lot of what makes a firm the right place to work is based on your instinct. The initial commission splits may not be as good at one company as at another, but if your gut is telling you that you feel more comfortable one place over the other—trust yourself.

You have to spend a lot of time working to succeed as a mortgage broker. Make sure that you like the team you join and the environment in which you will spend your days. Make sure that they share your code of ethics.

The Least You Need to Know

- Check out the company and owner's reputation before you interview at the firm.
- Study the corporate website to learn about the history and background of the owner and staff.
- Drive by the corporate headquarters before you interview to determine if you're comfortable with the location and the environment.
- A business mentor can help you develop your professional skills and expand your network.

Chapter 7

Where the Jobs Are

In This Chapter

- Resumé smarts
- The search begins
- Networking 101
- The perfect cover letter
- References that sell you

Look at a recent "help wanted" ad for an entry-level mortgage broker job that was posted online …

> At least one year experience—previous mortgage origination experience not necessary.
> Recent college graduates will be considered.
> Bachelor's degree or equivalent.
> Bilingual: English/Spanish, Chinese, Korean, or Polish a plus.
> Proven ability to build quality customer relationships.
> Maintain a positive, can-do attitude.
> Excellent presentation, communication, and interpersonal skills.
> Strategic thinker, with excellent time-management, problem-solving skills.
> Must have a valid driver's license and access to a motor vehicle.

Notice that the company wasn't looking for someone who could define second ratio (the percentage of a borrower's total debt to his gross monthly income). The ad was looking for someone with the potential to become a successful mortgage broker. The company wanted someone with some work experience—because you learn important life lessons from having the responsibility of any job.

What this ad tells you is that companies know you can learn the details of the industry, but if you don't have the other qualifications—strategic thinker, a positive, can-do attitude, good communication skills, time-management talents, a people person, a problem-solver—then you probably won't succeed as a mortgage broker.

In this chapter, you'll learn how to present yourself as a qualified, eminently hire-able, candidate for a mortgage broker job.

Tell Me About Yourself

Before you begin sifting through the classifieds, you need a resumé. Let me amend that. You need to develop a basic resumé that you can then adapt, as needed, to the character and culture of each mortgage broker company to which you apply. These aren't cookie-cutter jobs—and you don't want your resumé to look like it could apply equally to any company.

Tailor-Made Works Best

Computers and word processing allow you to tailor your resumé to change it from a boring recitation of facts to a powerful sales tool, selling you. Research each company and the position advertised, then highlight those qualifications that are a perfect match between the job description and your talents.

Yahoo! hotjobs (www.hotjobs.com) has templates to help you develop a resumé. There is also a template to build an online resumé to e-mail prospective employers.

A well-organized resumé includes a crisp description of the skills, strengths, and experience that you will bring to a company. This kind of resumé takes time, effort, and yes, creativity. Not in the sense of inventing experience or attributing to yourself skills that you don't have. Frankly that's lying, and besides being morally wrong, it can hurt only you in the long run. Dishonesty is one trait that can't be tolerated in the mortgage broker industry.

Technical and computer skills are critical in the mortgage broker industry. List programming languages, software, and operating systems you can use.

Stick to one page. Employers (or headhunters) have a limited amount of time to scan a resumé, so make every word count.

Don't bother to list references—an employer will ask for them.

Habla Español?

List the foreign languages you speak. Being bilingual (or more), opens up the job market dramatically. At the very least, with Hispanics now America's largest minority group, consider learning Spanish as a way of reaching out to an important market.

According to the U.S. Census, one of every seven people in the United States is Hispanic. Hispanics accounted for one half of the overall population growth of 2.9 million between July 2003 and July 2004.

> **Did You Know?**
>
> According to the U.S. Census, 28 million people in the United States speak Spanish as their first language; 2 million speak Chinese; 1.6 million speak French; 1.3 million speak German; 1.2 million speak Tagalog; and 1 million speak Vietnamese.

Proof, Double-Proof, Then (E-) Mail

Follow directions—especially for e-mail resumés. Most human resources specialists ask for exactly what they want: some will accept attachments, others want you to paste the resumé in the body of the e-mail. Some will ask for a Microsoft Word version of your resumé, others will ask for a text version only. Follow instructions. Here are a few other things to keep in mind:

- Don't get cute with the fonts. First, if it's an e-mail resumé, the personnel department may not have that font in their computer. But it's also distracting and unprofessional. Use a business font such as Arial or Times Roman, in 12-point type.

- Print your resumé on a laser printer for a clean—unsmudged—copy. To make duplicates, pay for a good-quality copy service.

- Proofread, proofread, proofread—then have someone else proofread again. Mistakes make you look amateurish.

No Experience? No Problem

Whether it's because you're just entering the job market or you're switching careers, the lack of job experience in the mortgage broker industry is less of a problem than in other careers. If being a successful mortgage broker requires mastering sales, marketing, and loan processing, you may already be a pro at the first two. Much of what you need to learn about loan processing can be accomplished through coursework, either in a classroom or online, as well as on the job.

The key is to translate those life experiences and accomplishments that are also business skills. Some of the qualities that make a successful mortgage broker include negotiating, communicating, marketing, selling, organizing, and computer literacy. You don't need to work in the business world to have accumulated those skills. You do need to emphasize how you have those skills on your resumé (and later in an interview).

If you've worked in sales, regardless of what you were selling, you've got some of the experience you'll need in this industry. If you've been an officer in volunteer organizations, then you may already have organizational, marketing, and communications experience. List your job experience and volunteer activities, then determine what skills you've needed to succeed in these roles. You can learn the "book" material, but you may already have much of the "street smarts" you'll need.

Where Do You Look?

You can find job leads in many places. Hunting for a job today generally starts at your computer—even if it means reading the newspaper classifieds online.

Some state chapters of the National Association of Mortgage Brokers (www.namb.org) include job listings on their websites.

Your college career center is another good place to check for job listings.

Here are some other good online sites to check. Use "mortgage broker" or "loan originator" as your search term.

America's Job Bank
www.ajb.dni.us
Offers jobs listings, resumé and cover letter help, training information.

Monster.com
www.monster.com
Large, private, global online network for careers.

Job Bank USA
www.jobbankusa.com
Jobs and resumé information.

Career Magazine
www.careermag.com
Jobs, resumé bank, and information.

CareerBuilder
www.careerbuilder.com
Jobs, resumé bank, career information, company profiles.

Employment Guide's Career Web
www.employmentguide.com
Job listings for major U.S. cities.

College Grad
www.collegegrad.com
Jobs, tips on resumés, interviews, salary negotiations, for recent college grads.

Networking 101

The best job is the one that someone recommends *you* for. It's a job that may not even be listed yet. Or it could be a position that the company hasn't quite decided they need to fill. And you hear about it because someone on the "inside" gave you an early heads up.

Welcome to the world of networking. The old adage, "It's not what you know, it's who you know," may not be totally accurate, but it certainly has more than a trace of truth to it. And it's even understandable. Given two perfectly qualified candidates, if you've been recommended by someone the employer knows and respects—it makes sense that you have the edge.

So who do you know? More people than you think. Convinced that you know no one in the mortgage broker industry? Maybe—but you probably know someone who does. Here's a quick guide to effective networking.

1. Make a list—the longer, the better. Put each name and contact information in an address book or electronic organizer. You'll be constantly adding to this list. Be inclusive at this point. Be sure to add any of the following people that you know:

    Realtors
    Contractors

> Bankers
> Mortgage brokers
> Lawyers
> Recent homebuyers or sellers
> Friends (of your own, as well as friends/relatives of your parents and siblings)
> Fellow congregants from your house of worship
> Members of clubs and organizations to which you belong

2. Prioritize the list. Determine who will be most helpful.

3. Take the first step. Call each person. For those in a related field, explain that you are beginning a job search in the mortgage broker industry and wanted their advice. Be specific about your experience and skills.

4. Ask each person for any suggestions or additional names.

5. Follow up each contact with a note of thanks. For those who have requested it, include your resumé.

6. Keep in contact regularly, even when you've already landed a job. You're now building your network of business relationships. In this field, word of mouth is one of the most powerful form of advertising you can have.

7. Return the favor. Be willing to listen and help when you get a call.

The Perfect Cover Letter

In many cases, the cover letter is an employer's first introduction to you. In a business where selling is key, this is your first sales opportunity and the product is you. The letter should be a clear demonstration of your communication and organizational skills.

◆ Less is more. Keep your cover letter brief and to the point. It's not a summary of your resumé, but rather a brief sales presentation of why you are the best candidate for the job. *Brief* is the keyword—hiring personnel don't have time to read lengthy presentations.

◆ Personalize each cover letter. You can use some of the same basic language, but each and every letter should reflect the effort you made to learn about the company. Go to the corporate website and under the heading "about us"—find the names of corporate officers to whom you can send your letter and resumé.

◆ Don't talk money … yet. Listing your salary requirements before you've even proved your worth is counterproductive. You may be eliminated before you even begin. Remember, mortgage brokers are paid on commission. Your salary is a result of your own efforts.

◆ Be specific. Include examples of those accomplishments which illustrate you have the skills a good mortgage broker will need. For example, if you've worked in sales, describe how you increased sales volume or developed the online website for your previous employer.

Like your resumé, proofread carefully.

The Interview Is Your First Sales Presentation

The interview is an opportunity to seal the deal. Especially in the mortgage broker industry, this is your opportunity for your first sales presentation. You need to be ready to impress by word and deed. Your attire and your body language will tell the interviewer a lot about you—make it all positive.

Homework Before the Interview

You need to prep for an interview. That means:

◆ Develop answers to tough questions you may be asked.

◆ Practice those answers so you speak confidently.

◆ Print out a resumé and make sure it's error-proof. If you're being interviewed by more than one person, bring extra resumés with you.

◆ Plan what you are going to wear. Try it on to make sure it fits and looks professional. For women, have an extra pair of hose on hand in case of a run.

◆ Skip perfumes or scented after-shave. Many people have allergies to perfumes or scents.

◆ Be on time—which means at least 15 minutes early.

Dress for Success

Being a mortgage broker is a professional job. You need to dress the part for the interview and the job. In my firm, I dress like a banker. I wear a suit and tie most days.

Sometimes in the summer, we have dress-down Fridays, but even then it's khakis and a dress shirt for the men; dress pants or a skirt and a conservative blouse for women. In this business, you never know when you're going to have to meet clients—and you have to dress like you might.

What a woman should wear to an interview:

- A conservative, well-fitted suit. The skirt length can be at or just above the knee. You have some flexibility in terms of color—but use good taste and, again, err on the side of caution.

- The blouse should complement the suit, with a neckline that is conservative.

- Light hose (no patterns, color, or fishnet), mid-heeled, and closed-toe shoes.

- Go easy on the fingernails—light colors, nothing flashy, and a moderate length.

- If you have many tattoos, consider using heavy spray-on makeup to cover them up.

- Remove any earrings that aren't in your ear—and limit the number of earrings to at most two in either ear.

- Hair should be recently cut, under control, and if long, pulled back from the face.

- Makeup should be subtle. Go easy on the eye makeup—no bright shadow or false eyelashes.

- Jewelry should be discreet and minimal.

Heads Up!

Women should wear a skirt or dress whenever possible. Pants are not the best choice for a job interview, even in a casual working environment. If pants are worn, they should be slacks that have a crease. Never wear stretch, form-fitting, or denim pants. (*Looking Your Best for Work*, University of Illinois Extension, www.urbanext.uiuc.edu)

What a man should wear to an interview:

- Buy the best suit you can afford. Wool or wool blend is best. It's an investment. Choose a conservative suit, both in terms of cut and color. Dark shades like charcoal gray, black, or navy blue work best. A thin, subtle stripe is fine, but avoid looking like a character from a '40s mobster film.

- Wear a dark, solid leather belt. Use suspenders only if the suit has the buttons to support them. The clip-on suspenders look tacky.

- A white or off-white, long sleeved shirt is the safest best. Make sure it fits well. A tight collar is unattractive and may make you feel uncomfortable during the interview when you're under pressure. On the other hand, a gaping collar looks like you borrowed your big brother's clothes for the occasion.

♦ Invest in a couple of good, conservative silk ties. No bowties, bolos, or string ties.

♦ Check the bottom of your shoes. As you cross your legs during an interview, a big turnoff is seeing holes in the soles. Worn heels say you don't pay attention to the little details. You want to wear dark, leather shoes. Go for either leather, laced shoes or well-made leather loafers. Avoid work boots or suede moccasins.

♦ Socks should match your shoes and suit. Black is always the safest choice. Calf length is preferable.

♦ Hair should be recently cut. Avoid the spiked or heavily gelled look. Be sure and clip ear hair, nose hair, and neck hair.

♦ Keep your moustache and beard neatly trimmed.

♦ Limit jewelry to a minimum. Remove any earrings not in ears—and consider removing those as well.

♦ Have neatly trimmed nails.

The Right Answers to Four Tough Questions

You'll feel more confident if you go into an interview prepared with answers to difficult questions. Here are some difficult questions and suggested answers.

Question #1: How do you handle stress?

The mortgage broker business is a tough, pressure-filled environment. An employer needs to know that you won't fall apart when you're in the midst of a dozen deals all demanding your immediate attention. This business isn't for the faint of heart.

A good answer might be: I do my best work under pressure. The first thing I do when things are going crazy is take a deep breath and then start prioritizing the tasks to determine what needs to be done first. That gives me a road map for how to handle the competing demands.

Then give an example of how you handled a particularly stressful situation: a new deadline for a big project; coordinating a team that was faced with multiple responsibilities; organizing the presentation for a major client; supervising the after-Christmas sale.

Finally, you might add what you do to de-stress—for example, working out at the gym, a daily walk, yoga.

Did You Know? _____

"There is growing evidence demonstrating that exercise can be effective in improving the mental well-being of the general public, largely through improved mood and self-perceptions."

—Dr. Kenneth R. Fox, "The Influence of Physical Activity on Mental Well-Being," *Public Health Nutrition*

Question #2: Give me an example of a challenge you faced at work and how you handled it.

Here the employer wants you to show him that you aren't intimidated by challenges and difficult situations. He wants to know that you're creative, can think outside the box, and will stick with a problem until it's solved.

A good answer might be: I like challenges. Last year, when our computer system went down the morning of our summer sale, I moved into high gear. I put in an emergency call to the corporate I.T. team to start troubleshooting the problem, but in the interim, I distributed calculators to every member of our sales team so they could add up customer purchases, was at the bank when it opened to get cash in order to make change since we couldn't get into our cash registers, set up coffee and donuts to thank our customers for their patience, and we were back online within 90 minutes of opening our doors. Our sales for that day exceeded the previous year's opening day totals.

Question #3: Why did you leave your last job?

Here the employer is trying to get a picture of the kind of employee you will make. You need to be honest, but diplomatic. Don't badmouth your former employer. It only reflects poorly on you and leaves the questioner wondering what you will say about his company in the future. You want to sound positive and focus on the future, not dwell on the past.

Heads Up! _____

In a survey of 600 hiring managers by CareerBuilder. com, major interview turnoffs include: bringing your mom and asking directions to another interview!

A good answer might be: I'm looking for new challenges and an opportunity to grow professionally. I learned a great deal from that job and appreciate the opportunities it offered. But I want to go in a new direction and will use the skills and experiences of that position to contribute to your company.

Question #4: Where do you see yourself in five years?

Here the employer is trying to gauge your commitment to a mortgage broker career and to his company. You want to demonstrate that you are looking for a place that will encourage your professional growth and financially reward hard work. You want to show that you believe this company is the place to do that.

A good answer might be: I want to grow professionally as a mortgage broker, building a strong network of referrals. I hope to be right here working as part of the team that makes this company a success. I like the idea of mentoring new members of the team and taking on more responsibility.

Four Questions You Have to Ask

The job interview is a two-way street. The interviewer wants to learn about you, but you need to learn about the company. Here are four topics that will help you decide if the company is the right place to begin your mortgage broker career. If these have not been discussed during your interview, don't leave without asking.

Question #1: What kind of support does the company offer to new brokers?

You will need supervision and help as you begin your mortgage broker career. While you have studied the material, on-the-job questions will arise on a daily basis. Who will you report to? Will an experienced broker be supervising your work? Can you help an experienced broker with their current deals? Will other brokers in the company refer business to you in exchange for a referral fee?

You're looking for a collegial atmosphere. While the mortgage broker industry is very competitive, you don't want to be working in a pressure-cooker environment, constantly looking over your shoulder worried that a co-worker will steal your clients.

> **Heads Up!**
>
> "Saying you have no questions means 'I have no interest in your company.'"
> —Rob Yeung, author of *Successful Interviews Every Time*

Question #2: What is the company's marketing plan?

You need to determine how the office promotes itself. While you understand that you will be expected to build up your own network of referrals, you want a company that is aggressively marketing itself to realtors, contractors, lenders, and the public, in order to bring in clients.

If the company is part of a national or regional corporation—how is the local office promoted? Does the local office have to pay for any of the national advertising?

If the company has a website (you can check that yourself before the interview)—how does it drive customers to it? What search engines is it listed with? If the company doesn't have a website—why not? Would they be interested in building one? Will you be able to have a page within the website to promote your services?

What other advertising (newspaper, radio, television) does the company do to promote its services? Ask the interviewer for some samples.

Will you be expected to do any cold calling for clients? If so, how does the company generate the lists (or rent them)?

Question #3: How far do I take a file before handing it off to the loan processor?

Every company has their own system for processing the paperwork and acquiring the necessary documentation. In some firms, you may serve as loan processor, as well as broker. In others, you may hand off the file once the initial client paperwork is completed and a rate is locked in. The loan processor will then handle getting the necessary documentation. At the beginning of your career, it's helpful to at least shadow the loan processor so you see each step.

Question #4: What is the compensation package for new mortgage brokers?

Some companies pay on *commission* only, others offer minimal salaries. The bottom line is that this is fundamentally a commission-based industry. Your income is dependent on your own efforts. Starting out, this can be difficult. You'll need to have some savings to help with the initial cash flow. Some companies offer a draw against future commissions. This isn't a salary. You're borrowing against future income, but it's helpful in terms of cash flow.

Sometimes, for entry-level mortgage brokers, I'll pre-pay up to half of the commission on deals that they bring in and look like they might close just to ease the cash flow crunch of a newbie.

def·i·ni·tion

Commission is the compensation that is paid to a mortgage broker based on a percentage of the loan amount.

Post-Interview Tips

When the interview is over, be sure to offer your thanks—and a firm handshake before you leave. Ask for the interviewer's business card.

Follow up with a thank you note (e-mail is acceptable) again expressing your appreciation for the interview, as well as your interest in joining the company. Offer to send any additional information they might need and that you look forward to hearing from them.

References That Sell You

You have to assume that potential employers will check your references. Some states require a background check in order to qualify for a mortgage broker license.

According to Allison Doyle, who writes "Your Guide to Job Searching" for about.com (www.jobsearch.about.com), on average employers check three references for each candidate. "It's essential to select the right people, and to talk to them in advance about using them."

Some employers will limit their references to merely confirming starting and ending dates and salary information. You should include among your references individuals who can be specific about your background and your performance. You can use former bosses, co-workers, colleagues, business acquaintances, professors/academic advisors, customers, and vendors, as well as leaders and members of organizations for which you volunteer.

Once you've landed a job, send your references a thank you note. Keep in contact with your references, whether you're searching for a job or not. You want an active network for both future job searches, as well as part of fulfilling current job responsibilities. For all you know, your reference will soon need a mortgage broker—and will think of you!

If you're worried about what former employers are saying about you, for a fee there are companies that will check your references and provide you with a report. These include:

- www.badreferences.com
- www.jobreference.com
- www.myreferences.com

Checking Up on You

Some states require a criminal background check to qualify for a mortgage broker license. It is a search of state and/or local government files to determine if you have had a past criminal conviction. Never lie on your resumé or any application about criminal convictions. Some states grant licenses if the conviction is more than 5 years old.

The Least You Need to Know

◆ When you are job hunting, customize your resumé and cover letter for each company.

◆ It's always wiser to dress conservatively for an interview.

◆ Practice answers to tough questions to avoid getting rattled during the interview.

◆ Ask specifically about mentoring and compensation if the interviewer doesn't cover those topics.

$$$$ and Sense

In This Chapter

- ◆ The inside scoop on commissions and splits
- ◆ Be prepared for the worst, hope for the best
- ◆ Planning for the future
- ◆ Expenses: who pays for what?

Congratulations! The owner of the mortgage broker firm has offered you a job. You like the boss, your co-workers seem collegial, and the company culture is supportive and energetic. You want to be a mortgage broker and this is a great opportunity. All this sounds terrific, but now let's get down to the nitty-gritty of the business side of a job.

How often are you going to get paid? How are you going to handle the slow months when the commissions are few and far between? Who's going to pay for your health insurance? How about your travel expenses? Who picks up the tab for all those donuts you're bringing to realtor open houses?

This chapter will help you sort out the details of your job before you start so there are no surprises—or disappointments—after you've joined the team.

The Money Talk

Woody Allen once said: "Money is better than poverty, if only for financial reasons." So even if you find it awkward to talk about money, you need to have answers to the questions of what are the splits (how much you'll earn on each deal); when you will be paid (weekly, bi-weekly, monthly); how long after a deal is closed you will get paid; and what kinds of bonuses you can expect at the end of the year. You also need to figure out how to handle your cash flow. Some months will be more lucrative than others—how are you going to deal with the months that are lean?

Although you will work on commission, you are an employee of the company, not an independent contractor. That's an important distinction for you financially, as well as legally. It will impact how you file your income taxes, what benefits will be offered (health insurance, Social Security taxes, retirement plans). It also protects you legally so that you are covered by the company's liability insurance.

Split in Your Favor

As we discussed in Chapter 2, you'll be paid on commission which consists of the origination points, discount points, broker fee, and yield spread premium (the fees paid by a lender to a mortgage broker for the delivery of a loan that carries a higher interest rate; see Chapter 17). The commission is paid to the mortgage broker company at the closing, and your percentage of it will be in your next paycheck.

The more loans you close, and the larger the amounts, the more you earn. It will take time to build up to the point where you always have deals in the pipeline. Your goal is to close between 15 and 20 deals a month.

The size of the loans will depend on the housing market in which you work. If it's a high-price district, the mortgages will be larger—and you'll earn a bigger commission. If you work in an area where housing prices are moderate, then you'll need to increase the number of deals you close in order to up your earnings.

You need to research the housing market in which you'll be working. Presumably, you did at least a cursory survey before going on the job interview. But you want to discuss the market in detail with the company owner so that you and he both have a reasonable understanding of what you can expect to earn.

Every company has their own method of determining splits (how much of the commission you'll receive, how much will go to the company). Certainly in those first few months, with no experience, your BPs (basis points, the term used to describe your percentage of the deal; see Chapter 2) will be significantly lower, especially for in-house generated business, maybe a one-third/two-thirds split. Even if you bring in a deal, given the level of supervision you need in that first month, you'll probably still get a reduced percentage.

Ask the owner …

◆ To spell out the splits for the first couple of months while you're still learning the business. In my company, I pay an entry-level new hire, working with an experienced broker on his deals, out of the company's portion of the fee. The experienced broker can help a new hire, get some assistance, and suffer no loss of his own income.

◆ At what point you can expect the splits to increase to reflect your growing experience. Ask for specifics. Is the benchmark measured in terms of months on the job or business generated? Some new hires hit the ground running and need a smaller time frame to learn the business. If you're tied to a certain number of months, rather than level of expertise, you could be losing money.

Draw Against the Future

Many companies, especially for the first couple of months, will give you a draw against your commission. It will be a minimal amount of money, but it should help your cash flow until you start generating and completing your own deals. Remember: The draw is a loan. You'll have to pay it back out of the commissions you earn.

Ask the owner …

◆ Will he agree to a cash advance? How much and for how long?

◆ How long will he give you to repay the advance? You need to be able to pay it back incrementally, especially in the first few months when your earnings are limited.

◆ Even after you are an experienced mortgage broker, there are still slow times in the business. Can you draw against commission at those times?

Bonus Time

I pay my mortgage brokers a year-end bonus based on the company's overall profit and their personal performance. Each broker and I set goals for how many deals they will close that year. It's based on a realistic appreciation of the housing market, as well as their plans for reaching new clients and bringing in business. If it's a depressed market, then the goals will differ from a period when houses are selling like hotcakes. Bonuses are therefore individualized and vary based on each broker's own record.

I pay holiday bonuses to staff who don't work on commission (loan processors, administrative help). I also pay an incentive to the loan processors if they complete more than a certain number of loan files.

Ask the owner …

◆ What bonuses, if any, are paid, and how they are calculated.

Cash Flow Tricks and Tips

Managing your cash flow is always a tricky business if your earnings are based on commission. Some months you're flush, other months are lean. Here are some ways to smooth out the year financially:

◆ Make a personal budget for the year and forecast your expenses. Include housing expenses, food, clothing, telephone, car (loan and maintenance), medical, long-term debt (student loans, credit card). That way you know the minimal amount of money you need to have each month.

◆ Track your expenses carefully so that you see where you're spending money and places you can cut corners.

◆ As soon as you can, begin a savings account so that you eventually have at least three months of liquidity to tide you over during the slower months. Develop a plan to save. For example, save half of any bonus, and use the other half to pay down bills.

◆ Avoid using cash advances on credit cards to supplement your income. The interest rates are ridiculously high for even brief periods.

◆ Limit the number of credit cards you have. It's better to pay off the balance each month, but if not, pay high-interest debts first, even if the balance is greater on other credit cards.

Heads Up!

Does your company have a probationary period? Be clear about how long it lasts and how you will be evaluated during that time.

In Sickness and in Health

No matter what your age, or how healthy you currently are, you need insurance: health, disability, and life insurance. You need to check what kind of coverage your company provides.

Health Insurance

I offer health insurance coverage to my employees. Even sharing the premium costs with my staff, the coverage is a huge chunk of my operating budget. Unless you are covered under your partner's benefits, lack of health insurance coverage should be a deal breaker for you in deciding whether to join a firm.

Carrying the premiums for an individual health insurance policy is too much of a financial burden. Even if you have to pay a portion of your health insurance, the cost of a group plan is usually significantly lower, and the coverage provided is usually more comprehensive.

Ask the owner:

◆ What percentage of the insurance premium does he pay? What will you have to pay?

◆ Examine the coverage carefully. See how much out-of-pocket expenses you will have to carry; what doctors you can use; any limitations on hospitals you can use.

◆ When does the coverage begin? You may not qualify for coverage for a few months. If so, then pay to continue the health insurance under your previous job (or if you were covered under your parents' health insurance) until your new plan kicks in. Under no circumstances should you go without coverage. Even a simple broken bone can mean thousands of dollars in medical bills.

Disability Insurance

Like many insurance policies, disability insurance is based on a dire "what if" scenario. You may not think you need disability insurance if you're young and healthy—but that's a bet you shouldn't make. A broken leg or a difficult pregnancy could put you on the disabled list and cut your income significantly. As you become more successful, long-term disability insurance, a more expensive option but which provides coverage in case of permanent disability, can be critical. Even though your income is commission-based, you are still eligible for disability insurance.

Ask the owner:

- ◆ Does the company offer short-term disability insurance?

- ◆ When does the policy become effective?

- ◆ At what point in an illness does it begin to provide coverage?

- ◆ How much of your income will it provide in the event of disability?

- ◆ What is the base income it uses?

- ◆ How long is the coverage?

As you become more successful, you may want to consider buying supplemental, long-term disability insurance. Prices vary, so shop around, but expect to pay between one and three percent of your annual income. Don't count on Social Security disability benefits. They are very difficult to qualify for and the income is minimal. To qualify for long-term "own-occupation" (see following bullet) disability policies, insurers may require applicants to have earned at least $50,000 a year for three years.

Look for ...

- ◆ a financially stable insurance company. The number of firms that offer disability insurance is limited, but you want to be sure that the firm you use will be around in the future if you need them. Check out their rating at moodys.com, standardandpoors.com, or ambest.com.

- ◆ non-cancelable insurance. That is becoming more difficult to get, but it guarantees a lock on benefits and rates. The next best is a guaranteed, renewable policy. Avoid conditionally renewable policies, as they are subject to an increase in rates and a change in the conditions required for coverage.

- ◆ an "own-occupation" disability policy. That means that you will be covered if you can't do the principal duties of a mortgage broker, even if you are able to work in some other field.

- ◆ residual or partial disability coverage. This will provide you with income if you've been disabled and you return to work on a reduced schedule. As a mortgage broker, if you're out of work for an extended period of time, you'll have to rebuild your network and await closings in order to get back your income stream. This policy would fill the gap.

- ◆ policies with inflation riders so that the income you would receive keeps pace with the economy.

◆ a policy that has a "future purchase" option. That lets you increase your coverage as your income grows.

Life Insurance

If you don't have a spouse or child dependent on you, then your life insurance needs are less demanding, although it is easier to buy whole-life (permanent) policies when you are younger. Your company may offer a small term policy and if you have no other dependents, then this could be sufficient for your needs.

If you are young and want broader coverage, you should consider term instead of whole-life (permanent) coverage. While term policies provide only death benefits, for a specific number of years, they have much lower premiums for younger, healthy applicants. Over your lifetime, though, whole-life policies are generally cheaper than term.

Ask the owner …

◆ Does he offer a life insurance policy?

◆ Do you need to pay any of the premiums?

◆ Can you take the policy with you if you leave the company?

Retirement Benefits

It may sound premature to discuss your retirement when you have just been offered a job, but you need to plan ahead. I offer my employees the opportunity to participate in a 401(k) retirement account.

A 401(k) is a personal pension plan. You will have the opportunity to decide how much of your earnings you want automatically deducted from your paycheck. Since the contribution is deducted from your earnings before federal, state, and local taxes are taken, you end up paying taxes on a lower amount of money. A 401(k) is a great tax-saver. You don't pay taxes on this until you begin to withdraw money at the time of retirement.

If your company doesn't offer a 401(k) plan, then start your own retirement program. Open a Traditional IRA or Roth IRA and contribute the maximum amount allowable under the law. The tax savings for today are a strong enough incentive to take action, but you're also being smart in planning for your future. For more information, check out the Internal Revenue Service guidelines or individual retirement plans: www.irs.gov/retirement/article/0,,id=137320,00.html.

Ask the owner ...

- ◆ Does he offer a 401(k) program?

- ◆ Does the company match your contribution? Over 80 percent of employers offer to match a percentage or set dollar amount that you put into your 401(k).

Who Pays for What?

As I've mentioned before, sometimes you have to spend money to make money. Promotional giveaways like magnets with the company's name, business cards, professional trade organization membership, networking lunches/dinners—all of these are reasonable expenses and you need to understand how many, if any, of these bills you'll be expected to pick up. For those that you do, you need to speak to a tax professional to see what is deductible.

Did You Know?

Have a separate credit card for business expenses. Whether your company reimburses you or not, it's a smart way to track your business expenses.

I provide my brokers with a wide variety of promotional giveaways. I buy magnets, calendars, pens, all embossed with the company's name. I also provide personalized business cards. I have subscriptions to a wide variety of financial and trade magazines, newsletters, and newspapers that come to the office so that all staffers can read them. I provide each broker with a desktop computer, but they are expected to provide their own laptops. I provide all software. I buy thousands of holiday cards with greetings from the company, and each broker then personalizes them for his own clients and contacts. I underwrite the cost of all open houses. I had a corporate website designed and pay for the server.

I'm always looking for new ways to promote the company and encourage my staff to discuss new ideas. Within reason, I'm willing to underwrite most outreach programs.

Ask the owner ...

- ◆ What business expenses will he underwrite?

And be sure to consult a tax professional about which, if any, business expenses you can deduct.

The Least You Need to Know

◆ Splits should increase as you gain experience, and should be greater for personally generated business.

◆ Consider carefully whether to accept a job without health insurance. The expense may be too high to carry on your own.

◆ Contributing to a 401(k) or other personal retirement plan is important for your future and also an ideal way to help reduce taxes now.

◆ Negotiate which business expenses your company will underwrite.

Part 3

Building Blocks of Success

To succeed as a mortgage broker, you've got to become an expert in the housing market and finance. In this part, I'll help you understand how to analyze economic trends and how they impact your job. Since this is a business that is built on word of mouth, I'll also give you tips on how to develop a strong network of referrals. I'll provide you with advice on the technology and software you'll need. You're definitely going to have to learn how to juggle competing demands in this business, and in this part, you'll learn the best time management tricks to do just that.

Becoming a Market and Financing Expert

In This Chapter

◆ An overview of the two mortgage markets

◆ The economic trends you can't ignore

◆ Financial markets beyond our borders

◆ What's happening in your local housing market

Being a mortgage broker is more than just crunching numbers. You've got to become a financial analyst, studying the local, national, and international economic trends that will impact mortgage rates. You need to understand your own local housing market so you can advise your clients about their eligibility, preferably before they begin shopping for a home in your area.

In this chapter, you'll learn how mortgages are financed and how to interpret the economic trends that affect rates.

The ABCs of the Mortgage Markets

As a mortgage broker, you are helping buyers find financing for their home purchases. Mortgages to home buyers are part of the *primary mortgage market*. These loans, in turn, are sold on the *secondary mortgage market* to investors. By selling the loans, funds are then made available for additional loans to be made in the primary mortgage market. It's a cycle that is critical to a healthy housing economy.

def•i•ni•tion

The **primary mortgage market** makes loans to home buyers. It consists of mortgage originators like commercial banks, savings and loans, credit unions, and so on. The **secondary mortgage market** buys and sells first mortgage trust deeds for investment from primary mortgage lenders through conduits like Freddie Mac, Fannie Mae, and Ginnie Mae, as well as private investment banks.

Let's Back Up a Little

A little history lesson will explain the importance of the primary and secondary mortgage markets. Changes in the underlying financial structure of the mortgage market over the last century have resulted in more home ownership, especially by those who would have previously been excluded.

Prior to the Great Depression, it was much more difficult to afford a home, and the result was that home ownership rates were low. Down payment requirements were about 40 percent of the purchase price and the loan had to be repaid within three to five years! (Contrast that to the current market that permits zero down payment, or more typically 10 to 20 percent, and some mortgages that don't mature for 40 years.)

Until the mid-1970s, mortgage loans were primarily originated and kept in the portfolios of the depository institutions (as well as the portfolios of insurance companies). Typically, a buyer went to his local Savings and Loan Association to get his mortgage. The S&L was then able to fund new mortgages based on its ability to raise funds by managing their portfolios, as well as attracting new depositors and loan applicants. Legislation and regulation encouraged *depository institutions* to confine their loans to the local housing market. In time, however, this resulted in an unbalanced mortgage market with

def•i•ni•tion

Depository institutions are commercial banks, savings and loans associations, savings banks, and credit unions.

some regions having an excess of funds and low rates, and others having meager funds and high rates.

The only way to mitigate this problem was to make the mortgage market less dependent on the depository institutions. But to do that you had to develop a strong secondary mortgage market that made it attractive to investors outside the depository institutions and insurance companies to invest. Mortgage-backed securities became the vehicle for attracting investors.

Enter Fannie, Ginnie, and Freddie

Again step back in time. In 1934, the federal government created the Federal Housing Administration (FHA), to help build or acquire single-family and multi-family properties. (After World War II, its mission was expanded to include urban renewal projects, hospitals, and nursing homes.) The FHA offered insurance against mortgage defaults, which reduced the credit risk for investors. But to get the insurance, the mortgage applicant had to meet certain standards. This is important because it was the first time mortgage terms were standardized—and standardization is essential for pooling mortgages, which is the underlying principal of a secondary mortgage market. (Later the Veterans Administration also insured mortgages.)

The second important change was that the FHA developed a new mortgage design: long-term, self-amortizing, fixed rate mortgage loans. Remember, previously, mortgage loans were short-term which meant that borrowers essentially had balloon payments at the end of five years, usually made by securing a new mortgage. But it also meant an increase in the possibility of default. To craft a liquid secondary market to buy these new FHA mortgages, Congress created a new government-sponsored agency: the Federal National Mortgage Association, Fannie Mae.

It was a start, but there were still problems. In periods of tight money, Fannie Mae couldn't ease the housing crisis. So in 1968, Congress divided Fannie Mae into two organizations: Fannie Mae and Ginnie Mae, the Government National Mortgage Association. Ginnie Mae was to use the "full faith and credit of the U.S. government" to support FHA and VA mortgage markets. In 1970, Congress created the Federal Home Loan Mortgage Corporation, Freddie Mac, to support conventional mortgages, those not insured by the FHA, VA, or the Rural Housing Service.

The secondary mortgage market was then much more appealing to investors. The securities issued by institutions that pool mortgage loans were guaranteed by government (Ginnie Mae) or quasi-government agencies (Fannie Mae and Freddie Mac).

Ginnie Mae securities had the backing of the "full faith and credit of the U.S. government." Fannie Mae and Freddie Mac, while not carrying the exact same backing, are still considered virtually risk-free. In effect, all of these mortgage-backed securities have the same credit risk as U.S. Treasury bonds but offer a higher yield.

Mortgage-Backed Securities

As a mortgage broker, you are interested in mortgage-backed securities because they reflect the current mortgage market. They don't affect mortgage rates, but mirror the strength or weakness of the market and the economy as a whole.

def•i•ni•tion

Securitization is the creation of a security by pooling mortgage loans purchased from originators. These securities are sold as bonds and their value is derived from the original mortgages from which they are created.

Here's how they work. Mortgage loans are purchased from banks, mortgage companies, and other originators, and assembled into pools by a governmental, quasi-governmental, or private entity. Then the entity issues mortgage-backed securities (MBSs) that represent claims on the principal and interest payments made by the borrowers of the loans in the pool. This is called *securitization*.

Most MBSs are issued by the Government National Mortgage Association (Ginnie Mae), the Federal National Mortgage Association (Fannie Mae) and the Federal Home Loan Mortgage Corporation (Freddie Mac). There are also some private institutions, such as brokerage firms, banks, and homebuilders, who securitize mortgages. These are known as "private-label" securities.

Let's take a simplified example of how mortgage-backed securities work.

♦ The home buyer takes out a mortgage from a local bank to purchase a home.

♦ The bank sells the mortgage to an investment banking firm that bundles a group of mortgages into a pool and then creates securities which are sold to a buyer like a pension fund. These securities are guaranteed by Freddie Mac.

♦ The local bank receives the value of the mortgage—which it can lend out to other borrowers.

♦ The home buyer continues to make monthly payments to the bank that originated the mortgage, but the interest and principal payment is passed through to the buyer of the mortgage-backed security.

◆ The local bank receives a small processing fee; the investment firm receives payment by offering a coupon on the bonds that is slightly less than the interest payments on the mortgage; and the securities buyer gets a return that is slightly higher than a corresponding 10-year Treasury note. The securities buyer doesn't own the mortgage, but gets his return from the payments on mortgages.

There is little risk of default since most home mortgages are guaranteed by the Federal Housing Administration.

The International Component

Mortgage-backed securities appeal to institutional investors throughout the world. American real estate is considered a safe, profitable investment. Whereas at one time your local Savings and Loan Association was the primary player in funding home mortgages in a community, today, it's just as likely that it's a foreign institutional investor.

Overseas investors believe that American real estate is a safe and wise investment. On a simple level, it means that while housing and mortgage rates are affected by American economic trends, you have to factor in to your analysis the effect of a strong international secondary mortgage market.

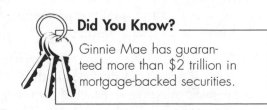

Did You Know?

Ginnie Mae has guaranteed more than $2 trillion in mortgage-backed securities.

The National Economic Trends You Need to Watch

If you talk to three different economists, you'll probably get three different economic forecasts. There is rarely universal agreement on what the various economic markers mean. What you want to do is get a feel for what is being measured by various national indexes and what those portend for the housing and mortgage markets.

For example, while there is not a direct cause-and-effect relationship between a rising unemployment rate and rising mortgage rates, you can see that if the economy is shrinking and layoffs are growing, then the housing market is probably falling, less new housing is being built, and less money is available. However, it's not quite that simple. All this is tempered by the effects of a strong international secondary mortgage market.

The Consumer Price Index

An *index* is the measure of the relative average of a group of items to a base value. An index is used in economics to combine and compare diverse measures. It uses a weighted average rather than a straight arithmetical mean and compares it to a base value or period.

def•i•ni•tion

An **index** is a method of combining and comparing diverse measures to a base value or period. The **Consumer Price Index** measures the change in the cost of basic goods and services in comparison with a fixed base period.

The *Consumer Price Index (CPI)*, as calculated by the federal Bureau of Labor Statistics (BLS), reflects spending patterns for each of two population groups: (1) all urban consumers (CPI-U) and a subset of that, (2) urban wage earners and clerical workers (CPI-W). The all urban group represents about 87 percent of the total U.S. population. It is based on the expenditures of almost all residents of urban or metropolitan areas, including professionals, the self-employed, the poor, the unemployed, retired persons, urban wage earners, and clerical workers. Not included in the CPI are the spending patterns of persons living in rural nonmetropolitan areas, farm families, persons in the armed forces, and those in institutions like prisons or mental hospitals.

The CPI-W subset, urban wage earners and clerical workers, is based on the expenditures of households included in the CPI-U definition that also meet two other requirements: More than one half of the household's income must come from clerical or wage occupations and at least one of the household's earners must have been employed for at least 37 weeks during the previous 12 months. The CPI-W's population represents about 32 percent of the total U.S. population.

The BLS has classified all expenditure items into more than 200 categories, arranged in eight major groups:

♦ Food and beverages (breakfast cereal, milk, coffee, chicken, wine, service meals, and snacks)

♦ Housing (rent of primary residence, owner's equivalent of rent, fuel oil, bedroom furniture)

♦ Apparel (men's shirts and sweaters, women's dresses, jewelry)

♦ Transportation (new vehicles, airline fares, gasoline, motor vehicle insurance)

♦ Medical care (prescription drugs and medical supplies, physicians' services, eyeglasses and eye care, hospital services)

- ◆ Recreation (television, pets and pet products, sports equipment, admissions)

- ◆ Education and communication (college tuition, postage, telephone services, computer software and accessories)

- ◆ Other goods and services (tobacco and smoking products, haircuts and other personal services, funeral expenses)

The CPI does *not* include investment items like stocks, bonds, real estate, and life insurance because these items relate to savings and not to day-to-day consumption. It also can't be used to compare levels of living costs or prices across areas. For example, if a family heats their home with solar heat, but fuel prices are rising more rapidly than other items, the family may experience less inflation than the general population. As the BLS explains, "a national average reflects all the ups and downs of millions of individual price experiences. It seldom mirrors a particular consumer's experience."

Most of the specific CPI indexes have a 1982–1984 reference base. That means the BLS sets the average price level for the 36-month period of 1982, 1983, 1984 as equal to 100. BLS then measures change relative to that period. So an index of 110 means there has been a 10 percent increase in prices since the reference period. An index of 90 means there has been a 10 percent decrease.

The CPI is one measure of inflation. The BLS defines inflation as the process of continuously rising prices (or equivalently, continuously falling value of money). The CPI measures inflation as experienced by consumers in their day-to-day expenses. Other measures such as the Producer Price Index (PPI), the Employment Cost Index (ECI), the BLS International Price Program, and the Gross Domestic Product (GDP) are all indexes that have been developed to measure different aspects of inflation.

How does the CPI impact on mortgage rates? The CPI is one of many indicators of economic trends. During periods of inflation, mortgage rates, like all other prices, tend to rise.

The Producer Price Index

Unlike the Consumer Price Index, which measures price change from the purchaser's perspective, the *Producer Price Index (PPI)* measures change from the perspective of the seller. It is a family of indexes that measures the average change over time in the selling prices

def•i•ni•tion

The **Producer Price Index** measures wholesale price levels in the economy.

received by U.S. producers of goods and services. Over 10,000 PPIs for individual products and groups of products are released each month. PPIs now cover products of virtually every industry in the mining and manufacturing sectors, and are gradually being introduced for the products of industries in the transportation, utilities, trade, finance, and services sectors. Like the CPI, the Producer Price Index has a 1982–1984 reference base.

The PPI differs from the CPI in two important ways: (1) the composition of the set of goods and services, and (2) the types of prices collected. The PPI measures the goods and services of U.S. producers—no imports are counted. The CPI measures goods and services purchased by consumers and includes exports. Furthermore, the price collected for an item in the PPI is the revenue received by its producer. Sales and excise taxes are not included because they don't represent the revenue to the producer. In contrast, sales and excise taxes are included in the price of an item included in the CPI because that is the out-of-pocket expenditure for the consumer.

> **Heads Up!**
>
> When the CPI, PPI, and Unemployment Rate rise, expect to see mortgage rates moving upward as well. That's because these indexes are early reflections of a change in the economic climate.

How does the PPI impact mortgage rates? As an economic indicator, PPIs capture price movements before the retail level (as measured by the CPI). It may foreshadow price changes for businesses and consumers. It can serve as a harbinger of a period of inflation in which mortgage prices may rise.

The Federal Reserve and Interest Rates

The Federal Reserve is the system of federal banks in charge of regulating the U.S. money supply, primarily by buying and selling U.S. securities and by setting the *discount interest rate*. That's the interest rate at which the Federal Reserve lends money to commercial banks. As the cost of money rises to the bank, the increases are passed along in rising consumer loan rates. The Federal Reserve fights inflation by raising the discount rate and decreasing the money supply.

> **def•i•ni•tion**
>
> The **discount interest rate** is set by the Federal Reserve. It is the rate at which commercial banks can borrow money from the Federal Reserve.

How does the discount interest rate affect mortgage rates?

The discount interest rate doesn't directly affect mortgages. Its greatest impact is on short-term loan rates. But as a mortgage broker, you pay attention to the discount interest rate as reflective of the overall direction of the economy. A growing economy, not riddled by inflation, is the best condition for mortgage rates.

The Stock Market

Risk versus reward. That neatly captures the dilemma faced by investors—both individuals and institutions. If the economy is growing, there's greater interest in stocks as an investment. Individuals and institutions are willing to take the risk of investing in stocks with a bigger payoff, rather than in the safer mortgage bond market.

How does the stock market affect mortgage rates?

There is no direct effect, but a rising stock market usually results in falling bond prices because investors are putting their money into the higher risk, higher reward of stocks. When Treasury and mortgage bond prices fall, look for higher mortgage rates. Why? In order to attract investors, the yield rates on these fixed-income securities must rise. When yields rise, mortgage rates, which are linked to yield rates, follow.

Ten-Year Treasury Bills

The U.S. Treasury sells bonds with different maturity rates. Generally the shorter the maturity, the lower the yield because the investor's money is under less risk. The basic idea is that if you tie up your money for a longer period of time, you should be rewarded with a higher yield for taking the higher risk. The investor has no idea what will happen in 30 years, for example, but if his money is tied up that long, he should see a bigger payoff.

The Ten-Year Treasury Bill is the one most associated with fixed mortgage rates. Most mortgages are paid off within 10 years (actually closer to 7½ years), even if they are 30-year mortgages. That's because within 10 years, the borrower generally sells the house or refinances, either way paying off the loan.

Adjustable rate mortgages (ARMs) are generally tied to Treasury Bills of equal length. For example, if the ARM will adjust its rate at the end of five years, it's tied to a Five-Year Treasury Bill.

How does the Ten-Year Treasury Bill affect mortgage rates?

It is the rate that is most closely associated with fixed rate mortgages. As it rises or falls, fixed mortgage rates generally follow.

Employment Numbers

The federal government conducts a monthly survey called the Current Population Survey (CPS) to measure the extent of unemployment in the country. A low unemployment rate, concurrent with strong level of new job creations, are indicators of a healthy economy.

How do the employment numbers affect mortgage rates?

The correlation between the two is not direct, but again gives you an idea of the general state of the economy. A healthy economy, with low unemployment, encourages home buying and investment.

Reading the Local Housing Market

Mortgage brokers need to understand the housing market where they are conducting business. On a very simple level, if the market is booming, hopefully so is your business; if the market is flat, you may need to work harder to get your share and expand your efforts into other communities.

A house appraisal is a key requirement for securing a mortgage. Familiarity with the housing market lets you know ahead of time whether the appraisal of the house's value will be approved. If you are concerned that it won't, then you have the opportunity to discuss possible options.

If there is a downturn in housing prices, owners who opted for "interest only" mortgages may be in serious trouble. For those who chose this type of mortgage because of limited finances, it can be a disaster. As an ethical mortgage broker you want to lay out all the options and explain the risks to your clients. Here's the concern: the payments on certain loans (commonly called "Option ARM" for adjustable rate mortgage) don't cover the full amount of interest due. The unpaid interest is added to the loan balance, effectively increasing the outstanding loan amount over time. These kinds of loans provide the borrower with much lower monthly payments, but the negative *amortization* means they are tacking on tens of thousands of dollars to their original loan. If housing prices drop, the homeowner faces the prospect of a mortgage that is higher than the value of the house.

def•i•ni•tion

Amortization is the gradual elimination of a debt, like a mortgage, with regular fixed payments over a specified period of time.

You need to know who is buying in your market: homeowners or investors. In 2004, nearly one fourth of house purchases were as investments. This phenomenon was primarily concentrated in a few areas. For example, in Las Vegas, 44 percent of home purchases were investments. The problem occurs if there is a hint of a downturn in property values. Owners who live in their homes may ride it out. Investors, who generally have little or no equity in properties, will sell quickly. A disproportionate number of investors versus residents in a community can skew the housing market in a tight economic period.

Mortgage brokers need to put together a complete picture of the area to judge if the housing market is on solid ground. Besides tracking gains in housing prices, you need to know what else is happening in your area: job growth, population growth or decline, median income, and affordability (who can afford to buy in your community).

For example, there is some concern that Boston is a risky housing market. According to PMI Group, a residential mortgage insurer, housing prices in Boston fell between 1992 and 2001, and then showed a relatively modest 7 percent annual appreciation. In contrast, nationally, the median price of an existing home rose 10 percent in the last year, and some areas saw a 15 percent or more jump. But Boston has other problems. The area has lost 200,000 jobs since 2000, and yet housing prices remain high (median home price is $398,000). Experts suggest that the area's housing bubble may soon burst—and as a mortgage broker, you'd want to be on the alert.

To get a good understanding of your housing market, you should …

- develop good working relationships with local realtors and builders.

- study closely real estate ads (online and in newspapers).

- track real estate closings on homes in your area.

- read regularly local and trade newspapers for realtors and mortgage brokers, as well as financial newspapers like the *Wall Street Journal*.

- familiarize yourself with local zoning regulations so that you are prepared for client questions on properties. Check with the local, county, and state zoning boards to get copies of their regulations.

The Least You Need to Know

◆ A strong secondary mortgage market is vital to a healthy primary mortgage market.

◆ Mortgage brokers need to keep track of national economic trends in order to forecast the health of the housing market and the future of mortgage rates.

◆ Mortgage brokers should familiarize themselves with the housing market they service.

◆ A disproportionate number of investor owners (versus residents) in a community can skew the housing market in a tight economy.

Chapter 10

Networking 101

In This Chapter

- ◆ Networking is more than collecting business cards
- ◆ Community groups that help others and you
- ◆ Volunteer opportunities that build business relations
- ◆ Working with realtors

The mortgage broker business is heavily dependent on referrals. You want to build a network of connections in the community you serve. You want your name to be the one that comes instantly to mind when someone asks "Do you know a mortgage broker?"

You clearly want to build good relationships with the real estate agents in your area, but they're not the only ones who will serve as the conduit to your business. Your company's name could just as easily pop up because someone sees it on the back of their kid's Little League t-shirt. Sponsoring a team, which can cost a few hundred dollars, brings incalculable name recognition and goodwill.

You're a professional who knows the business inside and out. But you need clients to succeed. This chapter shows you how to build a broad network of relationships.

Managing Your Networking Contacts

The quality of the networking connections you make is more important than the quantity. But you won't know quality until you've networked a lot. A stack of business cards in your drawer doesn't tell you anything. In fact, it doesn't matter if you gave out a ream of your own cards if there hasn't been any thought behind your distribution system.

The first rule of networking is to develop a method of organizing your contacts so that they're easily retrievable. Take the time to input the data into your computer and download it to your PDA. Ideally, you will record the following information: name, address, telephone numbers (including cell), e-mail address, company name, position, where you met them, and if there is a connecting link.

You want to be able to cross-file the data. For example, when you file Mary Smith, real estate agent at Jones and Taylor Agency, of Newburgh, New York, if you pulled up a list of realtors, her name would appear; if you pulled up a list of real estate agencies, the firm would appear; if you pulled up a list of businesses in Newburgh, the company would be listed. If you don't bother to file your contacts, then you might as well throw away the business cards you carefully collected.

Going Beyond Hello

Effective networking is knowing how to take advantage of an opportunity. While exchanging business cards collects the information, you need to be able to make a people connection as well. Not quite the love connection of a match service, but you do want to make a good impression on whomever you meet.

Learning to make small talk is an art. Even if you're not totally comfortable, here are some icebreakers that will jump-start the conversation. The key is to ask open-ended questions that can't be answered with a simple "yes" or "no." For example:

1. Tell me about your company.

2. How long have you been in business?

3. How can I help you?

4. What is the best way to refer someone to you?

5. Do you draw most of your clients from this area?

But remember, you must be prepared to answer similar questions. You want to get to know other professionals, but the key is to have an opportunity to let them get to know you.

Practice a brief explanation of what a mortgage broker does and how your services are different from a lender. Try to keep it light, but specific. For example, I always point out that using a mortgage broker rather than a lender to find a loan is like going to an ice cream store. Your firm offers 31 flavors; a lender is limited just to vanilla. It's not that vanilla is bad, it's that you might find something that suits you better if you had a choice.

> **Heads Up!**
>
> Be a good listener. You have to really pay attention to the person you just met to hear about their interests and abilities. If you're too busy scanning the room for a better prospect, you're likely to miss the valuable resource you have in front of you.

Be careful about how you differentiate your company from your competition. It makes people uncomfortable if you badmouth other local firms. Make your case without diminishing others. Your reputation will stand on its own.

Follow-up is essential. Make time within a day or two of first meeting, to send an e-mail or a quick call to those contacts that you thought were promising. You want to make the connection while it's all still fresh.

First Stop: Business-Oriented Community Groups

Your company may be the member or sponsor of a variety of activities in the community you serve, but you need to put a face behind the firm name. Some local civic groups have traditionally served as an opportunity to network with other local leaders, as well as serving their community.

Volunteer to attend meetings of the local Chamber of Commerce. Other groups to consider joining are the local chapters of:

- Rotary International, www.rotary.org
- Lions Club International, www.lionsclubs.org
- The Benevolent and Protective Order of the Elks of the USA, www.elks.org
- Kiwanis International, www.Kiwanis.org

There are usually monthly program meetings of these groups, and their fundraising efforts meet both local, national, and international needs. It's not enough to simply show up for the weekly or monthly lunches. Volunteer for committees or be responsible for a program or fundraiser. You want to build the reputation of your company and yourself. You want to be known as a good resource and someone to consult for ideas, names of other workers, and suggestions. This keeps you and your company visible. When people see that you're dependable as a volunteer, it teaches them that you're dependable in your business capacity as well.

You might also consider joining the local chapter of Toastmasters, www.toastmasters. org, to develop your facility in public speaking, as well as to network with other local business professionals.

These groups are an opportunity for you to make contact with the other business leaders of the region. You want to know what is happening economically to the area and any changes that other businesses are planning.

For Women Only

In addition to community groups, women mortgage brokers might also join groups aimed directly at female business professionals. To find a group in your area, run a web search for women business leaders + the name of your city.

While it's important to be involved in civic groups, many women find a more supportive, noncompetitive atmosphere in all-female groups. Groups that are co-ed, some women believe, tend to be too political, competitive, and sports-oriented.

Margarita Quishuis, former director of the Women's Technology Cluster, a San Francisco-based mentoring organization for women-owned businesses, explained that in all-female groups, women "aren't afraid to share their fears and anxieties … while many women in business agree this would be sudden death with male business associates."

Women also find these all-female networking groups are a wonderful resource for advice on all the usual business-related concerns, but with the bonus of being able to openly discuss the ways to bridge the chasm between men and women in the workplace.

Don't limit yourself to only female networking clubs, but don't exclude yourself either. Quishuis advises to "never rely on only one social circle for your contacts."

If your area doesn't have an all-women's business professional group, this is an opportunity for leadership on your part. Start one.

Minority Networking Groups

There are also networking groups for African Americans, Hispanics, Asians, and Native Americans. A local web search will help you discover organizations in your area. Their value is similar to that found by women in all-female networking organizations. It's an opportunity to encourage career development, discuss common problems, and build an important business network. They aren't the only groups you should belong to, but they are a valuable opportunity to reach out to others in a noncompetitive, supportive environment.

Did You Know?

Always keep a stash of your business cards in your wallet; always carry backup materials about your company in your briefcase.

Beyond the Boardroom

Some of the best networking opportunities take place away from the traditional meet-and-greet business lunches. I've met clients and made professional contacts while pursuing my hobby with the Sports Car Club of America.

Look for opportunities to get involved in the community in other venues. What are your interests? Find a community group that supports them. For example, volunteer for the executive board of the Little League or Soccer League. Or offer to chair the Red Cross blood drive or the holiday gift drive for the underprivileged. Meeting other community leaders outside the normal channels is an equally valuable way to make connections and give others an insight into your character.

Professional Associations

Join professional organizations and network with peers. The National Association of Mortgage Brokers, www.namb.org, is the only national trade association representing the mortgage broker industry. With 46 state affiliates and more than 24,000 members, NAMB promotes the industry through programs and services such as education, professional certification, and government affairs representation. NAMB members subscribe to a code of ethics and best lending practices that foster integrity, professionalism, and confidentiality when working with consumers.

You should become an affiliate member of your area's board of realtors. Affiliate membership is open to professionals in allied industries who are not actively engaged in the real estate brokerage business.

Similarly, you may want to become an affiliate member of your local chapter of the Appraisal Institute, www.appraisalinstitute.org. This is the trade organization of home appraisers.

Realtor and Builder Networking

Real estate agents and builders are key to connecting to home buyers. There are two kinds of open houses: those targeted to buyers and those targeted to other agents. Offer to provide refreshments for both kinds of events, in exchange for permission to sit in the house with your materials and talk to prospective buyers or agents.

But there is another kind of networking that helps real estate agents and you. Offer to host a coffee and dessert program for all the agents of a real estate company to provide them with an overview of the current mortgage market and your projections for the future. You've got to be thoroughly prepared for these meetings as you're talking to other housing professionals.

I prefer to build a strong, exclusive relationship with one agency so that I'm the go-to mortgage company for those realtors. You may prefer to spread yourself thinner and offer your services to several companies. Another option is to reach out to another agency or builder that is not being served by another broker in your firm.

The Least You Need to Know

♦ Keep up to date your filing system for managing your contacts so that they are well-organized and easily accessible.

♦ Before you go to any networking events, develop a brief description of your job as a mortgage broker to answer the question, "What do you do?".

♦ Women mortgage brokers may find all-female business groups offer support and advice in a noncompetitive environment. But women brokers should also be active in other co-ed community groups.

♦ Join organizations like the National Association of Mortgage Brokers to meet peers and support common professional goals.

Chapter 11

Get Connected

In This Chapter

- ◆ Technology simplifies and organizes your business
- ◆ Three products you can't live without
- ◆ Basic home office equipment
- ◆ Technology insurance and security

The mortgage business is rapidly becoming a paperless industry. While people skills are critical to becoming a successful mortgage broker, if you're not comfortable using a computer and other assorted gadgets—get over it. Your company office is just one place where you'll be working. You need to have the ability to work wherever you are. You need to be able to access current rates, return calls, check files, network, draft letters, and answer e-mail, whether you're at a realtor open house, in your car, or at a client's office or home.

You don't have to work 24/7, but you should always be connected. I like gadgets more than most, but these aren't toys. Computers, cell phones, and handheld organizers all let you work smart and fast.

In this chapter, you'll get an overview of how to use technology effectively to streamline, simplify, and optimize your time and work.

Cellular-ly Speaking

Choosing a cell phone for business isn't about color, ring tones, or games. This is probably your most important business tool, although it's a close call with your laptop and PDA. Cell phones have essentially eliminated the need for a pager.

Cell Phone Etiquette

Cell phone etiquette is more than just good manners. It's a reflection of you as a professional. Nobody likes a boor, and talking loudly on your phone in a restaurant, or not switching to the vibrate mode for your ringer when in a meeting, is just bad form. Remember:

- Never take a call during a business meeting.

- Maintain a 10-foot zone from others when talking on your cell.

- Keep business calls brief and to the point.

- Use an earpiece in noisy locations so you can hear the amplification and modulate your own voice.

- Tell callers where you are when on a cell phone so they can anticipate possible disconnections.

Do You Need a Cell Phone and a PDA?

If you're going to invest in a Personal Digital Assistant (PDA)—which I think you should—do you still need a cell phone? At this point in time, I'm going to say yes, you still need both. I'm the first to admit that I've got the fastest thumbs on earth from all the typing I do on my Blackberry, but I'm not ready to give up my cell phone yet. (Palm, Handspring, Blackberry, and Treo are all PDA brands.)

Heads Up!

Being able to discuss business anywhere doesn't mean you should. You need to be discreet and remember that when in public, you don't know who is listening to your end of the conversation and what they can do with the information.

Now part of my rationale is the suspenders and belt theory. I want some backup in case the network of either my cell phone or PDA is down. I also want an alternative if I lose one of the gadgets. I figure that would be some seriously bad karma if I lose both on the same day. I can insure for the loss of either unit, but by having backups in place, I can cover the loss of the data.

Here are some other reasons to have both:

◆ "Smart" phones that do many of the same functions as a PDA are very expensive. Incompatible technology among smart phones means if you switch carriers, you may not be able to take your smart—expensive—phone with you. You'll be able to take your number, but the phone itself probably will be unusable. If you buy a generic Treo that can be used with almost every carrier (but not all), you will probably forfeit the deals and rebates normally offered by a cell phone provider to get you to sign up. Currently, the cost of these multifunctional phones is high, as are the plans that support them.

◆ If you lose your smart phone, then you have neither a phone nor a PDA.

◆ I find the size of smart phones too bulky. Smart phone screens are smaller than PDA screens, and size matters. I think the size and weight of my PDA is easy to use, and coupled with a lightweight cell phone, very convenient to carry around.

No question that the technology is moving fast, and soon it will probably be one gadget for all functions. But for now, I keep a cell phone and PDA in my pockets.

Don't Cheap Out

Having just suggested that smart phones are too expensive, I'm going to say that you need to invest in a good-quality cell phone. You need to be able to reach—and be reached by—current and potential clients, the loan processors in your office, lenders, realtors, contractors, appraisers, title companies, attorneys, and more. A missed call is money lost.

◆ Look for a phone that uses lithium-ion batteries. They last longer, weigh less, and give better performance than nickel-metal-hydride batteries. Ideally you want a phone that has a rated talk time of five hours ($3\frac{1}{2}$ hours minimum).

◆ In addition to the desktop charger that comes with the phone, buy a charger that feeds off your car lighter socket to take advantage of travel time.

◆ Make sure the address book can handle at least 600 names (preferably 1000), with multiple entries per contact. Some phones permit you to add additional info like e-mail addresses, website URLs, and street addresses. Having all the information at your fingertips is always helpful. Get a cell phone that has the ability to sync with your PC. This avoids having to type in the data and makes updating easy for your cell phone, PC, and PDA.

◆ Conference calling is another helpful feature. It reduces the number of phone calls you need to make if you can get all the parties on the line at the same time. For example, sitting in my car on my way to a closing, I held a quick conference call with the bank underwriter and Bill K, one of my clients, who was buying his first house. Bill had recently bought the small printing company where he'd previously been employed. The lender was concerned about the profit and loss statement for the current year. Bill explained that because of the sale, the previous owner had allowed some of the older contracts to elapse. But within the last two months, new contracts had been signed, two of which were for multiple years. I suggested that Bill submit copies of the contracts. The underwriter agreed that if the documentation supported the explanation, he'd approve the loan. It was a 15-minute conference call with me sitting in the parking lot of a shopping center that saved the deal.

The Bluetooth Solution

Named for the tenth-century Viking king Herald Bluetooth (who says geeks don't have a good sense of humor?), Bluetooth is a short-range wireless technology that simplifies multiple tasks. You can leave your phone in your pocket or briefcase and still be connected using a Bluetooth headset. No wires! You can exchange contact and scheduling info with other Bluetooth-enabled phones or print directly to a Bluetooth printer (must be relatively nearby). Best of all, it gives your laptop or PDA wireless high-speed Internet access via your Bluetooth phone.

Personal Digital Assistant

Being a mortgage broker is not for the faint of heart. You have to believe in yourself, trust your judgment, and be able to multitask. Your days are chock-full of appointments, follow-ups, calls, letters, cajoling, networking, problem solving, marketing, and paperless paperwork. You need help and without sounding like a walking advertisement for PDAs, that's just what I'm going to do. My PDA is my office in my pocket.

With it I can keep tabs on interest rates (and notify clients if I think they need to lock in), send and respond to e-mails, text message, check websites, and organize my calendar. I use it to take notes at meetings (you need to be comfortable with the miniscule keyboards, but practice makes perfect).

There's a huge range of PDAs available and more coming on the market. You need to test-drive the different models to find one that feels comfortable to use, isn't too heavy, and easily syncs with your computer.

> **Did You Know?**
>
> Quick time saver! Be sure to load a program to track expenses on your PDA. You may be able to deduct office and travel expenses on your tax return (check with a tax professional). This will simplify your bookkeeping, although you will still need to save receipts to document expenses.

Computers

If you aren't comfortable with computers, then you need to find another profession. You will help clients complete and submit applications online, send and receive information over the Internet, do online research, keep track of the status of each mortgage by checking computer files, and much more. Computers will simplify many of your tasks, and probably drive you crazy sometimes when you hit a glitch.

When you first join your firm, you'll want to know if they provide you with a computer(s), what software is already loaded, and what training you'll receive (see Chapter 8).

I recommend a laptop as an integral part of your mobile office. I use mine as my primary computer so that I always have the most current information with me. I do a daily download of data from my laptop to the desktop computer in my office to keep both as a backup and so that others in the office can access the information as needed. I also synchronize with my PDA—and yes, this is the boring stuff, but absolutely necessary.

> **Did You Know?**
>
> Keep a basic computer reference book on hand to troubleshoot problems. *The Complete Idiot's Guide to Computer Basics* (Alpha Books), now in its third edition, by Joe Kraynak, is a great primer for tech novices and even those who think they're pretty computer savvy.

Just to be clear, synchronizing databases happens when you connect two pieces of equipment (for example, laptop and PDA, laptop and office computer), and electronically compare the information on each. A program will then automatically update both machines.

Which Laptop Is Right for You?

Laptops come in different weights, sizes, processor speeds, and memory. Buy the best you can afford, but with the full knowledge that tomorrow a new model will be available that will be faster, lighter, and able to do more. But the fact is, generally speaking, you don't need it to do much more. Most laptops are more than adequate to handle the mortgage broker software, word processing, and Internet functions that you'll require. If you don't overload your computer with games, music, downloads of movies, and so on—if you treat your laptop as a piece of office equipment—then don't worry about the built-in obsolescence of every computer.

But there are a couple of tips that I've found important in choosing a laptop:

- You're going to be lugging around the laptop, so make it as light and thin as you can afford.

- Be sure your laptop is wi-fi (wireless) compatible. This will give you access to the Internet in a wide variety of settings, including many corporate offices, restaurants, and airports.

- A long battery life is key to effective use of a laptop. Look for laptops that allow you to add an extra battery. Conserve the battery by plugging in when possible.

- Invest in a warranty/service contract. Laptop repairs are expensive.

- Check the availability of technical support by the laptop manufacturer. You're looking for a manufacturer that provides 24/7 support.

- Avoid laptops with built-in components. These are difficult to upgrade.

Did You Know?

By 2006, there are expected to be 89,000 public wi-fi network access points and more than 99 million wi-fi users worldwide.

Software for the Mortgage Broker

Your laptop should be loaded with all the software that you would find on your office computer. That includes:

- Copies of the mortgage broker software, such as Calyx, Contour, or Genesis, that your office uses. These software packages generate the following forms: Fannie Mae Uniform Residential Loan Application (forms 1003 and 1008), disclosure statements, authorization to release information, Truth in Lending document, Good Faith Estimate.

◆ Software program, like TCalc, that provides additional financial calculators. These include:

Rent vs. Buy—allows you to compare the costs of renting a residence and buying a house.

Mortgage Qualification Calculator—shows you how much income a borrower needs to buy a home, based on income and other factors.

Mortgage Payment Calculator—displays the mortgage payment for the term of a loan.

Refinance Calculator—helps borrower determine if it's the right time to refinance.

> **Heads Up!**
>
> Pay for expertise when you need it. If you need to hire a computer techie to teach you how to use the software programs, sync the programs between your laptop, office mainframe, and PDA, or install new software, do it. It's a good use of time and money. For additional computer training, check your local continuing education programs, community colleges, and private companies.

Debt Consolidation Calculator—shows borrower how to reduce monthly payments and save money with a home equity loan or refinance.

Monthly Payment Calculator—allows you to explore the outcome of changes to the loan balance, mortgage term, and interest rate on the monthly principal and interest payments.

◆ Word processing program. Check to see which program the office uses. Most businesses prefer Microsoft Word, but you also want to know which version so that you can sync with your office.

◆ A browser for Internet access. Check to see how you access the Internet when in a wireless location.

◆ Password manager. This is software that remembers the passwords for all the sites you contact. Each lender will require a password in order to access their site. These passwords expire at different times, and you're not permitted to use the same password twice. This software will prompt you with the correct password for each site. I use Outlook Express Password Recovery Master, but there is other software that does the same job.

◆ Firewall, antivirus, antispam protection, spyware protection. You need to protect your files with the most current antivirus protection, as well as a strong firewall to keep out hackers. You may need to consult a computer techie to make sure that you can access the company's files via your laptop. Sometimes the company security firewall makes remote accessing difficult. Given the nature of the information you have for clients, the need to protect their privacy is paramount.

◆ Automatic backup. Your company will probably have a built-in automatic daily data backup with information downloaded to a secure location. You need to develop your own backup system for your laptop. I think you should do it on a daily basis, if possible, but certainly no more than a week should go by between backups. Whether you subscribe to an automatic system or backup using CDs, zip drives, or even just floppy disks, the possibility of not being able to retrieve data lost is incalculable.

Heads Up!

I use an online, off-site, automatic backup system for my company's files. The backup is daily, at night (after office hours). Off-site is critical because in the event of fire or other disaster, no matter how many disks or zip drives you've used to back up, if the data is on-site, it's likely to be lost.

◆ PowerPoint. This program allows you to create and present programs with music and photographs, for use with realtors, builders, contractors, lenders, and clients.

◆ Excel. This program allows you to develop spreadsheets to track clients, loans, lenders, and so on.

◆ Accounting and check writing. You'll want a good program to manage your business accounts and keep clear records for tax purposes. These programs allow you to itemize as you go so you'll have a clear printout at tax time.

Home/Car Office Equipment

To complete your home office, mobile and fixed, there are a few other pieces of equipment you'll need.

Printers

This is a tough call, but I'm going to suggest you need both a printer for your home office and a portable one.

Manufacturers will often include a color printer as part of a package deal for new computers. Keep it at home.

The portable printer is an expense that is debatable but probably worth it. You will be on the road a lot and you'll want the ability to print applications, information sheets, PowerPoint pages, driving directions, web pages, and the like.

Look for these features in a portable printer:

◆ The lighter, the better. Portable printers range from two to five pounds, plus battery and paper. You're lugging enough already, so cut the weight if you can.

◆ You want a printer that can be battery operated, if necessary. It costs a little more, but the flexibility is worth it.

◆ A model with a Bluetooth adapter that permits you to print wirelessly is a good investment. You may be able to print directly from your Bluetooth-enabled cell phone.

Scanner, Copier, and Fax Machine

While your company office will probably have all these machines, it's worth it to have access to them at home as well. There are multipurpose machines that combine all three of these functions. Just a small heads up that sometimes combining so many functions limits the quality of the specific elements. Also, with prices coming down on all these products, you may find it cheaper to purchase them individually. Check *Consumer Reports* for product reviews.

Heads Up!

You may not need a free-standing fax machine, just the ability to get and receive faxes. Here's how. You can subscribe to a service that assigns you a local fax number. But faxes are actually forwarded to you as e-mail attachments. You can also send faxes from your computer (even your laptop) so that you have fax ability wherever you are. For under $10 a month (plus activation fee), you have the ability to fax or receive up to 100 pages a month—all tax deductible as a business expense.

Similarly, you want to be able to scan in documents and transmit them via e-mail, which a scanner will facilitate. Finally, for mass copies you'll head for the office copy machine or Kinko's, but it's helpful to be able to make single copies of documents at home.

You'll also need some peripherals and accessories to make your portable home office work. Make sure you carry extension cords and adapter plugs, power cable, and paper. Spend time investigating which carrying case works best to hold your laptop, portable printer, files, and accessories.

The Least You Need to Know

- ◆ Invest in the best laptop you can afford.

- ◆ Given the state of the technology, you should still have separate cell phones and PDAs.

- ◆ Hire a computer professional to help you learn and manage the software and technology you need.

- ◆ Printer and fax access in your portable office will permit you to work as effectively when you're on the road as when you're in the office.

Chapter **12**

Time Is Money

In This Chapter

- ◆ Costing out your time helps you prioritize
- ◆ Organize to maximize
- ◆ Toxic or pointless business relationships
- ◆ Spending money to make money

I'm taking an entire chapter to talk about time management, because it's that important. I know I keep telling you how busy you'll be as a mortgage broker, but I worry that you think I'm exaggerating. But if you're as successful as I know you want to be, then you're going to need some way to squeeze more minutes out of the day.

I've always got at least 30 deals in the hopper. My calendar is stuffed with realtor open houses, business lunches, lender meetings, realtor education sessions, and other networking opportunities. I've also got to make time for marketing, keep up with industry research, plus all the details of running a business with a staff of a dozen people … and by the way, my family is my first priority and I love to race cars. I'm not giving up any of it, so I've developed ways to work smarter, not less.

Time Management Saves $$$$

There are five basic goals of learning to use your time wisely:

1. To help you work more effectively and efficiently.

2. To determine which tasks are important to your business and which can be dropped or handed off.

3. To increase the amount of time you have for work (and play).

4. To control the distractions that waste time and interrupt your flow.

5. To reduce stress.

If organizing your time well makes such a difference, why doesn't everyone do it?

◆ Not everyone knows time management or organizational skills

◆ Some people insist that they work best when in crisis mode or under deadline

◆ They're too lazy

But don't fool yourself. I've certainly pulled my share of all-nighters and have worked three weeks straight without a day off. Am I at my best under those circumstances? Nope, not even close. For those who thrive on tight deadlines and crisis management, that only works for short bursts. As a way of doing business on a regular basis, it's ineffective. To be successful, you've got to be able to think clearly, make strategic decisions, and argue effectively. Overtired and burnt out are two conditions that are counterproductive.

Did You Know?

According to the Center for Religion, Ethics and Social Policy at Cornell University, on average, Americans work nearly nine full weeks (350 hours) longer than Western Europeans do.

Working Americans average a little over two weeks of vacation per year. Europeans average five or six weeks. Thirty-seven percent of women earning less than $40,000 get no paid vacation at all.

Cost Out Your Time

One helpful exercise will help you prioritize your time. Figure out your hourly pay. When you know what an hour of your time costs you, it will be easier to determine if a task is worth the effort or not. It might be something that you should hire someone else to do for you. That's one of the reasons we have loan processors in our office. They handle much of the necessary backup paperwork, while the mortgage brokers are working directly with clients and starting on the next deal.

But also remember, there's not always an immediate payoff for time spent. Here's an example, and it's happened more times than I can count. One Sunday, I spent the entire afternoon sitting in a realtor open house for a really lovely, new 4-bedroom ranch with a swimming pool. Price? $750,000. A young couple came in to look around. The realtor showed them the house, then the couple stopped in the kitchen where I'd set up my handouts, my business cards, and of course, some coffee and donuts. Business rule #1: Buyers travel on their stomach. Offer free food and they will come.

We chatted. It was quickly apparent that this couple was just spending the afternoon wandering through open houses for fun. They weren't interested in buying, although I ran their figures through some scenarios to see what they could afford, which quite frankly wasn't much. They each took one of my business cards and I went home that day without any new clients or, for that matter, any donuts. Three weeks later I got a call from someone whose name I didn't recognize. Turned out he was the woman's boss who was about to buy a house (more expensive than the one where I'd met them) and she had highly recommended me. Who knew chocolate glazed donuts with sprinkles could be so effective?

My point, and I do have one, is that figuring out how much you earn per hour is a starting point. But don't give up an activity just because you don't see immediate results.

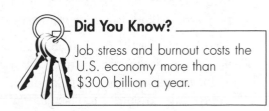

Did You Know?

Job stress and burnout costs the U.S. economy more than $300 billion a year.

Here's a simplified way of looking at this.

There are about 200 workdays a year—and that's just using the usual Monday–Friday, 37.5 hour workweek. That's about 1,500 hours in a year.

Now calculate your hourly rate—in two ways. First, what you actually earned this year; then, what you hope to earn within 3 years. For example, if you earn or hope to earn $60,000 a year, you're making $40 an hour!

The Pareto Principle (80/20 Rule)

There's a difference between being busy and being effective. You need to focus on the important things. You could work 12 hours straight, skip lunch and dinner, and still not accomplish what needed to be done that day to earn a living.

There's a theory called the Pareto Principle, or the 80/20 rule. Essentially it says that 80 percent of consequences stem from 20 percent of causes. When applied to business, it's interpreted to mean 80 percent of unfocused effort generates only 20 percent of results. Conversely, the other 80 percent of results are generated by the focused 20 percent of effort.

Time Management for Mortgage Brokers

There are a ton of time management books on the market, but nary a one that is written just for the mortgage broker. So I'm giving you my best tips for making your day work smoother and more efficiently, given the realities of a complex business.

Reading Effectively

On a daily basis, I'm confronted with loads of material that I have to wade through, and much of it is technical. Every day I read the *Wall Street Journal*, review the latest reports from the Federal government on the indexes I follow (see Chapter 9), study new mortgage regulations from Fannie Mae, Freddie Mac, or state boards, check the current interest rates from the 40+ lenders I routinely use, and learn about the latest loan products that these companies are offering. Of course, I also need to read *The New York Times*, as well as my local community newspaper, plus the realtor publications and mortgage industry newsletters.

Here's what I've learned about reading technical stuff. First, it's deadly dull. There's no attempt at any literary turn of phrase or entertainment value. It's the information, and if it's a government regulation, it's in legalese. I need to understand this material, but it's easy to skim it too fast and miss the important details that make a difference.

This book is written for busy people. There's a preview of what's ahead at the start of every chapter, a summary at the end of the most important points covered, a detailed Table of Contents so you can find what you need, and a complete index so you can zero in on specific topics.

But since most publications aren't as well organized, here's how I handle complicated, technical material.

◆ Set aside a specific time for reading. I have to read technical material in the morning when I'm fresh. The stuff is tough to get through and there's no chance of me remembering the important info after a long day. I take 45 minutes each morning to read before I go in to the office. Figure out when you're most awake and aware, then make reading/education a permanent part of your schedule.

◆ Before reading, figure out the key points you want to know. For example, if it's a news release from the Bureau of Labor Statistics on the Consumer Price Index, you want to know not only whether it went up or down, but what specific costs, if any, spiked or declined sharply. Those numbers will give you an insight into the future of the housing market. Let's assume that the energy index rose, you know that fuel prices continue to rise and stay high, and it will impact the cost of housing materials and construction. It also tells you that buyers will have to factor in the cost of the commute from your community.

◆ Don't get hung up on details, unless you have to. Obviously you have to remember the details of new loan products, but for economic trends, you're looking at the overall picture, not the exact numbers.

◆ Underline and make notes in the margin as you read. It's like when you were in school—those steps help you remember the info. Mark any terms, names, or companies you want to look up.

◆ Summarize at the top. For new regulations, descriptions of loan products, and technology manuals, make your own cheat sheet at the top of the page summarizing the pertinent info.

◆ Read and toss. Most magazines and newspapers can be tossed right after you finish reading them. The information you read will quickly be dated. So why do I want you to underline and make notes? Because it's a way of remembering what you read. You don't have the time to file articles, so rather than building a bigger and bigger file, toss them.

◆ If you have a pile of material, start with the most recent publications, then skim and toss the earlier versions. Most of the info will have been updated often; the info in the article has become old news.

Keep in mind that reading effectively will help you wade through and better understand technical and often dense material.

Taming the E-mail Monster

I know this is becoming a paperless industry, but it doesn't mean that you can't be inundated with "virtual" paper. The inbox of your e-mail account will be routinely swamped. If you don't filter and control it, the odds of missing an important message are sky high.

First rule: Don't mix business and pleasure.

With all the info from lenders, realtors, appraisers, title companies, industry sources, and so on, that will be flooding your inbox, you don't need to mix in jokes from friends or news from Mom. Keep a personal e-mail account and use that.

Master Outlook Express. This e-mail program is designed to organize, filter, file, and much more. It's probably one of the most underutilized software tools, but one that can save you time and money. For example, you can create multiple inboxes so that by setting "rules," for incoming mail, messages from individual lenders can go to their own inboxes. All newsletters can go to another inbox. The goal is to declutter your inbox. When you have hundreds of e-mail messages in your inbox, the temptation is to hit delete, increasing your risk of missing important info.

Less is more. While a single opening line of pleasantry is fine, learn the art of pith. Keep your messages to the point and focused. Run a spell check before hitting send. It makes you look less professional if there are typos in your mail.

Did You Know?

More than a quarter of all e-mail a company receives is spam or junk mail. According to a survey by the research firm Public Opinion Strategies, 9 out of 10 office workers would support legislation to can (e-mail) spam.

Schedule e-mail. Set aside a few times a day to check e-mail, rather than responding to every ping. It's disruptive to your concentration and focus (and an easy way to procrastinate). Be sure to include checking e-mail when out of town. The backup if you miss even a day can be overwhelming.

Use your PDA to check e-mail when out of the office. You can take care of routine e-mail while waiting for a meeting to start.

Telephone Tag and Other Wastes of Time

The telephone is a lifeline for mortgage brokers—and a huge waste of time, too.

When possible, set telephone appointments to avoid playing telephone tag. When you do have to leave a message, state a convenient time for callbacks so that you don't continue to swap voice mail messages.

Organize your thoughts before calling so that you can leave a thoughtful, specific voice mail message. Suggest that they leave the answers to your questions on your voice mail or contact you via e-mail if it would be easier.

Let your answering machine/voice mail pick up calls while you're in meetings or trying to concentrate. Don't be a slave to your telephone.

Time management expert and author Kate Kelly (*Organize Yourself!*, John Wiley & Sons, 2005) also suggests:

◆ Before making a call, make notes on what you need to cover and have materials you'll need at hand.

◆ Take notes as the call progresses so that you don't forget the details of what was decided.

◆ Establish at the outset of a call how long you have to talk. "I've got to go into a meeting in five minutes, but I wanted to check in with you first." This is especially helpful for long-winded contacts.

Here are six tips that will give the customer the message that he's called the right office:

1. Answer the phone by the third ring. No kidding. This may sound simple but more than three rings and the caller moves on to the next name on the list.

2. Put a person on the phone. Don't you just want to scream when you call a business and get trapped in an automated telephone nightmare? Don't subject your customers to that. Answer the phone yourself or have someone answer it for you. You want to establish a human touch to your business right off the bat.

3. Program your answering machine to work for you. When you can't answer the phone, make sure your answering machine message sounds professional. You want to give your callers pertinent information about your business, and most

importantly, the assurance that you'll call back within 24 hours—tops. If you can be reached by cell phone or pager, give those numbers. Update your outgoing message as needed. If your business will be closed for the holiday, change the recording and add that info.

4. Your voice speaks volumes. Answer the phone with a warm, enthusiastic tone (and train your office staff to do the same). Announce the name of your company, your own name, and then add a friendly, "how can I help you?" Remember, at this point, you're only a voice at the other end of the line. This is the first impression your caller gets of you and your business. Make it count.

5. Speakerphones send the wrong message. Callers recognize the tinny, distant voice that speakerphones produce—and the message is crystal clear: "I'm busy and doing something else while talking to you." If you want to free up your hands while answering calls, get a good-quality headset. Only use a speaker-phone when you need another person in the room to be part of the conversation at your end.

6. Return calls immediately. You want to get a reputation for being available. Make it your policy to return business calls within one day, preferably sooner. If you're not available, your competition probably is.

Toxic Business Relationships

Difficult business relationships complicate your life and can detract from your success. But they're also a fact of life. Coping with vendors and clients who are unresponsive, disorganized, or incompetent adds stress to a stress-filled job. Co-workers who take the "dog eat dog" concept too literally can make going to work a nightmare.

The sections that follow describe some tips for resolving common difficulties.

Clueless, Noxious Clients

This is a service business. Dealing with clients who don't "get it," no matter how many times you've explained it, is frustrating. Dealing with clients who would try the patience of a saint is par for the course. Your goal is to keep them as clients, while minimizing their impact on your blood pressure.

- ◆ Set clear expectations about what documentation or information they need to provide and the due dates, preferably in writing. Have a check-off system so that you both agree when they've completed their responsibilities. You can't chance that their memories will be reliable.

♦ If the phone calls and/or e-mails are becoming obsessive, suggest a specific time when you'll be able to talk to them, as opposed to responding to each and every call. But remember, good customer service means a fair amount of hand-holding.

♦ Be respectful and polite, even if they're not. Keeping your cool when those around you are losing it is the sign of the consummate professional. There will be screw-ups—hopefully not yours—but it helps no one if you lose your composure. Figure it out. What will resolve the situation?

Heads Up!

"It takes 20 years to build a reputation and five minutes to ruin it. If you think about that, you'll do things differently."
—Warren Buffet

♦ Firing the client is always a possibility, but always, always a last resort. You're losing money and they're likely to badmouth you to others. In 15 years, I've only once suggested that a client might find another company a better fit.

Outside Professionals and Lenders

I've had underwriters lose all the paperwork and then declare that they never received it. I've had title companies not complete their reports in time to meet a closing deadline. I've had the Internet connection for my office go on the fritz and couldn't process any loan applications.

And quite frankly, most of my clients would say, "who cares?" They came to me expecting me to help them get a mortgage, and they honestly don't care whose fault it is that things have gone haywire. They just expect me to fix it. So rule number one: forget the blame game. They don't care and they're blaming you anyway.

Heads Up!

Don't confuse friendship and business relationships. Be sure to offer the same level of professional behavior to your family/friends as you would to any other clients, even if you are taking a cut in your commission. Conversely, don't take friends or family for granted. Their goodwill has limits, too.

If you're consistently not getting the response or quality of work you need from an appraiser or title company or other provider, you need to spell out your issues. It does no one any good for you to remain silent. If after voicing your displeasure the situation continues, it's time to move on to another service provider.

Conversely, there are times you need to figure out how much the hassle is worth. I once worked with an appraiser whose analyses were outstanding. He was especially good about determining comparables in a wildly fluctuating market. But he was consistently late. I told him that his delays made it difficult to meet client deadlines, but despite his best assurances, nothing changed. So I did. I found other appraisers who worked more quickly. But there are still times when I'm concerned that a cursory appraisal may not take into account the full nature of a changing neighborhood, and I go back to my first guy. But when I do, I always build in extra time in the application process. Sometimes the hassle is worth it—most times it's not.

Generally you can't walk away from lenders if their products meet your clients' needs.

> **Heads Up!**
>
> "The most important persuasion tool you have in your entire arsenal is integrity."
>
> —Zig Ziglar, author and motivational speaker

- Build a "hassle factor" into your application time frame.

- Make duplicates and backups of all information you provide them.

- Ask for an acknowledgment in writing of the receipt of materials you send them.

- Speak to a supervisor or the account rep for the lender if you're having problems you can't resolve. They want your business. It's in both your interests to make the business relationship work.

Problem Co-workers or Bosses

The last thing on earth you need is a toxic co-worker or boss. Even if you like your job, if the work environment is poisonous, you're not at your best. But before you tender your resignation, try these ideas.

- If a co-worker is consistently sabotaging your work, either deliberately or unconsciously, you need to quietly, thoughtfully, and carefully document the incidents. Approach the co-worker with your concerns. He may have a different perspective that explains the situation. But if you can't resolve the issue between you, ask for a meeting with your boss.

◆ Pick your battles. It's not always smooth sailing and sometimes you're going to have to pick up the pieces for a co-worker or even your boss. Don't be a chronic complainer, but don't be a doormat, either.

◆ To avoid commission disputes, keep documentation of your work to back up your claims.

◆ If all else fails, consider a new job.

Spending Money to Save Money

You know what your own hourly rate is. Could you be more productive if you had help?

Are you spending hours doing your own taxes when you could hire an accountant to do them for you—and possibly take a deduction for the expense?

Would it help to hire a high school student to help with mass mailings to clients at the holiday times? Or to do filing for your home office? Or set up your computer?

Is there software that would simplify tracking your business expenses or a new computer that would speed up processing?

Consider hiring high school students or retirees part-time on a permanent or per-project basis. These workers can save you time especially if it's a clerical job that doesn't require significant training.

If time is money, then there are points in your career when you have to invest money in order to gain more time. It's a small example, but one I learned the hard way. The first year I owned my company, I handwrote the addresses on every holiday card I sent—and I sent over 600. It took me hours, and needless to say I wasn't in much of a holiday mood myself. The next year, in early November, I hired a teenager from the Youth Employment Service at our local high school to combine my client, vendor, and lender lists into one, create a mail merge, print out the labels using a calligraphy font, stuff, label, seal, and stamp the cards. It cost me $50 but was well worth the cost.

Be careful not to go into debt in order to get more real or virtual help. But spending money to regain valuable time is often worth it.

The Least You Need to Know

♦ Determining how much you earn per hour helps you figure out when to hire outside help as a time-saver.

♦ Learn how to maximize your e-mail program to file and filter your e-mail, as well as control spam, in order to better maximize your time spent on e-mail correspondence.

♦ Use the telephone judiciously. Plan what each conversation should accomplish and take notes while on the phone to keep a file of what was agreed upon and what needs to be done next.

♦ Consider hiring high schoolers and retirees to help with some clerical tasks.

Part 4

Here's the Deal

In this part, we get down to the nitty-gritty. You'll learn the importance of getting your clients pre-approved for a mortgage, even before they've found a house they want to buy. You'll discover the inner workings of the mortgage industry. I'll take you step by step through a mortgage application, so you're prepared to guide your clients through the process. Finally, we'll examine the different types of loans, focus on what makes one a better choice for a client than another, and discuss the value of paying points.

Chapter 13

Qualifying the Buyer: Before and After He Shops

In This Chapter

- ◆ Preapproval for a mortgage makes buying easier
- ◆ Taking the "guesstimate" out of how much a client can afford
- ◆ Understanding income, assets, and liabilities
- ◆ The good, the bad, and the downright ugly about credit

"Getting your ducks lined up in a row" is an old adage, but actually makes a lot of sense for buyers in a hot housing market. Mortgage brokers can prequalify shoppers to give them a nonbinding idea of how much of a loan they can expect a lender to approve. The mortgage broker will need to review information on the client's income and debt load, but the client doesn't provide any documentation to verify the data. It's an informal process, but gives the buyer a realistic idea of what he can spend for a house. It's good for you as a mortgage broker because it starts to establish a relationship with a client. He'll be more comfortable using you when he finds a home and needs to secure a mortgage.

Even better is the decision by some clients to go a step further and get preapproval for a mortgage. This process is similar to a real loan application without being tied to a specific property. Full documentation is needed to verify the information the client provides. For your purposes as a mortgage broker, it's good because it is a commitment by a client to use your services to secure a loan once they find a house.

Whether it's prequalification or preapproval, the focus is on the applicant's credentials as a borrower and is not tied to any specific property.

In this chapter, we'll review what is needed to preapprove a client for a mortgage. When the client has skipped the preapproval step (which is a purely voluntary stage), and has gone directly to applying for a mortgage for a specific property, then the lender requires information not only on the applicant, but on the value of the property as well. We'll cover those issues in Chapter 15.

The Value of Preapproval

As a mortgage broker, you want to advise clients to seek preapproval for a mortgage before they begin to shop for a home. Here's why:

♦ By getting preapproved for a mortgage, the buyer has a firm figure he can offer on a property. He avoids wasting time looking at homes he can't afford.

♦ A buyer with a preapproved mortgage may be more attractive to a seller, especially if there is a bidding war on a property. The seller knows that financing will not be an issue in the deal.

For the mortgage broker, preapproval means the customer has filled out the paperwork and provided documentation to verify the information he has provided, as if he were applying for a mortgage. He has paid for a credit report. At this point, it's unlikely that you will lose him as a client once he finds a property he wants to buy. This is an excellent way to build your client base.

When you first meet a client, you can prequalify him for a mortgage. This is an informal, nonbinding estimate of how much he can afford based on his current income and debt load. It's an opening gambit, but to lock in a firm offer, the client will have to provide documentation and authorize a credit report.

On the Plus Side of a Financial Profile: Income and Assets

Lenders want to know that their risk in lending money is minimal. The industry has developed formulas that calculate risk. Loan applicants must provide documentation to prove that the information they give is accurate. You will review the data and tell the client what documents they need to provide in order to substantiate it. You'll also pull a credit report to verify the applicant's history in paying their debts. We'll review each category that creates the financial profile of a loan applicant.

Income

It's all about the risk. To determine it, lenders need to know how much money the applicant earns and how much he owes. If the loan is to be in more than one name, then both parties must submit the necessary information and documentation.

For income, lenders want …

* to know how much the applicant has earned over a two-year period.

* to be able to verify that figure from a reliable source.

We'll talk about debt load in a few pages, but there is a rough ratio of income to debt that lenders use to determine how much money the applicant can spend to repay the mortgage.

For some of your clients, it's easy. They are salaried and can easily provide pay stubs and W-2 forms that verify their income. But other loan applicants will present a more challenging case to prove their income stream. You will need to advise them of how to build their argument to the lender that they are good risks.

Heads Up!

When evaluating the income level of an applicant, for salaried employees, lenders are interested in gross income (before taxes); for self-employed individuals, lenders are interested in net income (after taxes).

Income can be:

* earned from a salaried job

* earned as a self-employed worker

- earned by commission

- payments earned from a pension, retirement fund, or Social Security

- alimony and child support payments

- payments from an annuity or trust fund

- dividends or interest from bank accounts or stock

- royalties from a book or other intellectual property

- income from investment real estate the applicant owns

But in all cases, the lender wants to verify the income and see that it will likely continue:

- Income tax returns from up to three years can verify how much income has been earned from nontraditional sources and for how long.

- Awards statements from Social Security or pension funds should be attached (or if deposited directly into the bank account, a copy of the bank statement).

- Royalty or residual statements should be included.

This gives the lender an insight into the strength and durability of the income stream. The lender wants reassurance that the income from outside sources will continue for at least 12 to 36 months.

Bottom line? You need to make sure that your clients provide a complete picture of all their income sources. You may need to ask specific questions about possible income lest they forget or don't think it's pertinent.

Documentation for the Salaried Employee

The income documentation required of a salaried employee is:

- a month's worth of pay stubs showing year-to-date earnings

- most recent two years' W-2 forms

If the applicant has lost his pay stubs and W-2 forms, tell him to request duplicates from either his employer or from the IRS.

If the applicant has changed jobs within that time frame, ask him to provide all salary information and an explanation of why he switched positions. The lender wants to see a reliable job history. Certainly switching jobs for a higher-level job and increased compensation is a good sign for a lender. Changing jobs every few months, even for better pay and title, may trip a warning signal to the underwriter of the loan.

If the applicant has been a student for part of that time period, have him include his transcript and or a copy of his diploma.

Anticipate and then help your clients explain any potential problems.

Documentation for the Non-Salaried Worker

The income documentation required of a non-salaried worker is:

♦ two years' worth of income tax returns with full schedules

♦ a year-to-date profit/loss statement and balance sheet

Lenders understand that income for a non-salaried worker may vary from month to month, but the applicant should explain any discrepancies. For example, if the year-to-date income is significantly lower than the previous year's, the applicant might explain that his most profitable season occurs in the latter half of the year (if that's true). Lenders are looking for consistency of annual income.

Trickier is when it's difficult to verify income—for example, workers who earn much of their income from tips. In that case, some lenders will accept as verification bank statements that reflect regular monthly deposits.

Lenders are interested in the full unadjusted amount of income (before any payroll deductions), and that includes overtime pay, commissions, fees, tips and bonuses, and compensation for personal services.

♦ **Personal Services Income.** According to the IRS, personal services includes payments for contract labor; payments for professional services, such as fees to an attorney, physician, or accountant, if the payments are made directly to the person performing the services; consulting fees; honoraria paid to visiting professors, teachers, researchers, scientists, and prominent speakers; and generally, payments for performances by public entertainers.

♦ **Dependent Personal Service Income.** Dependent personal services are services performed as an employee in the United States by a nonresident alien. Dependent personal services include compensatory scholarship or fellowship income. Compensation for such services includes payments for wages, salaries, fees, bonuses, commissions, and similar designations for amounts paid to an employee.

Assets

What else does the applicant bring to the table? The lender wants to know the applicant's *assets*—what else he owns. An asset is an item of value; a *liquid asset* is something that can be quickly converted to cash.

While an asset would theoretically include the ugly vase from Aunt Dora, unless it's a vase from the Ming dynasty and worth thousands of dollars, the lender is more interested in the applicant's bank accounts, stocks, bonds, and mutual funds. Other assets include real estate, personal property, and debts owed to the applicant by others.

A liquid asset would be money in a checking, savings, or money market account. Non-liquid assets would include stocks, savings bonds, certificates of deposit, mutual funds, and certain retirement accounts. Access to their value is restricted. While the lender will consider the non-liquid assets in determining a borrower's financial circumstances, non-liquid assets won't be considered in terms of how much the applicant can repay on a monthly basis.

Again, the lender will demand verification of the applicant's assets. Advise your client to provide a paper trail of what he owns.

def•i•ni•tion

An **asset** is an item of value. A **liquid asset** is something that can be converted quickly to cash.

Bank, Savings & Loans, and Credit Union Accounts

These are liquid assets. The applicant needs to list his accounts and provide the current cash or market value of each. He should also provide up to three months of his current bank statements. Again, advise your client to explain any significant discrepancies or changes to his accounts. If there are significant deposits or withdrawals that are different from his usual exchange of business, have the applicant include an explanation. For example, if the applicant sells his vintage comic book collection, including Superman Number One, and deposits the sale proceeds into his account, he should include a copy of the bill of sale and a page from a reputable price guide for vintage comics verifying the value.

Stocks, Bonds, and Mutual Funds

The applicant will list all stocks and bonds (company names/number), a description of each, and their current market value. Advise your client to provide a brokerage statement verifying the amount and current value of these assets.

Heads Up!

Remind your clients that when providing documentation of bank accounts, they need to submit all the pages of their bank statements, even those that are primarily advertisements. Lenders often question missing pages and become concerned that the applicant is trying to hide something—for example, a major withdrawal. Bottom line: if the bank statement has seven pages, send in all seven.

Life Insurance

The applicant will need to provide the net cash value of any life insurance policies he carries.

Real Estate Owned

This is considered a non-liquid asset. It will include any real estate (for example, the applicant's current home if owned, as well as any investment property). The applicant should include the market value of the property(ies), as well as the carrying costs, for example, the taxes, insurance, and maintenance. If this is rental property, the client should enclose Schedule E of his tax return as verification of this info.

Retirement Funds

This is a non-liquid asset. The applicant will be asked to provide any vested interest in a retirement fund. Individual Retirement Accounts (IRAs) and Roth retirement plans are not considered liquid assets (there is a considerable penalty for withdrawing funds from these accounts). However, lenders do consider them in qualifying borrowers. Again, advise your clients to provide verification of these accounts.

If your client has a 401(k) account (a retirement plan made available by a company to its employees), he may be able to borrow against his vested amount. The borrower may wish to do that in order to get additional funds for a down payment; however, he should discuss this decision with his plan administrator. Some plans have limitations and restrictions on borrowing. Again, advise your client to provide verification of his 401(k) with his most recent statement.

Did You Know?

Banks will consider retirement funds in evaluating a client, but only at 70 percent of their value. That's because of the substantial early withdrawal penalty that would have to be paid in order to access the funds.

Businesses Owned

A non-liquid asset, the applicant should list the net worth of business(es) he owns and attach financial statements for each.

Automobiles

A non-liquid asset, the applicant should list the make and year for each automobile he owns and the current market value. Advise him to check the Kelley Blue Book, www.kbb.com, for value of cars.

Other Assets

The applicant should itemize any other assets of value. This would include significant artwork, jewelry, and hobby collections like baseball cards. Include documentation of a recent appraisal of market value for any item listed.

On the Minus Side of a Financial Profile: Liabilities

Just as lenders want to know all of your client's assets and income, clearly they need to know their *liabilities:* how much they owe. This includes monthly payments, for example rent, but also debt obligations, for example, credit card debt, car loans, and student loans. The applicant must provide the lender with complete information about all ongoing payment obligations, short- and long-term. As the mortgage broker, you will order a credit report that will verify much of this information, as well as give a rating of the individual's credit history.

def•i•ni•tion

A **liability** is a recurrent payment that the applicant owes. It includes monthly obligations like rent and utilities, but also credit-card debt, student loans, car loans, and child support.

On the loan application, the client must provide information on the name, address, and account number of each loan, the amount of the monthly payment, how many months are left to pay on the loan, and the unpaid balance. The applicant must also list alimony/child support/separate maintenance obligations, as well as job-related expenses such as child care and union dues.

Remind your clients that they must also list any other names under which credit has been previously received; for example, a woman might have credit cards using her maiden name. They must list creditor name(s) and account number(s).

In the Case of Divorce

The client should include a copy of his divorce decree, as well as any documents that pertain to child support, alimony, or separate maintenance.

Check with your client about any property previously co-owned with a former spouse. If the client has given the property to his former spouse, there's a potential problem. If his name is still on the mortgage loan, should it go into default, the lender may pursue your client for payment. He must take two steps: file a *quitclaim deed* to remove his name from ownership, and insist that the former spouse refinance the loan to remove him from any debt liability.

def•i•ni•tion

A **quitclaim deed** is a legal document that transfers all interests a person—for example, a former spouse—has in a property.

In the Case of Bankruptcy

If your client has ever filed for bankruptcy, finding a mortgage is more complicated, but still possible. The client will need to offer a detailed explanation of the bankruptcy circumstances. He'll also need copies of the bankruptcy schedules and the Discharge of Debtor.

For a conforming mortgage, the bankruptcy needs to have been settled between three and five years earlier. There are exceptions to this rule which shorten the time period, such as a catastrophic event that created financial havoc, such as the death of the primary wage earner in the family.

Heads Up!

Some nonconforming lenders will fund mortgages to applicants one month after discharge of their bankruptcy. There's a higher price to be paid, but loans of this sort are available.

Make sure that the client has re-established his credit successfully. Explain that he needs to show he is a good credit risk again. New credit needs to be repaid as agreed.

You should discuss lending options with your client. He may need to accept a higher-interest loan in order to qualify for a mortgage. However, should he be successful in re-establishing his credit, he could then refinance in a few years for better terms.

It Figures: Front End and Back End Ratios

Now that you have an idea of your client's assets and liabilities, you can begin to get a clear picture of what the lender is going to see when presented with a loan application. Lenders will verify the information presented by the client in the credit report you pull (refer to the section "The Credit Report"). But a very gross analysis will permit you to draw some quick conclusions on the type of loans for which your client will qualify.

Front End Ratio

The *front end ratio* determines what portion of the applicant's income will be used for monthly housing expenses. Typically, they want to see a front end ratio of no more than 28 percent. It is calculated as an individual's monthly housing expenses divided by his monthly gross income (pre-tax).

For example, if the client has an annual gross income of $48,000, his monthly income is $4,000 ($48,000/12 = $4,000). If his proposed mortgage payments, *PITI* (principal, interest, taxes, and insurance), will be $1,100 per month, the front end ratio would be 27.5 percent.

def•i•ni•tion

The **front end ratio** is calculated as an individual's monthly housing expenses divided by his monthly gross income. It is used to determine the percentage of an individual's income to be used for mortgage payments. **PITI** refers to the components of a mortgage payment: principal, interest, taxes, and insurance.

Back End Ratio

The *back end ratio*, also known as the debt to income ratio, is the percentage of an individual's monthly income that is used to pay debts. It is calculated as the individual's total monthly debt divided by his gross monthly income. It includes mortgage payments (PITI), credit card payments, child support, auto loans, student loans, and so on. Some lenders only consider the back end ratio when considering a mortgage.

For example, if a client has a monthly income of $4,000, and spends $1,150 on monthly payments (including mortgage payments), his debt to income ratio would be 29 percent.

$1,150/$4,000 = 29 percent

Lenders consider a good ratio as one be-tween 20 percent and 36 percent because it means the consumer has a better capacity to repay debts. Coupled with a good credit report, the consumer would likely qualify for a loan at the best interest rates, possibly even requiring less collateral.

def•i•ni•tion

The **back end ratio,** also known as the debt to income ratio, is the percentage of the individual's monthly income used to pay debt.

Let's Put It All Together

Here's a case study as an example, using Freddie Mac calculators:

- ◆ John Walden's annual salary, before taxes or deductions, is $48,000.

- ◆ He pays $300 a month on a car loan, and $100 per month on his student loan.

- ◆ He pays off his credit card debt each month and owes neither alimony or child support.

- ◆ His credit score is 724.

- ◆ He's hoping to get a 30-year fixed mortgage at 6.5 percent.

- ◆ In the community where he's looking, yearly property taxes are about $2,000, and yearly home insurance is about $200.

In order to have monthly mortgage payments of $1,040, which would be 26 percent of his gross monthly income (which is considered a good ratio), here's what works:

To have the monthly mortgage payment he can afford, at the rate he prefers:

Down Payment Percentage: 20%
Down Payment Amount: $33,883
Loan Amount: $135,534
House Price: $169,417
Principal and Interest: $857
Taxes and Insurance: $183
Total Monthly Payment: $1,040

If John puts down 10 percent, to have the same monthly mortgage payment:

Down Payment Amount: $14,269
Loan Amount: $128,423

House Price: $142,692
Principal and Interest: $812
Taxes and Insurance: $183
Mortgage Insurance: $45*
Total Monthly Payment: $1,040

*Because he is only putting down 10 percent, John will probably have to pay mortgage insurance (insurance protecting the lender against loss from a mortgage default). It is generally required of borrowers who put down less than 20 percent down payment. PMI premiums are based on the down payment amount and the terms of the mortgage.

But the ratios are only a rough estimate of creditworthiness.

You'll need to see the applicant's credit report and see his credit score to get a better idea of how a lender will respond to the client's loan application.

The Reality of Ratios

I'll give you the rule of thumb for ratios—and then tell you how it's often irrelevant.

Lenders traditionally use three different rules; the first number is the front end ratio and the second refers to the back end ratio:

- 5 percent down, the ratio is 25–33

- 10 percent down, the ratio is 28–36

- 20 percent down, the ratio is 33–38

Did You Know?

If your client has an installment loan, for example for a car, and is having trouble qualifying for a mortgage, it may be worth it to him to pay down his car debt. If an installment loan is down to 10 months or less, the lender won't include it when calculating his debt load.

The whole point of ratios is to limit risk by funding mortgages with applicants who are likely to be able to repay the loan in a timely basis.

But now that computerized approval engines, such as Desktop Originator and Loan Prospector, have replaced adding machines, lenders don't adhere as closely to the standard ratios. The approval engines take into account other elements, such as an applicant's credit and assets, when evaluating a loan application. For example, I had a client whose ratio was a whopping 65–70, but he was easily approved for a mortgage. Why? He was retired, had outstanding credit, and had a hoard of cash in his account. The approval engine could incorporate those facts into the evaluation process.

Why bother to learn about ratios? Because they're a quick assessment tool when meeting new clients.

The Credit Report

As part of the loan process, you will pull a credit report on each applicant. You will need their permission to do so. Credit reports track an individual's credit history.

There are three nationwide consumer reporting companies: Equifax (1-800-685-1111) www.cquifax.com; Experian (1-888-EXPERIAN [1-888-397-3742]) www.experian.com; TransUnion (1-800-916-8800) www.transunion.com.

Each company gets their information from different sources, so the reports may differ from each other. It's not a question of accuracy, but of which data is being reported. You should pull all three reports on a client. If you submit only two reports, lenders will use the lower credit score number; if you submit all three, the lender uses the middle number.

What's in the Report? What's Not?

Depending on the age and credit history of the client, a credit report can be quite large. It includes:

- ◆ Personal information: name, current and recent addresses, Social Security number, date of birth, and current and previous employers.

- ◆ Credit history: the details of all credit accounts that the client has opened, or that list the client as an authorized user. Even if the client has closed an account or not used it recently, depending on the manner in which the account was paid, the information can stay on the report for 7 to 11 years from their last activity. The credit report will detail the date each account was opened, the credit limit or amount of the loan, the payment terms, the balance, and a history of whether the client paid or time.

- ◆ Inquiries: There will be a record of each time the credit report is shown to another party, such as a lender, landlord, or insurer. Inquiries remain on the credit report for up to two years.

◆ Public information: Matters of public record from government sources remain on the credit report for seven years. This includes liens, bankruptcies, and over-due child support.

What's not included are checking or savings accounts, bankruptcies that are more than 10 years old, charged-off debts or debts that are more than seven years old, gender, ethnicity, religion, political affiliation, and medical history.

If the Client Disputes an Item

Make sure that the client reviews the reports to check for accounts he didn't open, charges he didn't make or disputed, or delinquencies he didn't cause. If there are any inaccuracies, the client should immediately take steps to correct them. Here's what happens.

◆ In writing, the client should tell the consumer reporting company what infor-mation that he believes is inaccurate. He should also tell the creditor, in writing, that he disputes the item.

◆ By law, the consumer reporting companies must investigate the items in ques-tion, usually within 30 days. The consumer reporting companies must forward all relevant data the client has provided to the organization or company that provided the original, allegedly inaccurate, information.

◆ Once the information provider receives notice of a dispute from the consumer reporting company, it must investigate, review the relevant information, and report the results back to the consumer reporting company.

◆ If the information provider finds that the disputed information is inaccurate, it must notify all three consumer reporting companies so they can correct the file.

◆ Once the investigation is complete, the consumer reporting company must give the individual the written results and, if the investigation results in a change, a free copy of his credit report.

◆ If an investigation does not resolve the dispute or your client does not accept the results, he can ask that a statement of the dispute be included in the file and in future reports. The client will have to pay a fee for this service.

Negative information can remain in a credit report for years. Most consumer report-ing companies include accurate negative information for seven years and bankruptcy information for 10 years. There is no time limit on reporting information about criminal convictions, information reported in response to an application for a job that pays more than $75,000 a year, and information reported because the client applied for more than $150,000 worth of credit or life insurance. Information about a lawsuit or unpaid judgment can be reported for seven years or until the statute of limitations runs out, whichever is longer.

What's the Score?

From all the information gathered, the consumer reporting companies develop a credit score, which is shorthand for how much of a credit risk they deem an individual to be: specifically, how likely is the person to make payments on a loan over the following two to three years? It's based on a complex mathematical model that evaluates the information. The scores range from 300 to 850, with most consumers landing somewhere between 600 and 800.

The top factors influencing a credit report are:

♦ How effectively the client uses credit. If a consumer's average balance of retail accounts is too high, it suggests to the lender that the individual is living beyond his means. If the client doesn't use his credit cards, the lender is concerned because there's no clear record to evaluate for creditworthiness. The best-case scenario is the client who has low balances on *revolving accounts* (credit cards), plus some *installment accounts* (mortgages, car loans), and pays off his debts in a timely fashion.

def•i•ni•tion

A **revolving account** is an account, like a credit card, that requires at least a specified minimum payment each month plus a service charge on the balance. An **installment account** is an account, like a mortgage or auto loan, in which the amount of the payment and the number of payments is prefixed.

♦ How long the credit history extends. Credit reports that are less than three years old are usually determined to be inadequate. If your client has a limited credit history, he may need to increase his down payment, accept a higher interest rate, include a co-signer on the loan, or provide other documentation to prove his creditworthiness.

♦ Asking for too much credit, too fast. Consumers who apply for too much credit at the same time (for example, multiple credit cards), may trip an alarm on the credit report. Each application for credit is noted on the credit report under "inquiries." While the consumer may just be shopping around for a good rate, all the credit report knows is that there have been multiple inquiries to the file. Multiple inquiries could also signal that the consumer has become financially unstable. A spike in the number of inquiries could result in a lower score.

Putting It All Together

All the numbers, ratios, and calculations give you a rough estimate about how much of a loan for which a client will qualify. But it's not that simple.

Mortgage loan software is complex and takes into account more than just the numbers plugged in. Plus, as the mortgage broker, you can help a client put his financial situation into perspective. A loan is dependent on good credit, the client's total financial picture, his job, down payment size, and more.

To prequalify a client, a quick calculation of front- and back end ratios, will give you enough to steer your client in the right direction in terms of what they can afford to buy. If a client is seeking preapproval of a mortgage, then the process is more complicated and may result in a higher or lower figure than the prequalification figures provide.

The Least You Need to Know

◆ Prequalifying a client for a mortgage gives the buyer a better idea of what he can afford to spend on a house. It's also an opportunity for you to establish a good working relationship so that when he seeks a mortgage, he comes to you.

◆ Preapproval for a mortgage is similar to a real loan application without being tied to a specific property. Full documentation is needed to verify the information the client provides. It's a commitment by the client to use your services to secure a loan once they find a house.

◆ Your client's credit report and credit score will play a significant role in their qualification for a mortgage. You can advise them if there are problems with their credit report.

Lenders, Documents, and Details

In This Chapter:

- ◆ Fannie, Freddie, and Ginnie set the standards
- ◆ Working with lenders
- ◆ Building relationships with lenders
- ◆ When banks undersell you
- ◆ Calling in a favor

You're the matchmaker in the mortgage world. Your goal is to find just the right lender and product for each of your clients. You then help your clients navigate the mortgage maze from application to closing. There are literally hundreds of lenders to choose from, but there is an advantage to limiting your relationships to 30 to 40. You want to build a strong connection with lenders because you want them to trust your judgment and work with you to get your clients approved for loans.

In this chapter, you'll learn about the powerful role that Fannie Mae, Freddie Mac, and Ginnie Mae play in the housing industry, as well as how to work with the lenders who fund the mortgages your clients seek.

Let's Start at the Very Beginning ...

Fannie Mae and Freddie Mac are not high school sweethearts, nor is Ginnie Mae their offspring. I can't begin to tell you how many bad mortgage broker jokes there are about these icons of the mortgage industry. Both Fannie Mae and Freddie Mac are publicly traded corporations, but chartered by Congress. Ginnie Mae is a government agency within the U.S. Department of Housing and Urban Development. These quasi- and fully governmental agencies are the backbone of the American mortgage industry and before we move into building your relationship with individual lenders, you need to understand how Fannie, Freddie, and Ginnie work. We touched on their roles in Chapter 9, but now let's really tackle how they impact your daily work.

The Grande Dame of the Mortgage Industry

The Federal National Mortgage Association, Fannie Mae, was created in 1938 as part of Franklin Delano Roosevelt's New Deal. As a result of the Great Depression, the housing market had collapsed. Fannie Mae was established to infuse federal money into local banks so they could afford to finance home mortgages. In turn, that would raise the level of home ownership and increase the availability of affordable housing.

For the first 30 years after its inception, Fannie Mae was the secondary mortgage market, with virtually no competition.

In 1968, it became a government-sponsored enterprise (GSE), which means it is a private company, generating profits for shareholders, but protected financially by the support of the federal government. It has:

 ◆ access to a line of credit through the U.S. Treasury

 ◆ exemption from state and local income taxes

 ◆ exemption from SEC oversight

Since 1968, Fannie Mae has helped more than 63 million families buy homes.

Fannie Mae makes mortgage funds consistently available and affordable to home buyers in every state by buying mortgages from the lenders. But in order to be sold to Fannie Mae, the mortgages must comply with certain guidelines and loan limits. These are called *conforming loans*. The loan limits are adjusted every year in response to changes in the housing market, but Fannie Mae's mission is to help low-, moderate-, and middle-income people buy homes.

You will use Fannie Mae Desktop Originator (software) to score online approval of applications for conforming loans. (Lenders use Fannie Mae Desktop Underwriter software.) While Fannie Mae does not fund mortgages, you must get their approval of an application before it's sent to a lender. The approval by Fannie Mae tells the lender that this mortgage meets the qualifications to be placed in a pool for sale on the secondary mortgage market. This is a critical step.

def•i•ni•tion

A **conforming loan** is one that meets all the requirements to be eligible for purchase by federal agencies such as Fannie Mae and Freddie Mac.

Freddie Mac Enters the Picture

In 1970, to curtail the monopoly that Fannie Mae held on the secondary mortgage market, the government created a second GSE, the Federal Home Loan Mortgage Corporation, Freddie Mac.

Freddie Mac is a quasi-governmental, federally sponsored company that acts as a secondary mortgage market investor to buy and sell loans. Freddie Mac buys one mortgage every seven seconds to help finance one in six homebuyers and more than two million renters.

Freddie Mac's mission is to stabilize the nation's mortgage markets and expand opportunities for home ownership and affordable rental housing. In addition to single-family homes, Freddie Mac also buys mortgages for multifamily buildings that offer rental housing to families, and in this way allow renters to have access to affordable homes as well.

Like Fannie Mae, Freddie Mac also has guidelines and loan limits for single-family houses, as well as limits on multi-family units. You will use Freddie Mac's Loan Prospector (software) to score online approval of applications for conforming loans. Again, you must secure Freddie Mac (or Fannie Mae) approval for a conforming loan before you send it to a lender.

Did You Know?

The Primary Mortgage Market Survey, a list of average interest rates compiled from Freddie Mac's weekly nationwide interest rate survey, can be accessed at the company's website, www.freddiemac.com.

Experience has taught me that Fannie Mae is more likely to approve applications from first-time homebuyers, while Freddie Mac looks more closely at assets. As you work in the field, you'll get a feel for which agency is right for different clients.

How Do Fannie Mae and Freddie Mac Differ?

While both organizations have the same charters, Congressional mandates, and regulatory structure, the two companies have different business strategies. It's sort of like Coke and Pepsi—same goals, but different ways to get there.

Congress believed that the competition between the two companies in the secondary mortgage market would translate into lower housing costs for the public.

In 2004, U.S. lenders made $2.6 trillion in home loans. Freddie Mac guaranteed $365.2 billion of the loans, while Fannie Mae guaranteed $527.2 billion.

Did You Know?

Freddie Mac and Fannie Mae set many of the guidelines for conventional (conforming) loans. Fannie Mae and Freddie Mac control about 90 percent of the nation's secondary mortgage market. The combined assets of Fannie Mae and Freddie Mac are 45 percent greater than that of the nation's largest bank.

Ginnie Mae's Role in the Housing Market

The Government National Mortgage Association, Ginnie Mae, was created in 1970, and is a government-owned corporation within the Department of Housing and Urban Development. Ginnie Mae securities are the only mortgage-backed securities with the full faith and credit guaranty of the U.S. government. Ginnie Mae securities pool packages of qualifying FHA and VA loans, as well as loans made by the Rural Housing Service (RHS) and the Office of Public and Indian Housing (PIH).

Working with Lenders

Now that we've seen the underpinnings of the mortgage market, and the companies that set the guidelines for most loans, let's talk about the lenders you will deal with on a daily basis.

You want to establish relationships with every bank in your area because these are the ones whose rates you're most likely to hear quoted by prospective clients. But the bank personnel you see at the branch in your community are actually your competitors. That's the retail division of the bank: they're trying to get the same clients you are with the lending products offered by the bank.

You will deal with the bank's wholesale division, whose personnel are more than likely not located in your area, perhaps not even in your state. But each bank has account reps. Their job is to sell the bank loan products. They'll be calling on you to make sure that you are familiar with their latest offerings.

You want to know the underwriters who will handle your applications. Where possible, you want to meet them face to face, but with the centralization of these departments, that may not be possible. As banks have merged, and especially for banks with branches in many states, the underwriters may be located in a central office hundreds of miles away.

Heads Up!

For a change, you're the one being wooed. Bank account reps want your business. But keep in mind, no matter how friendly the account rep, no matter how good the fruit basket he sends you at the holidays, this is a business relationship and your first priority is your clients. Choose the loan products from the lenders who best serve your clients.

But you need to introduce yourself, if only by phone and e-mail. You want them to know you and your company. You want to build a relationship of mutual trust and respect. The mortgage broker industry is competitive. You want to make your mark as a professional whose judgment can be trusted.

Lenders are in the business of making money by lending money. They can only do that if there is minimal risk of a mortgage default. Your job is to match your client to the right loan product that meets his needs and his current financial circumstances. The right match minimizes risk for the lender and maximizes the savings for your client.

What Do Each of You Bring to the Table?

For the lender, building a good relationship with you is important because:

- ◆ he needs you to bring clients that are good risks

- ◆ he wants you to sell his loan products, not another lender's

- ◆ he recognizes that if he is the lender for a mortgage, he may get the client for other banking needs

For you, a good relationship is key because:

◆ you need the lender to respond to you in a timely fashion, and occasionally even faster if the circumstances call for it

◆ you need to be able to work with the lender to make your marginal clients succeed, rather than be rejected

◆ you need lenders who respect and appreciate your business

What Makes a Good Business Relationship?

Good service and good business practices are, of course, essential to success as a mortgage broker, but you need to be able to deliver loans in a timely fashion or your clients will go elsewhere. And for that you need to have a good working relationship with the lenders.

Building a good relationship with the underwriters of a lending institution is a long-term process. You want them to believe that you consistently send them good files, in other words, applicants who meet their guidelines and are good risks. By building a level of trust, you hope that for those occasions when the file is marginal, they'll trust your judgment that it's worth approval.

Mutual respect is the key in any business relationship. You need to convey to each lender that you:

◆ share a commitment to high performance

◆ understand that you are dependent on each other

The lender needs you to bring in clients, you need the lender to supply the mortgages.

Heads Up! _____

Remember that the underwriter only sees what's on the loan application. Unlike you, the underwriter hasn't spent an hour with the client going over every detail of his finances and future. The underwriter doesn't know the applicant like you do. That's why it's critical that you write a cover letter to accompany each application. You want to make your clients come alive for the underwriter. You want him to see what you see. Take notes during your meeting with the client so that you can add in details. Also give the letter to the loan processor in your office so that he has the information in front of him when he gets questions from the lender, appraiser, title company, and so on.

This is most definitely a two-way street. Having satisfied customers is a win-win situation for both of you. The key to building trust is honest communication. Here are some other tips to build a good working relationship:

- Anticipate the underwriter's questions. You want to make his job straightforward and easy. He should have all the information he needs to make a (favorable) decision about your client. While you routinely look at applications from the underwriter's point of view, as you get to know each lender, you'll be able to see the "hot spots" for each lender and tailor the applications to answer the question before it's asked.

- Return calls promptly. I sometimes feel like my phone is an extension of my ear. It's permanently attached. But it's our lifeline as mortgage brokers. It may seem self-evident, but calls from lenders are a top priority. They hold all the cards when they're reviewing a client's loan application—and you want to answer any questions and let them get back to the job ASAP. But remember to return any business calls in a timely fashion, whether it's a client, realtor, appraiser, title company, etc. Responding promptly shows respect.

- "Honesty is the best policy …." Especially, as Mark Twain, added, "… when there is money in it." Insist on honesty from your applicants. First, because it's the right thing to do. Second, because the documentation the client provides will reveal the truth in any case. And third, and equally important, your reputation is on the line. You have to work with these lenders for other cases. If they can't trust you, your business career as a mortgage broker is over.

- Admit when you're wrong. Don't try to tap-dance your way out of a mistake. Apologize, correct it, and move on. Again, you want the lender to know you're a straight shooter who takes responsibility for errors.

- Don't forget the human touch. Take a moment to exchange pleasantries with the person on the other end of the phone or within an e-mail message. Express appreciation for their efforts. Acknowledge the pressures they are facing. It's way too easy in this technology-driven industry to forget the people aspect of this process.

Schedule regular meetings with the loan processor in your office to review all the files he's working on. You want to be kept current on the status of each application. Once you hand off the application to the loan processor, it's more likely that he is getting the queries from the lender, appraiser, title company, and so on. You want to know what's going on and if you need to intervene.

When Banks Undersell You

It happens. You get beat sometimes by a bank in your area that cuts the rate it offers to customers who work with them directly. Usually, your rate for loan products from lenders is the same as the ones they're offering, but not always. How do you compete?

◆ Remind your client that the bank is restricted to offering only their own loan products. You've got hundreds of different lenders who might meet or beat that particular bank rate.

◆ Point out that, at one time, there was an advantage to using the local bank because the underwriters and officers of the bank were all homegrown. But with today's mega-bank mergers, often there is little advantage to having a local bank fund a mortgage. Underwriters and bank officers often don't live in the area. It will be up to the loan originator (whether it's you or the bank loan officer) to answer any questions about local real estate. It's not a mom-and-pop operation anymore.

◆ Tell your client that the bank loan officer is not unbiased. He is paid to promote his bank's loan products. As the mortgage broker, you are compensated by whichever lender you use so you have no self-interest to promote only one particular company.

◆ Let your client know that if the bank declines his loan application, he starts over from scratch. In contrast, as his mortgage broker, you may submit his application to several lenders right from the beginning to ensure that you can close on time. Furthermore, if one bank declines an application, as a mortgage broker you are familiar with other lenders who will accept his circumstances.

Heads Up!

Bait and switch. That's what sometimes happens when a person goes to the bank and gets a rate quote. I've had clients quote me bank rates that I know aren't possible. And the reason I know is because I have the wholesale rates from the same bank and the quote is lower than that. Without actually calling the bank rep a bald-faced liar, remember you're a professional, and tell your client that before he accepts the bank quote he needs to get it in writing (which will never happen). Explain why you know the rate is higher and suggest he might want to review a variety of loan options.

Make New Friends ... and Keep the Old

If there are hundreds of lenders to consider, do you need to limit your business to a few ... and how many is a few? Over the years, I've done deals with hundreds of different lenders, but on a daily basis, I primarily focus on 15 different lenders.

Why? Because volume counts. Think about it. Why does Wal-Mart drive out the local hardware store? Because they can buy in a volume that the local guy can't. Send enough business to a lender and you become a preferred customer. You won't get a badge saying "top banana," but your calls will be returned a little faster, and when you need to call in a favor, it's more likely to be granted.

On the other hand, you don't want to concentrate all your business with just a few lenders. You don't want to be caught with all your eggs in one basket if their products aren't competitive enough with other companies or they change their guidelines for loans or they get bought out. With all the recent bank mergers, the number of lenders is reduced. For example, in the last year, four banks I worked with on a regular basis were bought out by the same institution.

Always take the time to meet the new guy in the neighborhood. Test-drive his products, but don't forget your old friends. You spend time cultivating these relationships.

> **Did You Know?**
>
> Washington Mutual bought out six different banks in the last two years. If you had limited your business relationship to just those six lenders, you'd be down to one now. Make sure you keep a wide array of lenders in your arsenal.

The Least You Need to Know

- The government-sponsored enterprises, Fannie Mae and Freddie Mac, set the industry standards for conforming loans.

- Ginnie Mae, an agency of the Department of Housing and Urban Development, pools qualifying FHA, VA, RHS, and PIH loans.

- Keep in touch with the underwriters of the lenders you use so they learn to trust your judgment.

- Don't concentrate all your business with too small a group of lenders, but don't scattershot your business as volume is rewarded with additional attention by lenders.

The Mortgage Application Process: Step by Step

In This Chapter

- ◆ Down payment strategies that work for the client and the lender
- ◆ Determining the value of the property
- ◆ Title searches are a critical part of the process
- ◆ Government monitoring of potential bias
- ◆ Truth-in-Lending reveals the actual rate
- ◆ Locking in the rate

The preapproval process discussed in Chapter 13 covered many of the steps your clients will take to secure a mortgage. But preapproval only covers the buyer's financial qualifications. In this chapter we'll assume that your client has found a house he wishes to buy. If he has not been preapproved for a mortgage, your client must provide the financial information previously discussed, and you will need to order a credit report.

We'll also review how the size of the down payment plays an important role in determining the rate and the lender's approval. We'll talk about different down payment strategies.

Moving beyond the information about the prospective borrower, we'll focus on the property for which a loan is sought. Before the lender makes a decision on approving a mortgage, it must verify the property's value and legal status. You'll need to order a property appraisal, as well as a title search.

We'll also review two other parts of the application that are designed to provide your clients with full disclosure of the actual price of the mortgage (Truth in Lending); as well as prevent possible bias in mortgage lending (Information for Government Monitoring Purposes).

Finally, we'll tell you how to help your client determine when is the best time to lock in a rate, even if it costs him for the privilege.

As the mortgage broker, your job just got a whole lot more complicated.

The Lowdown on Down Payments

The size of the down payment will affect the type of mortgage your client can secure. It also determines the amount of money that he will eventually repay. The larger the down payment, the less money he borrows and the smaller the repayment. Lenders see mortgages with larger down payments as more secure because the buyer has more of his own money invested in the property.

Traditionally, homebuyers were expected to put down 20 percent of the sale price. Those expectations are long since gone. Today there are programs to help buyers who have limited funds and can't afford to put 20 percent down. There are programs to help buyers who can't even afford any down payment.

But even for the average homebuyer, given the high prices of today's housing, it's a struggle. In this section, we'll review some strategies you can suggest to buyers who want to boost their nest egg, as well as what you need to know about mortgages with minimal down payments.

VA loans permit zero down payments with limited closing costs, while down payments for FHA loans can be as low as 3 percent. While this helps qualified buyers who don't have enough in savings for a down payment, you should remind these clients that they still must be able to afford the monthly payments.

Increasing the Nut

Hopefully your client has carefully calculated how much money he has for a down payment before he walks in your door. But despite his best number crunching, you may be able to point out other sources of funding he hasn't considered.

- ◆ Betting against the future. Your client may be able to borrow from his retirement plan. He will need to consider the tax consequences, early withdrawal penalties, and repayment terms, but he may be able to borrow from his 401(k) plan or from his Individual Retirement Account (IRA).

- ◆ Friends and family. Your client may be able to ask family members or friends to loan or give him money toward a down payment.

- ◆ Reduce high-interest debt. Paying off high-interest credit card debt may initially deplete some of your client's savings, but saves money in the long run.

- ◆ Adopt cost-cutting strategies. Moving into less expensive housing, forgoing vacations, or taking a second job can all help boost the down payment savings account.

- ◆ Sell investments. While stocks and bonds in your client's portfolio certainly strengthen his creditworthiness to a lender, it might be wiser to sell some investments to increase the down payment he can make.

- ◆ Work with the seller. The seller may be interested in lending your client the funds for a down payment, taking a second mortgage on the house. Usually the interest rate on this type of mortgage is higher than the first mortgage. The seller might also be willing to pay part of the closing costs.

Private Mortgage Insurance

Lenders require buyers to pay for *private mortgage insurance (PMI)* if they can't put down at least 20 percent. The insurance is the lender's protection against the mortgagor's default. The rates range from ⅓ to 1 percent of the loan balance per year.

Calculating the Real Cost of Mortgage Insurance

While at first glance it appears that the cost of mortgage insurance is minimal, you need to explain the financial ramifications. It may be your client's only option since his finances are limited, but full disclosure is essential.

def•i•ni•tion

Private mortgage insurance (PMI) protects the lender from loss in case of default by the borrower. It's generally required for loans with less than 20 percent down payment.

Let's assume that your client wants to buy a house for $100,000, but only has $5,000 for a down payment. He can get a 15-year, fixed rate mortgage of 6 percent for $95,000, but will have to pay mortgage insurance of .56 percent of the balance per year for the first four years or until the owner's equity or LTV (loan-to-value ratio) in the home drops below 80 percent and the insurance is no longer mandatory.

In simple terms, although he only needs an additional $15,000, he will end up paying a higher fee on all $95,000. Because he must borrow an additional $15,000, your client must pay an additional fee on the whole amount, not just the amount needed to make up the difference between a 5- and 20-percent down payment.

But if he doesn't have the money, doesn't plan to remain in the home for long, or even if he has the cash and can get a better return on his investment in other ventures, then the mortgage insurance may be a good option.

Mortgage Insurance Termination

The first few years of paying a mortgage, the owner is paying primarily interest. His equity in the home is slowly growing. But once it reaches at least 22 percent, the lender, by law, should terminate the insurance. However, the borrower may initiate termination of the insurance premium when the loan balance hits 80 percent of the original value.

Given amortization schedules, it usually takes about 10 years for a 30-year fixed rate mortgage to reach 80 percent of the property value; or almost 4 years if it's a 15-year fixed rate mortgage.

To reach the 80 percent target sooner, the borrower could increase his monthly payments (which are applied directly to the principal). For a client who is short on cash for a down payment, but is expecting a steadily increasing income, this may be a good alternative.

The lender is not required to accept a request for cancellation if:

 ◆ the borrower has a second mortgage

 ◆ the property has declined in value

 ◆ the borrower has been late in paying his mortgage by 30 days or more within the year preceding the cancellation date or late by 60 days or more in the year before that

If the borrower's loan was sold to Fannie Mae or Freddie Mac, the basis for cancellation is on the current appraised value of the property, rather than the value at the time the loan was made. Under these rules, the borrower can request cancellation after two years if the loan balance is no more than 75 percent of the current appraised value, and after 5 years if it is no more than 80 percent. The borrower must request termination and must secure an appraisal that is acceptable to the agencies and the lender.

If the borrower has a second mortgage, the property is held for investment rather than occupancy, or if the property is not a single-family residence, the ratios required for termination are lower.

Late payments will jeopardize early termination efforts.

Piggyback Loans

If your client can only afford to put down less than 20 percent, you might advise him to consider a piggyback loan instead of paying mortgage insurance.

Again, let's suppose that the price of the home is $100,000. The borrower puts down $5,000, and then takes out two loans: a first mortgage for $80,000; and at a higher rate, a second mortgage or home equity loan for $15,000.

Why is this preferable to mortgage insurance? Under this system, the borrower only pays a higher rate on $15,000. Mortgage insurance is calculated on the whole loan ($95,000). Furthermore, mortgage insurance premiums are not deductible, whereas the interest on the second mortgage is tax deductible.

The downside of piggyback loans, if tapped, is:

- they slow the buildup of equity in the home

- they prevent borrowers from getting a home equity loan or line of credit to pay for home improvements or to consolidate debts

- the second mortgage often has variable rates which may be a problem for the borrower if rates go up

- the borrower has to pay closing costs if he decides to refinance the first mortgage in order to pay off the piggyback loan

Heads Up!

Second mortgage rates are based on the prime rate. When the prime goes up, so does the mortgage rate.

I always advise my clients to apply for a piggyback loan even if they don't plan to use it immediately. You already have all the paperwork from the first mortgage application completed so the effort is minimal. I explain that the time to get a home equity loan is before you need it. It will be more difficult to secure one if you apply in the midst of a crisis—for example, if the client has lost his job. Instead, if you have it in reserve, it is there when you need it. There are no interest charges if you don't use the money. As the mortgage broker, you earn a commission on both the first mortgage and the piggyback loan.

SingleFile Alternative

The mortgage insurance industry, in an attempt to stem the rise of piggyback loans that avoid PMI, has developed an alternative product. MGIC, the largest mortgage insurance company, now offers SingleFile. The borrower doesn't pay a monthly mortgage insurance premium—instead the lender pays for the insurance.

Of course, the borrower does pay, but there isn't a separate, nondeductible premium. Instead, the lender charges a higher interest rate (a quarter-point to half-point higher).

What's the advantage over PMI? The mortgage business is very competitive, so lenders are more likely to cut the cost of the insurance charge to keep their rates attractive to borrowers. Cost comparisons reveal that the monthly payments of loans made with SingleFile are less expensive than comparable loans with PMI.

> **Heads Up!** _____
>
> Lenders like SingleFile because they make more money. The borrower pays a higher rate for the life of the loan. In effect, the borrower is locked in at that rate for 30 years—unless he refinances. In contrast, PMI can be cancelled after two years or if the equity in the house increases.

What's the advantage over piggyback loans?

- The borrower has only one payment to make.
- Closing costs are lower.
- Since SingleFile's insurance is part of the interest rate, the interest is tax deductible.

There are two drawbacks to this product. It is limited to low-risk borrowers who have excellent credit. It can't be cancelled by having the house reappraised or by reaching a certain level of equity in the house. The only way to terminate the SingleFile loan is to refinance the house or sell.

The Bottom Line

Here are some points your client should consider when looking at piggyback loans, loans with PMI, and SingleFile.

◆ While the cost is initially lower on a piggyback loan, private mortgage insurance can be cancelled once there is sufficient equity. (This is not true of SingleFile.)

◆ The borrower needs to consider how long he plans to hold on to the home to determine which of these products, if he has a choice, he should consider. The longer he plans to be in the home, the greater the advantage of the single loan with PMI since the insurance will be cancelled at some point. If he plans to sell or refinance the home in less than five years, then a piggyback loan makes more sense.

◆ The advantages of the piggyback loan are dependent on the homeowner's tax situation (PMI isn't deductible, piggyback loans and SingleFile are), the speed of home value appreciation (if homes are rapidly appreciating, then the borrower may be able to terminate the PMI sooner), and any additional costs and fees associated with each product.

The Appraisal

You must arrange for the house to be appraised as part of the loan application. The lender will not approve the mortgage until it is established that the house is worth the amount of the loan. The fee for most *appraisals* is between $200 to $400. The purpose of the appraisal is to support the loan to value.

Appraisals must conform to Federal Reserve guidelines, but it is still a subjective process. The appraiser must determine the current market value of the house. This is especially difficult in a volatile housing market where prices are moving quickly and properties vary widely.

def•i•ni•tion

> The **appraisal** is a third-party estimate of the value of the property at a specific point in time.

Appraisers can only use houses that have gone to closing as comparables. So they are working in effect 90 days behind. In a volatile housing market, when prices are rising rapidly, this can be a problem. The appraiser can note in his file Time Value Adjustments to indicate the rising prices of the houses.

The appraiser will compare the house to at least three other comparable homes in the area that have sold within the last six months. He must adjust for differences in the homes since clearly a completely renovated home will sell for more than one that hasn't been touched in 25 years. The appraiser will physically measure and inspect the home. This is not a substitute for a home inspection. He will take photographs and will include them, along with floor plans (he may hand-draw them), and a site map in his report.

It's a problem if the appraisal is lower than the sale price of the house. This happens if prices are rising quickly and comparable sales don't reflect the change yet.

Make sure you use experienced, well-trained appraisers approved by the lenders you use. Ask the appraiser for his resumé, which should include the list of lenders for whom he is approved. Check credentials and ask for references. Appraisers are certified by the individual states under federal guidelines, but only half the states require licenses. Most states do require appraisers to pass a written exam, have 75 hours of continuing education, and serve 2,000 hours of direct experience through an apprenticeship.

By law the lender is required to give the client a copy of the appraisal. Here are some suggestions for dealing with a low appraisal:

♦ Have the client review the report and point out any valuable features of the house that the appraiser missed.

♦ Review the comparable sales and point out if the appraiser missed a recent comparable sale for a higher price.

♦ Ask your client if he wants a second appraisal. While he will need to pay an additional fee, he may be willing to do so in order to buy the house he wants. You will have to make a decision (check with your manager) if you are willing to split the fee with him. If you believe that a second appraisal will be substantially different, it may be worth it to save the deal.

♦ The client can go back to the seller and ask for a reduction in the sale price to reflect the appraisal. The seller may be willing to do that to avoid having to put the house back on the market.

If the appraisal is lower than the sale price, the lender accepts the lower number. They may still do the deal, but based on the appraisal figure. Ask the client if he is willing to increase his down payment or accept a higher interest rate. The lender may be willing to accept a low appraisal if the borrower has more equity in the property and the loan is smaller or pays off at a higher rate. If the client is convinced that prices in the area are going to rise (and that he's just ahead of the curve), he may be willing to invest more and buy the house.

A Clear Title Is Essential

As part of the mortgage application process, you will need to order a *title search* of the property. It is a thorough examination of all public records that involve title (ownership) of that specific property. It is to guarantee that there are no liens or other claims against it except for those that will be cleared at closing.

def•i•ni•tion

A **title search** is a thorough examination of all public records that involve title of a specific property. It is to guarantee that there are no outstanding claims against the property except for the liens that will be cleared at the closing. **Clouds** on the title are defects or problems that throw into question the title of the property. They should be resolved prior to closing.

Title searches usually go back 30 to 40 years (sometimes more). They involve researching past owners and deeds, wills, trusts, mortgages, judgments, and other liens to make sure that the title has passed correctly to each new owner.

Clouds, which are problems with the title, should be resolved prior to closing. For example, if a couple were both listed on the deed, but only the husband signed off at closing—even if the closing was 20 years previously and two sales had occurred in the interim—that would be considered a cloud on the deed and the wife's interest in the property must be removed to clear the title.

Title searches should reveal rights held by others (for example, right of way, view easements, power line easements, mineral rights), claims by prior undisclosed heirs, and pending legal action.

Title Insurance to Cover the What-Ifs

Both the lender and the buyer generally purchase title insurance. This protects against losses that might occur after closing in the event that a previous owner's rights were overlooked during the title search. Like most insurance policies, it's rarely used, but is invaluable if a situation arises where title is in question.

The mortgage policy covers the lender for the life of the loan. If a new loan is issued and the current mortgage is paid off, then a new policy is required. The mortgage policy covers the amount of the mortgage.

The owner's policy is also valid for the life of the loan. It covers the property's full sales price, legal fees in defending the owner's rights, and insures the owner against loss.

The policy covers problems that did not show up in the search or that were missed by the examiner. The insurance also covers errors in public records.

The policy does not cover defects that occur after the property is purchased. Unlike casualty insurance like for fire or flood, which protects against catastrophic events that might occur in the future, title insurance protects only against damaging events in the past.

Usually the policy doesn't cover problems with easements, mineral and air rights, and liens. The borrower should ask for an explanation of all exclusions, and a recommendation for which ones should be resolved prior to closing.

Title insurance would cover hidden hazards, including forgeries, fraud, errors in recording the deed, defective foreclosures, faulty surveys, misinterpreted wills, conveyances by a minor or someone mentally incompetent, an undiscovered heir or ex-spouse who claims interest in the property, or a deed delivered after the death of the property owner.

Who Pays and How Much

Who pays for the owner's title insurance varies from state to state and is based on local custom. There are no laws requiring either side to pay. For example, in Southern California, the seller usually pays for the owner's policy for the buyer, and the buyer pays for the title insurance for the lender. In contrast, in Northern California, the buyer typically pays for both policies. However, like everything else in the sales contract, it's open for negotiation.

The premiums are paid in full with a one-time fee, which is usually part of the closing costs. Typically, the fee is .5 percent of the purchase price, but this varies from state to state.

The rate also depends upon the kind of policy that is being issued.

+ The basic rate covers a policy issued on a purchase transaction and is usually calculated on the purchase price and the mortgage amount.

+ The re-issue rate (generally lower than the basic rate) depends on whether the seller can provide backtitle to the purchaser. It's based on the age of the seller's title policy.

+ The refinance rate covers a policy issued to the current owner on a mortgage loan. The rate may be dependent on the previous mortgage amount, but varies from state to state.

+ New construction rates cover the builder during construction before construction is completed. This is usually a significantly lower rate than the basic rate. New construction rate does not cover the buyer purchasing a completed new home from the builder.

Heads Up!

Your client should ask about an inflation rider for the policy. It increases the coverage amount as the property's value increases.

Government Monitoring

As part of every mortgage application, your client will be asked to complete a short survey on race, gender, and ethnicity. It is designed to provide the government with data that monitors a lender's compliance with the Equal Credit Opportunity Act. It's against the law to discriminate on the basis of race, religion, age, color, national origin, receipt of public assistance funds, sex, or marital status.

The client has the option of refusing to provide the information (and can't be discriminated against for refusing). But the law also requires that if the applicant doesn't provide the information, the person taking the application, on behalf of the lender, is required to note the information on the basis of visual observation or surname.

The borrower and co-borrower are asked to check the following boxes:

❏ I do not wish to furnish this information

Ethnicity/Race: (for race, may check more than one designation)
❏ Hispanic or Latino
❏ Not Hispanic or Latino
❏ American Indian or Alaska Native
❏ Native Hawaiian or Other Pacific Islander
❏ Asian
❏ White
❏ Black or African American

Sex:
❏ Female
❏ Male

The interviewer (who is taking the application) must provide his name, signature, telephone number, address of the interviewer's employer, and answer the following question:

This application was taken by:
❏ Face-to-face interview
❏ Mail
❏ Telephone
❏ Internet

Truth in Lending Is Complicated

The federal government requires under the *Truth in Lending (TIL) Act* that within three days of a loan application, the lender provides a statement containing "good faith estimates" of the costs of the loan. The estimate will include the total finance charge and the *annual percentage rate (APR)*. The APR expresses the cost of the loan as an annual rate. It's higher than the stated contract interest rate on the mortgage because it takes into account points paid, mortgage insurance, and other fees that add to the cost of the loan.

As the mortgage broker, you may provide your clients with a TIL, and then the lender will provide one as well. There may be a difference between your estimate and the lender's. This is usually because the client is uncertain which loan he wants when he applies. By the time the application is submitted to the lender for approval, the loan is designated.

def•i•ni•tion

The **Truth in Lending Act (TIL)** requires lenders to provide loan applicants a statement containing "good faith estimates" of the true cost of the loan. It will include the total finance charge and the annual percentage rate. The **annual percentage rate (APR)** is the cost of the loan as an annual rate. It includes points paid to secure the loan, mortgage insurance, and other fees.

Step by step, let's review each part:

Federal Truth-in-Lending Disclosure Statement

Lender:

Borrower:

Property Address:

❑ Initial disclosure at time of application

❑ Final disclosure based on contract terms

Part One: Overview of the Loan

◆ **Annual Percentage Rate.** Remind your clients that this is not the same as the interest rate and will be higher than the interest rate. The APR, in addition to the amount of interest to be paid over the life of the loan, includes prepaid finance charges (points), mortgage insurance, other fees, computed at annual rate.

◆ **Finance Charges.** This is the cost of the loan. It is the total dollar amount the borrower will pay over the life of the loan. It combines the amount of interest, plus mortgage insurance, plus points.

◆ **Amount Financed.** This is not the same as the amount borrowed. It is the amount of credit available to a customer. It includes the mortgage amount, minus points and certain closing fees as shown in the Good Faith Estimate of Closing Costs.

◆ **Total of Payments.** This is the amount of payment multiplied by the number of payments the borrower will make over the life of the loan.

Part Two: The Payment Schedule

◆ **The Number of Payments.** If it's a 30-year mortgage, there would be 360 payments; a 15-year mortgage would have 180 payments.

- ◆ **The Amount of Payments.** This is the estimated dollar amount of the borrower's monthly payments.

- ◆ **When Payments Are Due Monthly.** This is the date on which payments will be due.

The lender will check the points that are applicable to the borrower's loan:

- ❑ **Demand Feature.** This loan transaction has a demand feature that permits the lender to demand full repayment of the loan before its due date.

- ❑ **Required Deposit.** The annual percentage rate does not take into account the required deposit.

- ❑ **Variable Rate Feature.** The loan contains a variable rate feature. Since the loan's rate may vary, the annual percentage rate and minimum payment may change as a result.

Disclosures about the variable rate feature should have been provided earlier.

SECURITY INTEREST: The borrower is being given security interest in:

- ❑ the goods or property being purchased

FILING OR RECORDING FEES:

LATE CHARGE: If a payment is more than 15 days late, the borrower will be charged $ / % of the principal and interest past due.

Part Three: Prepayment

If you pay off the loan early, the borrower:

1. ❑ may ❑ will not have to pay a penalty
2. ❑ may ❑ will not be entitled to a refund of part of the finance charge

The first question concerns penalties for paying off the loan early. Some loans charge a prepayment penalty. This section details whether a fee will be charged for paying off the loan before it is due.

The second question details whether the borrower will receive a refund for interest paid in previous years if the loan is paid off early. Although the borrower will not owe any additional interest, he will also not get a refund for prepaid finance charges and interest already paid in previous years.

Part Four: Insurance

This section details what insurance is required for the property.

INSURANCE: Credit life insurance, accident and health insurance, or loss of income insurance is not required in connection with this loan. This loan transaction requires the following property insurance:

❏ Hazard Insurance ❏ Flood Insurance ❏ Private Mortgage Insurance

Borrower(s) may obtain property insurance through any person of his/her choice provided said carrier meets the requirements of the lender.

Part Five: Assumption

ASSUMPTION: If this loan is to purchase and is secured by your principal dwelling, someone buying your principal dwelling,

❏ may, subject to conditions ❏ may not assume the remainder of your loan on the original terms.

Very few modern mortgages permit a buyer to assume the mortgage of the seller at the same rate and conditions. The lender will determine if the mortgage is transferable.

Locking In the Rate

If mortgage rates are stable, your clients may be less concerned about locking in their rate. It's more of a concern when rates are in flux and starting to rise. Part of your job as a mortgage broker is to keep close tabs on the trends in the economy (see Chapter 9). If you believe that rates are about to take off, you need to alert your clients and urge them to lock in.

Make sure your clients understand the difference between a rate quote and a rate lock. A lock is only valid if it's in writing.

Locking in is a legal commitment. The lender guarantees a loan at a specific rate; the borrower agrees, under some circumstances, to pay certain points and fees to lock in that rate. Both parties agree to close on the loan by a specific date.

def•i•ni•tion

Locking in is a legal commitment between the lender and the borrower. It guarantees a specific interest rate for the loan.

Most lenders don't charge a fee to lock in a rate within 60 days or less of closing. But if the borrower wants to lock it in for a longer period, the lender will charge for that privilege. While the fees vary from lender to lender, generally lenders charge between a quarter and a half of a point for an additional 30 days.

Make sure that the fee is a refundable one. Since you can lock in a rate before a mortgage is approved, which might be preferable if rates are shooting up quickly, having a refundable lock-in fee is important in case the loan is denied. Even for those whose loans are approved, you want a refundable fee since it's possible that circumstances could change; for example, the client could lose his job, and have the loan approval rescinded.

The lender will probably include a rate cap with the lock. It's a margin, about a quarter of a point above the day of the lock-in's rate, and if interest rates are higher at closing, the lender can charge the lock plus the margin. For example, if a borrower locks in a 30-year fixed mortgage at 5.5 percent with a .25 percent cap, at closing, even if rates have risen to 9 percent, the loan rate would only be 5.75 percent.

def•i•ni•tion

If interest rates fall after a borrower has locked in, most lenders permit a one-time **float down,** which allows the borrower to secure a lower interest rate.

Many lenders also permit a one-time *float down* within 30 days of closing. In that case, if rates have fallen, the borrower can grab a lower rate at closing.

The Least You Need to Know

- ◆ The amount of down payment the borrower can provide affects the type of loan and the likelihood of loan approval.

- ◆ The borrower with limited funds for a down payment may want to consider a piggyback loan in order to put down 20 percent.

- ◆ If the appraisal doesn't match or surpass the sale price of the house, the lender is unlikely to fund the loan.

- ◆ Title insurance does not cover problems that arise after the property is purchased, but can be invaluable if a defect in the title from years past surfaces.

16

Fixed Rate, Adjustable, Hybrid: Matching Mortgages and Clients

In This Chapter

◆ Finding the right mortgage is much more than finding the lowest interest rate

◆ Adjustable rate mortgages carry inherent risks

◆ Fixed rate mortgages are safe and predictable

◆ The hybrid mortgage becomes the hot new thing

Mortgages come in an infinite variety of shapes and sizes. As a mortgage broker, you'll need to explain the advantages and disadvantages of each type of loan so that your client can make an informed decision about what works best for him. On the other hand, avoid information overload. That's where, in your zeal to present options, you overwhelm the borrower with so many choices he doesn't have a clue where to begin to make a decision.

A big part of your job as a mortgage broker is as an educator. You'll need to explain the underlying premise of each of these types of loans: fixed rate, adjustable rate, and hybrid. Then you can offer the details that differ from lender to lender.

Your role is not to make the decision for your client. But out of 50 different loan products, you need to make an assessment of what you think would work best, present the choices to him, and explain your reasoning. He's counting on you to be the expert on financing. I mentally run through the various loan products and present my clients with five or six that might work for them. Generally I'll suggest a couple of loans from each type of mortgage. I can always offer more, but I haven't scared the client off with my initial presentation.

In this chapter, we'll get down to the nitty-gritty of loan products currently available on the market. I'm offering an overview of the most popular options, with the understanding that there are variations that crop up constantly. But if you have a firm understanding of these basic types of loans, you'll see that the variations don't fundamentally change how the mortgage works.

Comparing Apples and Oranges

When you present your client with alternative loan products, you need to present the full picture. The client may be tempted to reach for the loan with the lowest interest rate. But you know that the number may not be an accurate representation of the loan. For example, a 30-year mortgage with an interest rate of 8.0 percent and four points would have an APR of 8.44 percent, while a mortgage with an interest rate of 8.25 percent and only one point would have an APR of 8.36 percent.

In order to accurately compare the true cost of each loan, you need to provide the APR, the interest rate when it is calculated to include other costs of the credit. But not all lenders use the same formula to determine the APR. Some APRs are based on the loan amount, interest rate, and points, but others may include other costs including mortgage insurance, application fee, closing fee, title fee, and other costs. Make sure you are comparing similarly defined APRs when discussing loan costs.

You need to list the components of each loan product and how that impacts the short-term and long-term payments. Only then can the client make an informed decision.

Adjustable Rate Mortgages

There has to be a bit of a risk taker in the client who opts for an adjustable rate mortgage. In most cases it's not a big threat, but clients must accept that risk is the underlying premise of an ARM. With a fixed rate mortgage, the client's payment is the same for the first month and, 15 or 30 years later, for the last payment. In contrast, the interest rate of an ARM is periodically subject to change. How much of a change and how often is part of the loan specifics.

Let's define a few terms important to understanding how adjustable rate mortgages work.

The Index

Momentarily ignore the initial rate of the ARM. The lender can set that at whatever level he chooses. And almost always, that initial rate is lower than a fixed rate mortgage. It's one of the selling points of an ARM.

If this is a three-year ARM, at the end of three years the ARM's interest rate is subject to change. What do they base the new rate on? An index rate.

Lenders use different indexes as the bases for their interest rates. Some choose a Treasury Rate Index (one-, three-, or five-year T-bills); others use the Cost of Funds Index (the average cost of money to the San Francisco Federal Reserve); the London International Bank Offering Rate (LIBOR); while still others use their own cost of funds as an index, CDs index, PRIME rate, and others. The name of the index the lender uses is part of the loan papers.

That's part one of the ARM interest rate. The second part is the margin.

The Margin

Lenders then add to the index a certain number of percentage points—called the *margin*. The number of points varies from lender to lender, but is usually constant over the life of the loan. For example, the lender uses the One-Year Treasury Bill as the index, and let's assume it's at 7 percent. The lender then uses a 2 percent margin. That would make the interest rate 9 percent (7 percent index + 2 percent margin = 9 percent interest rate). Buyers can often buy down the margin. Like points, this is a good investment if the buyer plans to hold on to the property for the long term. It's paying money now to save money over the life of the loan.

def•i•ni•tion

The **margin** is the number of percentage points a lender adds to the index to determine the ARM interest rate. The **adjustment period** is the period during the life of an ARM between one rate change and the next.

Two lenders can use the same index, but use different margins resulting in different rates.

The period between one rate change and the next is called the *adjustment period*.

"Cap" Talk

Since the ARM interest rate is subject to change, lenders build in certain protections that limit some of the risks of an adjustable mortgage.

Almost all ARMs have a *rate ceiling*, also referred to as a lifetime cap. This is the highest interest rate that a borrower can receive under an adjustable rate mortgage over the life of the note. It is usually a specified number of percentage points above the initial interest rate.

Many ARMs also have *periodic caps*. This limits how much the interest rate can increase from one adjustment period to the next.

Monthly ARMs have *payment caps* that limit the increase of the monthly payment at the time of adjustment, usually to a percentage of the previous payment.

Here's an example:

Type of Mortgage	**Points**
7/1 ARM mortgage, LIBOR Index	.875
Amount of Mortgage	**Periodic Cap**
$100,000	2 percent
Initial Rate	**Lifetime Cap**
5.75 percent	5 percent

How does it work? These calculations are simplified for the sake of illustrating how points and caps work. Actual payment figures would include amortization of the mortgage, taxes, insurance, and so on.

- It's an adjustable rate mortgage with an initial rate of 5.75 percent and .875 points ($875). The monthly payment (without taxes and insurance) is $583.

- Interest rate changes are tied to the LIBOR index.

- For the first seven years, the interest rate is constant, at 5.75 percent.

♦ At the first interest rate adjustment, beginning with year 8 of the loan, the rate cannot increase or decrease by more than 2percent (the periodic cap). Worst-case scenario: the highest interest rate permitted at that first adjustment is 7.75 percent. The monthly payment, without taxes and insurance, would be $716.41.

♦ At the second interest rate adjustment date, one year later, now the ninth year of the loan, the interest cannot increase or decrease by more than 2 percent from the interest rate in effect immediately prior to the interest rate adjustment date. The lifetime cap of 5 percent limits the top rate that can ever charged. That means at no point can the rate be more than 10.75 percent (5 percent above the initial rate of 5.75 percent).

♦ If it were a monthly ARM, it could have a payment cap. Let's say it was 7.5 percent. That would limit how much the monthly payment can increase at the time of adjustment. For example, on a $583 monthly payment, this cap limits any increase to no more than $43.73 ($583 × .075 = $43.73) in the first adjustment, for a total of $626.73. The second adjustment could increase to no more than $673.73 ($626.73 × .075 = $47; $626.73 + $47 = $673.73).

Carryover Increases

Some ARMs permit rate increase carryovers so even if there is no change in the index rate at the time of adjustment, if the increase at the previous adjustment was limited by the periodic cap and did not cover the actual index increase, it carries over to the next adjustment period.

For example, using the same loan described here:

Initial Rate: 5.75 percent

First Adjustment: LIBOR increases 1 percent, loan interest rate is 6.75 percent.

Second Adjustment: LIBOR increases by 3 percent, but with periodic cap, loan's interest rate can only increase by 2 percent, so loan rate is now 8.75 percent with one point carryover.

Third Adjustment: LIBOR has 0 percent increase. But the extra point that wasn't included in the second adjustment carries over and the loan rate is 9.75 percent.

Bottom Line: The loan rate can increase at any scheduled adjustment date when the index plus the margin is higher than the rate currently being paid before the adjustment.

Interest Only ARMs

As borrowers look for financing solutions to help with cash flow problems, interest only ARMs have grown in popularity. They meet the needs of the borrower who has limited funds at the onset of the loan, but anticipates an increase in his earnings. For example, a 5-year ARM, interest only option, has a fixed interest rate for the first five years of the loan. Years 6 through 30, the interest rate is adjusted every year to the sum of the LIBOR index plus a margin rounded to the nearest one eighth of one percentage point (.125 percent). The margin doesn't change throughout the term of the loan. During the first five years of the loan, the borrower is offered an interest only payment option or an interest and principal payment option. For those who pay the interest only, the principal is obviously not reduced during that period. Years 6 through 30 require a principal and interest payment, but obviously the payments are significantly higher if no principal has been reduced for the first five years.

This option appeals to the borrower with limited funds, but a strong certainty that his income is going to increase enough during the life of the loan to pay the interest and principal. For example, the borrower who has just finished school and is beginning his career.

Heads Up!

Interest only loans have gotten a lot of press lately. There are concerns that some clients have gotten in way over their heads with these loans and end up with nothing to show for their years of mortgage payments. But for the right client, interest only loans can make sense. They are an excellent tool for maximum tax deductions. Remember you have 400 different loan products. Your job is to find the right one for each client.

There Is No Free Lunch: Negative Amortization

Most mortgages are designed to amortize: through monthly payments, the borrower reduces his debt to a zero balance by the end of the loan. In order to do that, the monthly payments are divided between paying down the interest and the principal. In the beginning of the loan, most of the payment goes towards interest.

The problem with payment caps is, while they limit sticker shock from skyrocketing interest rates, they can lead to *negative amortization*. The payments don't cover the rising interest rate, so the difference is added to the loan balance. The borrower could end up owing more than the market value of the home. Most loan papers limit the amount of negative amortization to 110 to 125 percent of the original loan amount. If the loan balance exceeds this amount, the borrower is required to accelerate principal payments until it reaches the recommended loan to value.

def•i•ni•tion

> **Negative amortization** occurs when the monthly payments are insufficient to cover the interest accruing on the balance. The difference is added to the remaining principal due.

If home values are increasing, then by selling the home, or refinancing, the borrower can repay the now larger debt. If home values have fallen, then the borrower is in trouble. The borrower can avoid negative amortization if he pays the additional interest owed monthly.

Negative amortization sounds scary—and for some homebuyers it's a tragedy. But again, for some clients, it may be the right choice. It's made for the buyer who is banking on the property appreciating in value, wants to minimize his monthly payments and the amount of money he puts down, and wants the interest deductions. Again, you need to understand your client's financial circumstances and plans and then you can help him choose the right loan product.

Here's a simplified example.

1/1 ARM loan with an initial rate of 5.75 percent, 2 percent rate cap, and 7½ percent payment cap.

Year One

Loan Amount: $65,000 @ 5.75 percent

Monthly Payment—$379

Of the $4548 paid, $3715 is for interest and $833 is for principal.

Year Two

Loan Amount: $64,167 @ 7.75%

Monthly Payment—$459

Of the $5508 paid, $4,952 is for interest and $556 is for principal.

But there is a 7½ percent payment cap. Monthly payment is $407.43 ($379 × .075) = $28.43 + $379 = $407.43 × 12 = $4,889.16.

Since interest for that year is actually $4,952, that results in a shortfall of $62.84. The borrower begins year three of the loan having not paid down the principal at all and the shortfall is added to the principal, which is now $64,229.84.

Negative amortization also occurs with option ARMs, also known as payment-option adjustables. This form of financing gives borrowers the option of several different monthly payment plans ranging from full amortization of interest and principal to minimum payments as low as 1 percent. Borrowers who opt for the minimum payment plan that doesn't even cover the interest due may quickly find themselves in deeper debt, the result of negative amortization.

This kind of loan may appeal to:

◆ the homeowner who is buying more than he can afford at that time, but who envisions an increase in his income

◆ the self-employed borrower whose income fluctuates and who wants the flexibility to make lower payments in some months

◆ the owner of rental properties who wants the payment flexibility to avoid negative cash flow should the properties not be leased.

Most option ARMs have built-in periodic conversion or reset rules that adjust the monthly payments at fixed points in time. The sticker shock that comes as the borrower transitions from minimal payments to dramatically higher ones (sometimes 70 to 90 percent) can be overwhelming. The borrower is forced to find a cheaper alternative, find the cash, or default. If the borrower has limited equity in the house, which is likely since these loans generally appeal to those with inadequate cash reserves, and if housing values have decreased since the purchase, the owner is left with a mortgage that even the sale of the house won't pay off.

Industry leaders are tightening the reins on these option loans because of fears of a rising tide of defaults. This isn't acceptable to bond investors (in the secondary mortgage market) who have purchased *option ARM* pooled mortgages. Your client may still need and want an option ARM.

Like any loan, you should advise him to consider:

◆ the advantages and risks of such financing

def•i•ni•tion

Option ARMs give borrowers a choice of monthly payment alternatives, including some that do not cover the interest due. This can result in negative amortization. The popularity of option ARMs has resulted in this form of financing quintupling its market share.

- whether he would be better off renting until he builds up his cash reserve

- whether, if he chooses this type of loan, he has the self-discipline to make higher payments when he can.

Prepayment and Conversion Considerations

ARMs come in many configurations. Some permit the borrower to pay off the loan in full without any prepayment penalty whenever the loan rate is adjusted. Others charge a fee. Still others permit the borrower to negotiate to eliminate or reduce the fee. You want to review with your client the specifics of the loan he is considering.

There can be a *soft prepayment clause*, which permits prepayment without penalty, or a *hard prepayment clause*, which requires the borrower to pay a penalty for prepaying the mortgage. Check the laws of your state because some have restrictions on prepayment penalties.

def•i•ni•tion

A **soft prepayment clause** in a loan agreement that permits the borrower to repay the loan before it's due without penalty; a **hard prepayment clause** requires the borrower to pay a penalty for paying off the loan before it's due.

Some ARMs permit the borrower to convert his ARM to a fixed-rate mortgage at designated times. The new rate is generally tied to the current market rate for fixed-rate mortgages. There may be a fee for the conversion. The interest rate and upfront fees may be higher for convertible ARMs. Again, as the mortgage broker, you want to review each of the loan's requirements with your client.

ARMs Are Good Choices for ...

Adjustable rate mortgages generally offer lower interest rates, at least for the initial period, than fixed rate mortgages. But ask your clients the following questions before they elect an ARM:

- If interest rates rise, will your income also be increasing enough to cover the additional costs?

- Are you anticipating any other large-ticket expenses, such as a car purchase or school tuition, in the short term?

- How long do you plan to own this home?

That last question, length of ownership, is critical. Especially for clients who anticipate remaining in the house for a relatively short term, rising interest rates may not be a problem. If your client opts for a 7/1 ARM that has a lower initial interest rate than a fixed mortgage, if he plans to sell the home before the adjustment period, he may not care if interest rates rise.

ARMs make sense for the client who doesn't mind a certain level of risk, needs (or wants) a lower interest rate for cash flow purposes, anticipates his income rising so is confident he can cover any increase in interest rates, or needs a larger loan.

Electing an adjustable rate mortgage with a lower interest rate may qualify the borrower for a bigger loan. Lenders sometimes grant a larger loan based on current income and the first year's payments rather than on the payment schedule if there is an increase in interest rates.

Even negative amortization may be an acceptable risk for some clients. In a rapidly appreciating market, the borrower may be able to cover the increased loan balance because the value of his house has appreciated as well.

Make sure your client understands all the provisions of his loan, what each of the caps mean (and their consequences), and what his payment schedule will be.

Fixed Rate Mortgages

The *fixed rate mortgage* is the traditional home loan. The borrower is guaranteed that the interest rate will not change during the entire life of the loan. That can be good news if interest rates are low and the borrower can lock in a good rate. It can be less appealing if rates are high and the borrower is looking at 15 or 30 years of a high rate even if at some point interest rates fall.

Variations on a Theme

Fixed rate mortgages generally run for either 15 or 30 years. Here are the pros and cons of each option.

The advantages of a 15-year fixed rate mortgage:

- equity built up sooner
- lower amount of interest paid
- loan finished faster

The disadvantages of a 15-year fixed rate mortgage:

♦ higher monthly payments

♦ may only qualify for a smaller loan amount

> **def•i•ni•tion** _____
>
> A **fixed rate mortgage** is a loan with an interest rate that does not change during the entire term of the loan.

The advantages of a 30-year fixed rate mortgage:

♦ smaller monthly payments

♦ may qualify for a larger loan

♦ more flexibility and cash flow

The disadvantages of a 30-year fixed rate mortgage:

♦ pay more interest over the life of the loan (as much as double the amount of a 15-year loan)

♦ takes longer to pay off

Let's compare the costs of the same loan under a 15-year plan and under a 30-year payoff:

$100,000 @ 6% for 15 Years
Monthly payments: $843.86
Total interest paid over lifetime of loan: $51,894
Total payments: $151,894

$100,000 @ 6% for 30 Years
Monthly payments: $615.72
Total interest paid over lifetime of loan: $121,656
Total payments: $221,656

Which Option Is Best?

There really is no "right" decision on whether to choose a 15- or 30-year fixed rate mortgage. Your client needs to determine what works best in the short and long term. While he undoubtedly would save money in the long run by opting for the 15-year loan, he may find himself cash strapped by undertaking such a large monthly payment.

Ask your client to review his current and foreseeable monthly obligations.

◆ Does his income cover the larger payment?

◆ If he anticipates new obligations, such as tuition, automobile purchase, or even a new baby, will he be short each month by choosing the 15-year option?

◆ Is he confident that his income will not be reduced during the course of the loan? Is he planning to retire?

A good alternative, if he has any doubts about assuming the larger monthly payment, is to choose a 30-year mortgage, but increase the amount he pays each month. He can double up payments and the additional checks will go directly to principal. That way he reduces the amount of interest he pays, but isn't contractually obligated to make the higher payments every month.

Hybrid Mortgages: The Best (and Worst) of Both

This loan is a combination of a fixed loan and an ARM. It starts out as a fixed rate loan, but morphs into an ARM. It generally carries a lower interest rate than a fixed rate loan, and less risk than a 1-year ARM.

Hybrids are available in varying time lengths. For example: 3/1, 5/1, 7/1, and 10/1.

Here's how it works. The 3/1 hybrid is a 30-year loan, with a fixed rate for the first 3 years. At that point, the interest rate and payment rate changes once a year for the life of the loan. Initially, the rate is less than for a fixed rate loan.

The other combinations work similarly, but a 3/1 will have a lower initial rate than a 10/1 because the higher the delayed adjustment period, the higher the initial rate.

There are 15-year hybrid loans with the same characteristics as the 30-year versions, but a shorter loan term.

There are hybrids that have longer adjustment periods. For example, there is the 3/3, which means that after the initial period of three years, the interest rate and payment rate change once every three years.

Hybrids Score Big

The popularity of this new mortgage is the result of several trends.

◆ Serial refinancing is much more common. Homeowners are comfortable with having a succession of loans and not intimidated by the mortgage process.

♦ As homeowners refinance or move frequently, the average loan is paid off in three to five years. So a homeowner may seize the hybrid's initial rate with the thought of refinancing or moving before the ARM portion begins.

♦ With mortgage rates so low for such an extended period, adjustable rates just aren't scary. Of course, any ARM carries a risk that the market will change and rates will rise.

Did You Know?

According to Freddie Mac, ARMs, including hybrids, have held a 14 percent share of the new mortgage market for the first six months of 2005.

♦ With rising home prices, the initial lower rate of the hybrid permits borrowers to leverage their income to buy a more expensive home.

Hybrids are likely to get more popular now that Fannie Mae has standardized terms for the 5/1 hybrids that it pools for mortgages. This will expand the money from the bond market for hybrids. Lenders are likely to push these loans harder and may lower initial rates even more to attract customers.

Fannie Mae's standard for a 5/1 is:

♦ 5 percent cap on first interest rate adjustment.

♦ 2 percent cap on subsequent annual adjustments.

♦ the interest rate can never be more than 5 percentage points higher than the initial rate. For example, there would be a 9.5 percent lifetime maximum on a loan initiated at 4.5 percent.

With a 30/5/1, the difference of 1 percent between a 4.75 initial rate for the first 5 years of the hybrid versus 5.75 percent for a fixed rate mortgage means a savings of $8,940.

The Pluses and Minuses of the Hybrid

As with any loan, there are advantages and disadvantages of taking a hybrid mortgage.

On the plus side:

♦ a lower initial interest rate than a fixed rate mortgage

♦ less risk than a 1-year ARM

♦ good option if homeowner plans to be in house for a limited time and moves before ARM component kicks in

♦ lower initial interest rate may permit borrower to qualify for a larger loan

♦ rates could decline, in which case ARM rate would be even lower than initial fixed rate

On the negative side:

♦ rates are generally higher than 1-year ARM

♦ rates could rise, resulting in higher payments when ARM component begins

♦ harder to plan finances with the threat of higher rates always a possibility during ARM component

♦ if market is rising significantly, then ARM rates could be significantly higher than initial fixed-rate period

The Least You Need to Know

♦ Use the annual percentage rate (APR) of loans to more accurately compare rates.

♦ Serial refinancing has changed the way homeowners approach the mortgage process.

♦ Negative amortization can be a dangerous result of payment caps on ARMs.

♦ Adjustable rate and hybrid mortgages both offer a borrower a way of leveraging his income in order to obtain a bigger loan.

What's the "Point"?

In This Chapter

- ◆ Myths and misconceptions about points
- ◆ When points make sense for your client
- ◆ Who pays the points?
- ◆ The tax implications of points
- ◆ Points = pay for you

Points get a bum rap in the mortgage business. Most clients complain bitterly if you suggest a loan that has points, and I've never understood that. If you know you're going to be in a house for at least five years, points are the best thing since sliced white bread. For the mortgage broker, each point paid means more money in your pocket. It's a win-win situation.

So before your clients rule out any loan that has points attached to it, you need to educate them about the advantages—and yes, disadvantages—of points.

In this chapter, you'll learn how, when, and why to advise your clients to use points.

Points: Upfront and Unashamed

Buying a house is an expensive proposition. Tell your clients that they need to put even more money up front at the closing and they're likely to balk. But if they understand that these up-front charges will actually save them money in the long run, it's likely to make a difference.

def•i•ni•tion

Points are the up-front charges, levied by the lender, to obtain a certain mortgage. Each point costs 1 percent of the loan. The **par rate** is the lowest interest rate at which a lender will make a loan without charging discount points.

Points are charges levied by the lender, payable at closing, to obtain a certain mortgage. Each point costs 1 percent of the loan and is considered, for tax purposes, prepaid interest. Points may also be called loan origination fees, loan discount, or discount points.

Every loan has a par rate which is the lowest interest rate at which a loan will be made without charging discount points. If a loan is procured at less than par, discount points are charged. So if the *par rate* is 5.625 percent, zero points, to get a loan at 5.25 percent, the borrower would have to pay at least 1 point.

Here's how it works.

Start with the loan options offered by one lender for a loan of $100,000:

15-Year Fixed Rate Loans

0 Points	1 Point*	2 Points**
5.625 percent	5.250 percent	5.125 percent

* Points owed were actually 1.125
** Points owed were actually 1.750

Would a client be willing to lower his interest rate by .375 percent (1 point) or up to .5 percent (2 points) over the course of a 15-year mortgage for less than $2,000?

What would his monthly payments be for a loan at each rate?

Assume the loan is for $100,000, with a down payment of 20 percent or more:

5.625%	5.250%	5.125%
$823.73	$803.88	$797.32

On a simple level, it would take a little more than six years to recoup the cost of the points. After that, the buyer would be saving $26.41 a month or $316.92 a year choosing the lowest interest rate. And that's not even including the reduced loan balance over the lifetime of the loan for having a lower interest rate.

Does It Work with ARMs?

Now let's look at a 7/1 ARM and see the effect of paying points. Does it still pay?

0 Points	1 Point	2 Points
6.500%	5.625%	5.375%

Assume the loan is for $100,000, with a down payment of 20 percent. For this loan, there is no prepayment penalty and the interest rate is constant for seven years and then adjusted every year thereafter. The interest rate cannot increase or decrease by more than 5 percent on the first interest rate adjustment date. Starting with the second interest rate adjustment date, the interest rate cannot increase or decrease by more than 2 percent from the interest rate in effect immediately prior to the interest rate adjustment. There is a life of loan interest rate ceiling equal to the sum of the initial interest rate plus 5 percent.

Bottom line: the rate can't go higher than 11.5 percent if the borrower takes the loan with an interest rate of 6.5 percent, with no points; 10.625 percent if he pays one point; and 10.375 percent if he pays 2 points. In other words, by taking an ARM, the borrower is gambling that the rates will not go up, or at least not much. But in any case, while the rate reduction from paying points applies only to the starting rate, a lower starting rate usually means a lower maximum rate, too.

So for the first seven years, when the interest rate cannot be adjusted, here's what he would pay.

0 Points	1 Point	2 Points*
$871.11	$823.73	$810.47

* The actual point is 1.875 percent.

On a simple level, it would take not quite three years to recoup the cost of two points ($2,000). After that, the buyer would be saving $60.64 a month or $727.68 a year choosing the lower interest rate. And that's not even including the reduced loan balance over the lifetime of the loan for having a lower interest rate.

Here's the Hitch

But, and here's where the calculations get more complicated, these calculations haven't considered equity growth and lost interest earnings. Those calculations are more complex and must include a borrower's tax bracket in the calculations and the current investment rate, what the borrower can earn on his money. There is software that can run limitless scenarios that can provide your client with figures customized to his circumstances.

On my website, www.facmortgage.com, you can practice with different factors (rates, tax bracket, investment rates) to get a feel for how points can pay off.

Paying points is generally a good thing, but it does require an additional outlay of cash. And there's no marketability of having a lower interest rate. The buyer has used some of his liquid assets to secure the lower interest rate, but he can't sell that rate to raise immediate cash should he need it.

Here are the basic rules of thumb:

- It generally takes about 4½ years to recoup the cost of paying points, depending on a borrower's tax bracket, current investment rates, and the amount of down payment and loan. If a homeowner remains in the house for longer than that, it's worth it to pay points.

- If the borrower plans to sell the house within a short period of time, then paying the points to get a lower rate isn't cost effective.

- It's almost never cost effective to pay points to reduce the rates on a 1-year ARMs.

- In general, if a borrower plans to stay in his home for more than four years, it's worth it to pay points for a lower interest rate for any fixed rate mortgage. It's certainly worth it for any 10-year ARM, generally for a 7-year ARM, and questionable for 5-year and 3-year ARMs.

Should the Client Finance the Points?

One way to avoid a cash outlay for the points is to roll the points into the loan. But of course, it increases the loan balance. The amount of time needed to hit a break-even point and then benefit from a lower interest rate is longer. But there are important caveats:

◆ Will financing the points by adding them into the loan trigger any additional costs to the borrower? If so, then you must discuss with your client if financing the points still makes sense.

◆ Will financing the points increase the loan amount above the maximum size loan eligible for purchase by Fannie Mae and Freddie Mac? This threshold changes annually. In 2005, the average single-family first mortgage loan was $359,650 (higher in Alaska, Hawaii, Guam, and the U.S. Virgin Islands). A mortgage above the Fannie Mae/Freddie Mac limit results in higher interest rates.

◆ Will financing the points push the mortgage into a higher mortgage insurance premium category? Mortgage insurance is assessed on loans in which the down payment is under 20 percent. The premium is based on the ratio of loan amount to property value: 80–85 percent; 85–90 percent; and 90–95 percent. Will adding in the cost of the points push the loan into another category and increase the cost of the insurance?

Points get a bad rap. Be sure and discuss the very real advantages of points if the buyer intends to remain in the house.

The Tax Implications of Points

Paying points often pays off in the long run, but their tax value is immediate. According to the IRS, a borrower can deduct the points in full in the year they are paid, if all the following requirements are met:

◆ The loan is secured by the primary home (where the borrower lives most of the time).

◆ Paying points is an established business practice in the area in which the borrower lives.

◆ The points paid were not more than the amount generally charged in that area.

- ◆ The borrower uses the cash method of accounting, in other words, the borrower reports income in the year he receives it and deducts expenses in the year he pays them.

- ◆ The points were not paid for items that usually are separately stated on the settlement sheets such as appraisal fees, inspection fees, title fees, attorney fees, or property taxes.

- ◆ The borrower provided funds at or before closing that were at least as much as the points charged, not counting points paid by the seller. The borrower cannot have borrowed the funds from the lender or mortgage broker in order to pay the points.

- ◆ The borrower uses the loan to buy or build a primary home.

- ◆ The points were computed as a percentage of the principal amount of the mortgage.

- ◆ The amount is clearly shown on the settlement sheet.

Points that do not meet these requirements may be deductible over the life of the loan. Points paid for refinancing generally can only be deducted over the life of the new mortgage.

Refinancing and Points

We'll talk more about refinancing and home equity loans in Chapter 21, but it's worth noting that paying points to refinance a mortgage or take out a home equity loan also makes sense. Again, the first question has to be: How long is the borrower planning to be in the house? If the intention is to stay at least five years, then points generally are worth it, certainly on a 15- or 30-year fixed mortgage.

But the tax implications are different. In most refinancing cases, the homeowner deducts the points over the lifetime of the loan. In general, here's how it works.

Assuming a $100,000 loan, a borrower refinances his mortgage and pays $2,000 for 2 points for a 30-year mortgage. A 30-year mortgage has 360 payments. The borrower could deduct $66.72 each year of the mortgage ($5.56 per payment × 12 = $66.72).

The Exception to the Rule

If the borrower uses part of the refinanced mortgage proceeds to improve the primary home and meets the first six requirements we described above when discussing a first mortgage, then the borrower can fully deduct that part of the points related to the improvement in the year that the borrower paid them with his own funds.

But if the borrower uses the refinancing to pay other expenses, such as college tuition or to buy a new car, then he must amortize the points deduction over the life of the loan.

The Serial Refinancer

When mortgage rates continue to drop, some homeowners may decide to refinance a second (or third or fourth) time. What happens to the remainder of the points being amortized on that first refinance?

It gets complicated.

Let's go back to the example above. The borrower has decided to refinance after four years. He's amortized the $2,000 he paid in points from the first refinance, and has deducted a total of $266.88 over the four years. That leaves $1733.22 remaining. He paid another 2 points, $2,000, for a new, 30-year refinance.

- ◆ If the refinance is with the same lender, then the remainder of the first refinance points ($1733.22) gets added to the points from the new refinance ($2,000). These two (for a total of $3,733.22), are then amortized over the life of the second refinance. He would then deduct $126.60 per year over the life of the loan.

- ◆ If the refinance is with a different lender, then the borrower can deduct any remaining balance of the points in the year the mortgage ends, either due to a prepayment, refinancing, or even foreclosure. So the borrower would deduct $1733.22 for the year of the second refinance, plus $126.60 of the second refinance (or portion thereof depending upon when the refinance is completed). The borrower would then amortize the points of the second refinance over the life of the mortgage. However, if the borrower uses the refinance proceeds to improve the primary home, then the exception discussed previously applies.

If a client refinances a second time, he can take a tax deduction of the leftover points from the first refinancing. For example, let's say he paid 2 points the first time he refinanced. Two years later, he refinances again. Since the tax deduction of refinancing points is amortized over the length of the loan, he is limited to deducting only $\frac{1}{30}$ of the points each year (presuming a 30-year mortgage). After just two years, he would still have a significant amount of undeducted interest on the original points. At the time of the refinancing, however, he can deduct the entire remaining portion of the original points. If he has paid new points for the second refinancing, he begins to deduct that amortized amount as well.

Remind clients of this tax deduction when working with them on their refinance.

> **Heads Up!** _____
>
> NY CEMA (New York Consolidation, Extension, and Modification Form) is a program that may save your clients the cost of mortgage taxes when refinancing. If a lender will assign the old mortgage to the lender of the refinance, mortgage taxes, worth hundreds of dollars, can be waived. Lenders are more interested in doing this when they hold the old mortgage and are handling the refinance. They lose interest when the refinance is with one of their competitors. Check your state laws to see if a similar program is available in your area.

A Few More Variations

Let's suppose that the borrower refinances his home, with a 15-year $100,000 loan, with three points. Two of those points were for prepaid interest, but one of them was charged for services, charges that would normally be stated separately on a settlement sheet, like the mortgage recording fee or appraisal. In this case, the borrower can deduct $2,000 (two points) over the life of the loan, but the remaining point is not deductible. It was a fee for services.

Or the same borrower refinances, is charged 3 points, but one is for services so it's not deductible. He uses $25,000 of the loan for home improvements and $75,000 to repay his existing mortgage. In this case, the borrower deducts 25 percent of the deductible points ($25,000 ÷ $100,000 = .25) in the first year, $500. He then prorates the rest of the deductible points ($2,000 − $500 = $1,500) over the life of the loan ($1,500 ÷ 180 months). That equals $8.33 per month or $100 per year.

While it's important that you understand the basic parameters of tax deductions for points, you are not a tax professional. Advise your clients to speak to a tax expert about their personal circumstances.

Who Gets the Deduction: Seller or Borrower?

Sometimes, to facilitate a deal, a seller will offer to pay the points. But the seller cannot deduct them as interest on his return. They are considered a selling expense and can be used to reduce the amount of gain realized.

If the seller pays the points, the buyer may deduct them provided the buyer subtracts the amount from the basis, or cost, of the residence.

Negative Points

Unlike the points we've been discussing, which are paid by the borrower to the lender in order to secure a lower interest rate, *negative points* are paid by the lender to the borrower in order to secure a higher interest rate and cash rebate.

In exchange for originating these loans, the lender pays the mortgage broker a *yield spread premium*, a rebate for bringing in a higher-interest, and therefore potentially more lucrative, loan. Mortgage brokers must disclose to the customer the yield spread premium. Like the points paid to secure a lower interest rate, each negative point is equal to 1 percent of the loan. For example, for a $100,000 loan with negative 2.5 points, the broker would earn $2,500.

> ## def•i•ni•tion
>
> **Negative points** are cash rebates offered by lenders to consumers as part of a higher-interest-rate loan. The rebate may only be used to defray settlement costs. The **yield spread premium** is the payment from a lender to a mortgage broker for originating a loan at an "above par" rate. It's also known as a lender rebate.

Why would you, in good conscience, steer a customer to a higher interest rate? Because it's the best deal for the client.

For the cash-strapped client, negative points can be the difference between buying a home or not. In exchange for a higher interest rate, the lender gives the borrower a cash rebate that can be used for settlement costs. But since these funds are limited to paying settlement costs, the client should never take more negative points than he can use to defray those costs. The remainder of the rebate is lost to the client.

For example, a lender might have the following rate/points programs on a 30-year fixed rate mortgage:

> 7.5% with 3.5 points
> 8% with 0 points
> 8.75% with -2.5 points

If a customer's settlement costs on a $100,000 loan are $2,500, then the negative points in the aforementioned programs could be fully used. But if the settlement costs were only $1,800, the client would not pocket the remaining $700.

Another borrower who might be interested in negative points is the client who doesn't intend to hold on to the loan for long. The rebate, even with a higher interest rate, may be a selling point. He uses the cash to pay settlement costs, flips the property quickly, and is in and out fast.

But for those who intend to keep the mortgage for an extended period, a higher interest rate is less appealing, even with a rebate.

The Least You Need to Know

- ◆ Points can be financially profitable for both the customer and the mortgage broker.

- ◆ If a homeowner plans to remain in his home for at least five years, then paying for points makes sense.

- ◆ The tax implications of paying for points is complicated.

- ◆ A cash-strapped buyer or a client who intends to flip the property quickly may be interested in loans with negative points.

Part 5

Niche Markets Pay Off

Within the mortgage industry, there are important niche markets. In this part, we'll review the way mortgage brokers can help low-income and minority clients join the ranks of homeowners. We'll also examine the growing business of reverse mortgages: a way senior citizens can stay in their homes and take advantage of their home equity in order to get a steady income stream. Last, I'll give you an insider's look at the profitable mortgage market of co-ops, condotels, multi-family housing, and refinancing.

Serving the Public Interest and Earning $$$

In This Chapter

- ◆ Low-income clients become homeowners
- ◆ Federal grants add dollars to the mix
- ◆ Nonprofit groups fund down payments
- ◆ Subprime loans are a (risky) alternative

No one should be denied the opportunity to fulfill the American dream and own his own home. There are programs designed to help low-income and minority groups become home buyers. As a mortgage broker, you will still earn fees for each of these loans, and there is the added satisfaction of helping others.

In this chapter, we'll review the requirements that low-income borrowers must meet and the programs that are available, and look closely at the subprime mortgages that have become an alternative method of financing.

A Complex Problem Just Got Tougher

Helping low-income and minority clients buy a home is more complicated, but also an incredibly satisfying experience. Don't get me wrong. I absolutely relish finding the right loan to help a client buy a mansion with a putting green in his yard, and I earn every dime of the deal. But I also take pride in helping families navigate the tricky path to home ownership when at first glance they don't seem to qualify.

Fannie Mae's 2003 National Housing Survey sheds light on the complexity of the problem. It found four critical areas that must be addressed in order to reach the underserved and close the minority homeownership gap.

Information Gap

There is a significant difference between the general public and the minority communities in their levels of accurate understanding about buying a home. It's especially pronounced among Spanish-language dominant Hispanics. This group is referred to as Spanish Hispanics; English-language dominant Hispanics are called English Hispanics.

This information gap showed up in their responses to the survey that questioned respondents on the home-buying process. For example:

◆ One third of Americans overall claim an above average understanding of the home-buying process. In contrast, only 23 percent of African Americans and 18 percent of Spanish Hispanics claim such knowledge.

◆ 55 percent of English Hispanics and 51 percent of African Americans know that it's not necessary to have stayed in the same job for at least five years to qualify for a mortgage, while only 39 percent of Spanish Hispanics knew this.

◆ 64 percent of English Hispanics and 57 percent of African Americans knew that it's not necessary to have a perfect credit rating to qualify for a mortgage, but only 22 percent of Spanish Hispanics understood this.

Affordability Gap

Not only is there a real difference in how much minority groups can save for a house, there is also a perception that they can't afford to buy a home, despite various programs designed to help.

◆ More than half of all "seekers" (those who began the home-buying process, but did not take it to completion) said that the reason they failed was because it was more expensive than they initially thought, or they had concerns about qualifying for a low-cost mortgage because of their credit history.

◆ Affordability worries are primarily driven by a lack of savings. "Seekers" save only 7.6 percent of their monthly income, half of what the nation saves on average (13.7 percent).

◆ Many immigrants cluster in "traditional gateway" cities. These areas have high housing costs, so affordability is even more difficult.

> **Did You Know?**
>
> 52 percent of all immigrants live in the 10 metropolitan areas with the largest immigrant populations. Nearly 50 percent of immigrants who arrived in the 1990s were living in the gateway cities in 2000.

Credit Gap

While cost is the number-one reason why renters report they haven't bought a home, credit concerns is the second leading reason (39 percent). Credit concerns are an even bigger issue for minority households: 49 percent of English Hispanics, 46 percent of Spanish Hispanics, and 42 percent of African Americans cite credit concerns as the number-one reason they haven't bought a home.

Confidence Gap

Minorities have less confidence in their abilities to complete the home-buying process than the general public. The confidence gap is magnified because minorities are especially concerned about discrimination and future home price increases.

Measuring confidence on a scale of 1 to 5, English Hispanics were nearly as confident as the general public (3.8 as compared to 3.9) that they could complete the home-buying process, but African Americans (3.6) and Spanish Hispanics (3.4) were definitely less confident.

African Americans were more concerned that they would encounter discrimination during the home-buying process (3.4 as opposed to 4.0 for the general public). Spanish Hispanics were the least confident group about obtaining a mortgage (3.2 compared to 3.9 for the general public) and worried more about finding a real estate professional (3.1 compared to 3.5 for the general public).

Fannie Mae's Commitment to Closing the Gap

Fannie Mae is committed to investing $2 trillion over the next 10 years to create 6 million new homeowners, including 1.8 million minority families. It's part of the company's American Dream Commitment, which also has goals of helping families keep their homes, and expanding the supply of affordable homes where they are needed most.

Fannie Mae's Community Home Lending mortgage products are designed to help borrowers overcome two barriers to home ownership: lack of down payment funds and qualifying income.

Remember: Fannie Mae does not make these loans directly. They come from traditional lenders. Fannie Mae sets the guidelines for qualifying for these loans and guarantees to buy pools of these loans on the secondary mortgage market.

The Community Home Buyer's Program

This mortgage product has an expanded debt-to-income ratio:

- Borrowers can use a greater amount of their monthly income toward housing costs compared to other standard mortgage products. Conventional mortgages require that no more than 28 percent of the borrower's gross monthly income be used for housing costs (principal, interest, taxes, and insurance). The Community Home Buyer's Program allows the borrower to use up to 33 percent of his gross monthly income for housing costs.

- Borrowers can use up to 38 percent of their income for monthly debt expenses, compared to the standard 36 percent.

The borrower only needs to put down 5 percent. The loans are for fixed rate mortgages only (no ARMS). It doesn't waive, however, the mortgage insurance that loans made with minimal down payments require.

To qualify for the loan, the borrower must earn no more than the area median income for his Metropolitan Statistical Area (MSA) or county. That income level differs from state to state, as well as within each state depending on the locale. Specified high-cost areas permit borrowers to qualify even if they exceed the median income. For example, borrowers in Hawaii can earn more than 170 percent of the median income and still qualify for the loan.

However, the maximum income limit is removed and the down payment requirement is reduced to as low as $500 or 1 percent from the borrower's own funds, if the mortgage is combined with FannieNeighbors, a mortgage option for eligible properties located in HUD-designated central cities, underserved areas, and eligible minority and low-income census tracts.

The borrower is not required to have cash reserves after closing, although we'll discuss later how having cash reserves may waive another requirement.

A compulsory home buyer education session is a built-in component of this program. That requirement, however, can be waived if the borrower meets all three of the following conditions:

- he has previously owned a home
- he can make at least a 5 percent down payment from his own resources (not a gift, loan, or grant)
- he has at least two months' mortgage payments in reserve after closing

Forty-Year Mortgages

This is a new Fannie Mae mortgage product that may serve to make home buying more affordable. By increasing the standard loan term from 30 to 40 years, monthly payments are lower and borrowers' purchasing power is enlarged. First-time home-buyers, or those living in high-cost areas seeking manageable monthly payments, may find this amortization term attractive.

The 40-year mortgage is eligible on both standard fixed rate products as well as standard 3/1, 5/1, 7/1, and 10/1 hybrid ARMs.

Other Fannie Mae Products Helping Low-Income and Minority Borrowers

Here are some other loan programs that have been developed to encourage home ownership among low-income and minority communities. Some are designed to focus on specific communities that need revitalization, others are directed at nonprofit groups that are focused on this issue.

FannieNeighbors. FannieNeighbors is a nationwide, neighborhood-based mortgage option designed to increase home ownership and revitalization in areas designated as underserved by HUD, in low- to moderate-income or minority census tracts, or in central cities. The FannieNeighbors option adds underwriting flexibility to Fannie Mae's Community Lending mortgage products by removing the income limit if a property is located in one of these areas. You can use the Fannie Mae Property GeoCoder, https://commlend.efanniemae.com/PropertyGeocoder, a free, online application, to determine whether a property qualifies for the FannieNeighbors option.

Lease-purchase. Lease-purchase is an option that nonprofit organizations can use to help borrowers who have successfully managed their credit obligations in the past, but have insufficient savings for a down payment. With lease-purchase, nonprofit organizations can purchase homes that can be leased with an option to buy. Part of the rent payment is saved for the purpose of accumulating the down payment and closing costs needed to buy the home. The mortgage may then be assumed by the borrower from the nonprofit at a later time, usually three to five years after the initial lease date.

Community land trusts. Community land trusts are established by nonprofit organizations to provide and preserve long-term affordable housing for low- and moderate-income families. Typically, a nonprofit organization acquires and holds land for the benefit of a community. The community land trust retains title to the land, but sells the homes under long-term ground leases to low- and moderate-income families at affordable ground rents. Community land trust properties are eligible for Fannie Mae's Community Lending mortgages.

To find out more about community land trusts, check out the website (www.iceclt.org/clt) for the Institute for Community Economics (ICE), which provides more detailed information on CLTs. This includes a CLT model, examples of CLTs, a list of current CLTs, and frequently asked questions. Members of ICE developed the CLT concept in the 1960s and continue to be among the industry leaders in this field.

Down Payment Gift Assistance Programs

There are several grant programs that help potential home buyers who can afford the monthly payments of a mortgage, but don't have the funds for a down payment and closing costs. Typical assistance ranges from 1 percent to 7 percent and does not have to be repaid. Funds can be used for the down payment or closing costs. They can be used for new or existing homes, but cannot be used to refinance or make home improvements.

HUD doesn't issue formal approval of gift programs by charitable organizations. The burden is on the lender to work with a reputable program that meets HUD requirements. If your client is working with a down payment gift assistance program, check with the lender to make sure that it is acceptable.

Here's how these programs generally work:

- ◆ The underlying principle is that the home seller gives a portion of the proceeds back to the buyer at closing. The amount is dependent on the type of loan the buyer is getting. But since sellers are not allowed to give homebuyers down payment funds, that is where the gift assistance program resolves the problem.

- ◆ The seller enrolls his home into a down payment assistance program. He agrees to contribute the amount equal to the assistance plus a fee (usually .75 percent of the sales price).

- ◆ At closing, the down payment funds are wired from the gift assistance program to the closing agent. The seller has no part in the transference of funds, thereby avoiding any infraction of the law.

Why would a seller want to participate in this kind of program? He's hoping for a better deal. My mother used to say, "Sometimes you got to spend money to make money." Let's look at it this way. Most sellers build in some leeway in their asking price, but have a bottom line that is where they want to end up when they walk away from the closing table. By participating in this kind of program, the seller is hoping that he'll attract a buyer who is more willing to pay closer to the asking price in return for this kind of down payment help. Hopefully, it's a win-win for both sides. While the seller can't claim the gift as a charitable contribution, he may be able to deduct it as a selling expense. He should consult a tax professional.

Some other guidelines to consider:

- ◆ The gift funds can't result in a loan that exceeds the appraised value of the home.

- ◆ Ask the lender, on behalf of your client, the wording for the offer to purchase so that it meets underwriting guidelines.

- ◆ The home buyer must qualify for a loan that allows gift funds.

- ◆ There may be limits on the sale price of homes in these programs.

◆ There are no minimum or maximum income requirements for buyers.

◆ Unused funds must be returned to the gift program.

Five Programs That Work

For the following programs, the seller pays in the amount of the gift plus a processing fee: AmeriDream (www.ameridream.org), GiftAmerica Program (www.sbrnetwork. com/giftamerica), Homes for All Program (www.ezdownpayment.com/gift/services/ buyers.asp), Nehemiah (www.getdownpayment.com/buyers/homebuyers.asp), RealtyAmerica.org (www.realtyamerica.org).

Check the websites for more information about these seller-pays programs. In the next section, we'll discuss a federal program that offers down payment assistance but does not involve the seller.

The American Dream Downpayment Act

This federally funded HUD program began in 2004. It is different from the seller pay-in programs described previously. The seller is not involved at all.

The American Dream Downpayment Act makes grants to participating jurisdictions for down payment assistance to low-income, first-time homebuyers. HUD estimated that the $200 million in grants in 2004 and 2005 would enable as many as 40,000 families to become homeowners each year.

Here are some other points to consider:

◆ The program lowers closing costs by approximately $700 per loan.

◆ The annual income of a grant recipient must not exceed 80 percent of the area median income.

◆ The maximum down payment grant is $10,000 or six percent of the purchase price of the home, whichever is greater.

◆ The average subsidy is $7,500, to be used for down payment, closing costs, and other home-buying transaction fees.

The Subprime Market

We know that lenders are interested in minimizing their risk when they make loans. The whole approval process for conventional mortgages is to give the lender a clear picture of how likely it is that the loan will be repaid in a timely fashion. In most cases, if the risk is too high, the application is rejected.

But what if the borrower were willing to pay a higher interest rate—a significantly higher rate—in order to secure the loan? Would a lender be more interested in taking the risk?

The answer is the *subprime market*. These are loans that do not meet the prime market underwriting standards. Subprime borrowers represent a higher risk because they fall into one of these categories:

def•i•ni•tion

> **Subprime market** mortgages are high-risk, high-interest loans. Borrowers may seek out these mortgages because they have poor credit histories, the loan has a high LTV ratio, or the borrower is unable to document all the information on his loan application. Subprime mortgage loan originations rose by 25 percent per year from 1994 to 2003, nearly a tenfold increase.

- ◆ Poor Credit Histories. Their credit score is typically below 650. Research has shown that loans made to borrowers with credit scores below 650 have higher delinquency rates.

- ◆ High Loan-to-Value Loans. These mortgages have an LTV over 90 percent, and may be as high as 125 percent. The value of the loan is higher than the value of the property.

- ◆ Failure to Document Loan Application Information. These borrowers, the self-employed or those whose income is dependent on tips, often can't or don't want to document all of their income. Therefore, their documented income is lower than that reported on their application.

Let's be clear. This is an established financial market with national lenders. While you may recognize Champion Mortgage and The Money Store, two subprime lenders, many divisions of commercial banks also make subprime loans.

The underwriting guidelines for the subprime market are not standardized like the ones for conventional loans. Lenders can evaluate the risks based on their own guidelines which makes it more difficult for a borrower to shop around for a good rate.

It is a market that is growing fast, but it is also under increasing federal and state scrutiny because of the huge potential for abuse. Minority borrowers are dispropor-tionately represented in this pool and there is concern that it's because they are tar-geted for these high-interest loans, even when they could qualify for a conventional loan. The National Predatory Lending Task Force (U.S. Department of the Treasury and U.S. Department of Housing and Urban Development) found that on average, the frequency of subprime lending nationwide was three times higher in low-income neighborhoods than in upper-income neighborhoods and five times higher in pre-dominantly black neighborhoods than in predominantly white neighborhoods.

According to a study by the Fannie Mae Foundation, "the high cost of subprime credit has prompted concerns that its rapid growth may be due in part to the sales tactics of lenders ("targeting") or to a lack of financial sophistication that leads some classes of borrowers to pay more than necessary for credit. At the same time, high default and foreclosure rates among some subprime borrowers have prompted concerns that it may not be in the best interest of some borrowers or of the neighborhoods in which they reside for such loans to be extended in the first place."

As a mortgage broker, your job is to provide your clients with the best deal for their circumstances. Only after you have exhausted the possibilities of a conventional mort-gage should you consider the subprime market. And for some clients, a subprime mortgage or refinance may be their only opportunity for homeownership. If it is, take the time to advise your clients of all the ramifications and risks of taking a high-interest loan. Provide them with the information they need to plan for the future and develop a plan to refinance within a few years to a conventional mortgage at a better rate once they've restored their credit rating.

The Least You Need to Know

- There is an information, confidence, affordability, and credit gap that impacts home-buying decisions among minorities.

- Fannie Mae has a group of programs designed to encourage low-income and minority home buying.

- There are federal and private down payment assistance programs that help low-income home buyers.

- The subprime market is a rapidly expanding industry that can offer money to otherwise credit-risky borrowers, but at a significantly higher interest rate.

Co-ops, Condotels, Multi-Family Housing, and More

In This Chapter

◆ Co-op financing requirements

◆ Condotels and their potential for big bucks

◆ The market for multi-family housing

◆ A word about the commercial real estate market

Mortgages—and mortgage brokers—are needed for all kinds of properties. In this chapter, we'll examine the nonconforming mortgage market. These are mortgages for properties that don't fit Fannie Mae/Freddie Mac regulations for conforming loans of single-family housing. They include cooperative housing units (commonly called co-ops), large-scale, multi-family housing (which provides rental units), and condotels (the newest craze in vacation homes). We'll also touch briefly on commercial real estate mortgages.

Each of these markets can be lucrative for the mortgage broker but the process may be more complicated. Don't miss out on the opportunity to cash in.

Co-ops: Where Home Is a Share of the Whole

A housing *cooperative (co-op)* does indeed provide housing for the owner, but he doesn't own the house. The owner buys shares or membership in a corporation which owns all the multi-unit real estate. The shareholder gets a stock certificate and a proprietary lease to the specific unit he's purchased. Cooperative housing tends to be found in urban areas.

def•i•ni•tion

A **cooperative (co-op)** is a multi-unit housing complex in which owners have shares in the cooperative corporation that owns the property. Each shareholder has the right to occupy a specific unit or apartment.

As a shareholder, the owner has the exclusive right, through an occupancy agreement or proprietary lease, to live in a specific unit. The owner has to agree to live by the rules of the corporation. The co-op board usually requires approval of any renovations to the unit (beyond painting and wallpapering), and will need to approve any buyer of the shareholder's unit. Some co-ops have rules on whether pets or children are allowed to live in the building. Each shareholder has a vote in the affairs of the corporation.

The co-op has a governing board that oversees maintenance and repairs for the building, as well as manages the finances of the cooperative. A shareholder has a mortgage for his own unit, but also pays a monthly maintenance fee to the co-op corporation. The fee covers the building's maintenance, insurance, taxes, and other expenses.

On his income tax, the shareholder deducts part of his maintenance fee because it goes toward the co-op's tax payment, as well as the interest on the mortgage for his own unit.

While some things about buying a co-op are the same as buying a conventional single-family home, some are different and it's that difference that concerns the lender. Even if the borrower is a sound financial risk, the lender is also concerned with the financial health of the entire co-op. Lenders will first approve the co-op before it approves the borrower.

The ABCs of Co-ops

The price of the individual unit is determined much like that for a house: location, location, location—and size. But the price can also be affected by whether the co-op limits the resale price of individual units (done in order to keep the housing available for a certain income group) and whether the co-op has an underlying mortgage for the entire property. Remember, as a shareholder, the buyer is responsible for the mortgage of his own unit and a portion of the whole building's mortgage.

There are three kinds of co-ops that affect the amount of equity an individual shareholder can accumulate:

◆ Market-rate housing co-op. In this type of co-op, the shareholder can buy or sell membership at the price the market will bear. The equity accumulation is similar to a single-family ownership.

◆ Limited-equity co-op. These types of co-ops limit the amount an outgoing shareholder can get from the sale of his unit. This is because these co-ops are intended to provide "affordable" housing. The co-op may have received below-market interest rate loans, grants, real estate tax abatements, or other features to make the property "affordable." There may be maximum income limits for new members.

◆ Leasing cooperative (or zero equity). These types of co-ops are owned by an outside investor, usually a nonprofit corporation. The cooperative corporation leases the property from the owner. The co-op corporation doesn't own the property so no equity can be accumulated. Sometimes, the co-op corporation buys the property from the nonprofit corporation and converts it to a market-rate or a limited equity co-op. Some leasing co-ops permit outgoing members to take part of their share of the co-op corporation's cash reserves that were built up while they lived there.

Financing the Purchase of a Co-op Share

Instead of a mortgage, the buyer applies for a share loan. The process is similar, but the lender will require much more information. Your client will be required to provide the usual documentation of his finances. But the lender is equally, if not more, interested in the financial health of the co-op as a whole. The lender fears that the underlying mortgage of the building could be foreclosed and then the lender's interest in the specific unit will be affected.

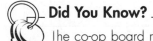

Did You Know?

The co-op board may set the requirements for the minimum down payment a buyer must provide.

The borrower's shares in the co-op and proprietary lease are essentially the collateral for the loan. But the lender can't dispose of them as easily as real estate. Should the lender foreclose, the co-op's board of directors could put conditions on the sale of the share. And if the building is not in good financial or physical condition, it would be even more difficult to dispose of the share.

The lender also worries about how much of the building is still *sponsored* owned. The sponsor is the person (or company) that owns all the shares in the cooperative when it's first formed. It might be the builder of the structure or the converter of the building from a rental building. The sponsor sells shares for the apartments, and those who buy the shares are cooperators. The sponsor owns all unsold shares. The more shares the sponsor owns, the more control the sponsor has over the fiscal and physical plan of the building. But it also means that if the sponsor gets into financial trouble, the lender may assume the sponsor's shares, and not the other cooperators.

def•i•ni•tion

The **sponsor** of a co-op is the individual or company that built the co-op or was responsible for its conversion from a rental to co-op building.

If the sponsor owns a majority or significant number of shares, a default by the sponsor could jeopardize every shareholder. Lenders are reluctant to grant loans to purchase a co-op apartment in a building that is less than 80 percent owner-occupied or in which a sponsor still holds a majority of shares (once a sufficient time has passed since the conversion plan was passed).

Co-op mortgages may have higher interest rates because of these risks.

The lender will demand that an officer or representative of the co-op board provide detailed information and documentation of the financial stability of the co-op.

Did You Know?

Both Fannie Mae and Freddie Mac purchase co-op loans as part of the secondary mortgage market.

You will need to expect that the process of securing funding for a co-op purchase will take more time than for a single-family residence. Your client will need to build that into his schedule. Not only does he have to get his own required documentation together, but he is at the mercy of the co-op board's representative in providing the following information.

Co-op information:

- The total number of units in the co-op

- The total number of co-op shares

- Whether any shareholders own more than 10 percent of the shares

- How many of the units are owner-occupied

- How many are shareholder sublets
- How many are sponsor owned
- How many are commercial units
- How many are vacant units

Underlying mortgage information:

- The lender name
- Principal balance
- What kind of rate (fixed or adjustable, and if adjustable, the index, the margin, the annual rate, the lifetime cap, and the next adjustment)
- Monthly payment
- Maturity date
- Whether all payments are current

Heads Up!

When considering a loan for the purchase of a unit in a co-op building, lenders are concerned about the underlying mortgage. If it's long term and at a favorable rate, the lender is more comfortable granting a loan for the individual unit since the lender can judge if the borrower can make the loan and maintenance payments for the term of the loan. However, if the underlying mortgage is due within a short time, there is no guarantee that it will be at favorable rates and the lender may be concerned whether maintenance costs will rise and the borrower will be able to meet the new obligations.

Cooperative financial information:

- Monthly maintenance per share
- Any special assessment, and if so, how much
- Total number of shareholders who are more than 30 days delinquent, and the total amount of money in arrears
- Total balance of replacement reserve

def•i•ni•tion

Some co-ops levy a **flip tax** if a shareholder re-sells the unit within a set period of time, often three to four years. This is to discourage buying and selling a unit for investment purposes. Co-ops may also impose a sales transfer fee on the shareholder when he sells his unit.

♦ Whether the cooperative imposes a *flip tax* and how much (a charge for re-selling the unit within a set period of time, like three or four years) or sales transfer fee (a charge levied for any unit sold, and if so, how much)

♦ Whether the payment of real estate taxes is current

♦ Whether the co-op is a limited equity co-op or has income provisions

♦ What percent loan/value financing the cooperative allows

Recent sales information:

♦ What units have sold in the co-op

♦ The number of shares

♦ The sale price and date of closing

♦ How much was financed and how much was cash

Investor information:

♦ Whether one or more entities own 10 percent or more of the total project shares

♦ The total number of investor/holder shares

♦ The total number of investor/holder units

♦ The investor's monthly maintenance

♦ The investor monthly rent collected and cash flow

♦ Whether the investor's maintenance obligations are current

♦ Whether the investors control the cooperative board, and if not, when control was relinquished

Additional information:

♦ Is the cooperative owned in fee simple title? If not, is the cooperative subject to a ground lease? If the cooperative is subject to a ground lease, a copy of the lease has to be provided.

◆ The expiration date of the unit proprietary lease/occupancy agreement.

◆ Whether the cooperative is Fannie Mae approved. If so, a copy of Form 1028 must be provided.

◆ Whether shareholders are allowed to pledge their shares as collateral for a loan.

◆ The name and contact information of the insurance agent/broker.

◆ Whether the cooperative maintains the right of first refusal.

◆ Whether the cooperative is involved in or currently expecting any litigation.

> **Did You Know?**
>
> The closing costs for a co-op are different than for a single-family home because it's not real property. For example, the buyer doesn't pay title insurance or mortgage tax. Generally, the closing costs for a co-op are less expensive than for a single-family home.

> **Heads Up!**
>
> Shareholders are responsible for both their own co-op loan, as well as a pro rata share of the building's underlying mortgage. The share is generally determined by dividing the amount of the underlying mortgage by the number of shares in the building and multiplying the per-share amount by the number of shares held by an individual apartment. That number is divided by either the appraised value or purchase price of the apartment, whichever is lower.
>
> Most lenders will not approve a loan where the unit's pro rata share is greater than 30 percent of the purchase price of the apartment.

In addition to providing the information listed here, an officer of the co-op would have to attach copies of the following cooperative documents:

1. Proprietary lease, shareholder lease, occupancy agreement, or the like

2. Articles of incorporation and by-laws

3. Rules and regulations

4. Actual budget of receipts and expenditures for previous year and proposed budget for current year

5. Stock certificate, membership certificate, or the like

Heads Up! _____

Each co-op has a reserve fund for major capital improvements or unexpected repairs. Lenders want to see a reserve fund that is at least $1,000 per unit with a minimum of $25,000 per building.

Heads Up! _____

In most cases, reverse mortgages (see Chapter 20) are not permitted on co-ops.

6. Ground lease (if applicable)

7. Master mortgage documents (if applicable)

8. Recent property inspection (if available)

Co-op buyers probably need a mortgage broker as much as, if not more than, the buyer of a single-family home. Lenders are skittish about placing co-op loans. It's easier to say no. But the market for cooperative housing is strong in urban areas and finding the lenders ready, willing, and able to do the deal can be a potentially lucrative niche. Build up a network of lenders who are interested in this type of loan. Find the institutions that are willing to work with you in overcoming the financial stumbling blocks that many lenders won't take on.

Condotels: Vacationing in Style

Condotels, part condominium, part luxury hotel, have become a new part in the lexicon of vacation home properties. Popular in Hawaii, Florida, and Las Vegas, these units are generally located in a hotel environment. A condotel unit can be occupied by the owner or available for rental. It's an individually owned condominium that can be rented out as part of a hotel when the owner is not in residence. Typically, condotels are sold furnished and have amenities like indoor and outdoor pools, spas, health clubs, bars, and restaurants. These types of properties are generally governed by the same state laws as conventional condominiums.

Most condotel properties have on-site rental/management offices that charge as much as 40 percent of the overnight fee. The property may require the owner to use the on-site group, or may permit the owner to handle their own management/cleaning or subcontract it to an off-site group.

In popular resort areas, condotel prices have risen rapidly. When prices were lower, a buyer could use the unit during at least part of the peak season and by renting it out the rest of the time, still break even on his expenses. Now with unit prices so high, it's more difficult for new buyers to be able to enjoy their property during the peak season and still break even on the expenses of a mortgage, taxes, and monthly assessments.

Advise clients that condotels, like other vacation homes, need to be seen as long-term investments.

Mortgage brokers are especially useful in finding lenders who are interested in this niche market. Buyers will need to document their ability to carry the expenses of this type of property (including maintenance fees), as well as their primary residence.

Even though the individual unit is part of a larger hotel complex, your client applies for a residential mortgage, not a commercial loan. He may qualify for second-home financing, but if the unit will not be owner-occupied, he will apply for a residential investment property mortgage. (The only exception would be if the buyer wants to close the loan in the name of a corporation and does not want the mortgage to appear on his personal credit report; he would then apply for a commercial loan.)

Lenders may offer condotel financing, but limit which properties they will fund. Lenders will vary in the requirements they set for approving a mortgage for this type of purchase. For example, lenders may offer different interest rates depending on whether the unit will be owner-occupied or available for rental. Lenders may also place other restrictions before approving a mortgage. For example, some lenders require …

- the project be located in a vacation/resort area.

- the unit have a minimum square footage (at least 600 square feet).

- the project can't require *mandatory rental pools* where the owner is required to make his unit available for rental.

- the type of amenities offered.

- how long the property has been in existence.

def•i•ni•tion

> **Mandatory rental pools** require the owner of a condotel to make his unit available for rental, at least part of the time, when not in residence.

Both ARMs and traditional fixed rate mortgages are used to finance condotels, but not all lenders offer all products. Again, if you're interested in this market, you'll build a network of those lenders who are interested in financing this type of property.

Interest rates will vary and are based on the borrower's credit score, down payment, and whether it's a second home or investment property. Investment properties generally carry an interest rate that is 1 to 1.5 percent above that for a primary residence.

Multi-Family Housing: Small and Large

There's the dictionary definition of *multi-family housing* and the mortgage broker's definition. Both mean living space for more than one family, but for Fannie Mae, Freddie Mac, and lenders, multi-family housing refers to properties that contain five or more residential units.

def•i•ni•tion

Multi-family housing refers to properties that contain more than one unit. Housing with five or more units is financed with commercial loans.

We're going to talk about the smaller, two- to four-family homes, which are funded with conforming mortgages; and multi-family housing which can be apartment buildings, condominiums, and cooperatives. While the mega-structures, requiring millions of dollars, are usually negotiated by the owners directly with the commercial side of lending institutions, you may be involved in projects requiring financing of $3 million or less (up to $5 million in high-cost areas). Both Fannie Mae and Freddie Mac are heavily committed to developing affordable multi-family housing for low-income renters. Fannie Mae has higher limits for conforming loans for multi-family housing than for single-family homes.

Two- to Four-Family Properties

Once favored by investors or those with extended families, now two- and three-family homes have become the entry point for many individuals who want to buy, but are cut out of the single-family home market by the high prices. A home buyer may qualify more easily for a mortgage for a two-family home because most lenders will include 75 percent of the income from the rental unit(s) (or fair market value) as part of the buyer's income stream. Buyers interested in two- to four-family homes basically apply for the same type of mortgage as for a single-family home. It's an opportunity to start to build equity, and with the tax savings, may actually prove less expensive than renting a similar-sized property. In some communities, selling prices for two-unit homes are rising faster than for single-family properties.

Two- to four-family homes may qualify for the various low down payment programs discussed in Chapter 18. While a buyer who qualifies for those programs is required to put down $500 or just 1 percent of the purchase price from savings for a single-family home, he will be required to put down 3 percent from savings for a down payment on a two-family home. Other programs directed at encouraging low- or moderate-income homebuyers generally will qualify two- to four-family homes as eligible properties.

> **Heads Up!**
>
> Fannie Mae lenders will require landlord education before approving loans to first-time landlords if the borrower includes the rental income as part of their qualifying information. For information on landlord education, check with your lender or the Fannie Mae website, www.fanniemae.com, for a counseling agency in your area.

The tax savings on two- to four-family homes includes not only the mortgage interest, but also the maintenance on the tenant(s)' part of the house. For example, if a two-family house is painted, half the paint job is deductible. Similarly half the heat and water bills are deductible. Advise your clients to check with a tax professional.

In addition, advise your clients, just like the lender checked their income prior to approving a mortgage, that they should check at least two consecutive pay stubs of prospective renters. Tenants should not be paying more than 40 to 45 percent of their take-home pay for rent. If the rent for the unit is higher than that percent of their income, the risk of default on the lease is increased. As an extra service, you should offer to run a credit report on prospective tenants.

> **Heads Up!**
>
> Remind your clients to check that the property has a certificate of occupancy that matches the current zoning. If the certificate of occupancy is not for multi-family housing, you will be in violation of the law if you rent a unit.

Multi-Family Housing: More Than Five Units

Mortgage brokers are rarely involved in the financing of large-scale, multi-family housing. Those deals are handled directly between the builder (or converter) and the commercial lender.

You may have opportunities to work on smaller projects that are under $3 million (up to $5 million in high-cost areas). Fannie Mae and Freddie Mac are both targeting multi-family units as a means of providing affordable rental housing for low- and moderate-income people. New rule changes should expedite these smaller loans. Previously, commercial lenders and savings banks had to keep the loans on their books until they could get enough volume to sell them as a pool to the GSEs. Now, new rules permit the lenders to sell their smaller loans as they write them.

Fannie Mae has opened a small-loans channel that will offer products and processes designed to help lenders originate and sell loans of up to $3 million (or $5 million in high-cost areas). These products will offer flexible terms and streamlined processing, including reduced documentation that should decrease approval times and cut transaction costs.

Fannie Mae projects to spend over $5 billion per year on multi-family lending, while Freddie Mac will spend more than $3.9 billion. The multi-family market, specifically the rental section of the market, is the way these two government-sponsored enterprises can meet their affordable housing goals set by the Department of Housing and Urban Development.

Both Fannie Mae and Freddie Mac have programs in three affordable housing categories: mortgages for low- and moderate-income people, mortgages for geographically targeted areas, and mortgages for very low-income people and neighborhoods. Still that is not sufficient to meet the needs of providing enough affordable housing, so the GSEs are looking to increase the supply of affordable rental units.

Commercial Mortgages

This is going to be a very short section. Very few mortgage brokers handle commercial real estate. These types of projects, like office buildings, shopping centers, factories, warehouses, and so on, are handled directly by the lenders.

The Least You Need to Know

- ◆ Lenders evaluate both the borrower and the co-op when considering a loan for a share in cooperative housing.

- ◆ Condotels, which combine the characteristics of a condominium and a hotel, are a fast-growing market in resort and vacation areas.

- ◆ A buyer may qualify more easily for a two- to four-family home because up to 75 percent of the rental income is counted as part of his income stream.

- ◆ Banks and other lending institutions handle the mortgages for most commercial real estate.

20

For Seniors Only

In This Chapter

◆ A market you can't afford to ignore

◆ Looking ahead with a reverse mortgage

◆ Federal versus private funding

◆ Other loan options for seniors

For senior citizens, their homes can be an important source of equity. For those who owe little or nothing on their mortgages, a reverse mortgage may be an ideal way to provide the owners with a steady source of income. Seniors might also be interested in home equity loans as a means of meeting unplanned expenses. As a mortgage broker, you earn commissions, albeit reduced, but more importantly, you offer these homeowners a better financial option and steer them clear of scams and scam artists who prey on the elderly.

In this chapter, you will learn about the loan programs that are designed for senior citizens.

Seniors Are a Growing Market

In the 2000 census, 35 million people 65 years of age or older were counted in the United States. That's a 12 percent increase over the 1990 census. The most rapid growth of the older population occurred in the oldest age groups. People are living longer. In 1900, the average life expectancy was 47.3 years. In 1960, life expectancy was 69.7 years. The most recent statistics now show the average life expectancy to be 77.4 years.

Did You Know? _____

According to the most recent census, these are the ten places in the United States with populations of 100,000 or more, which have the highest proportion of their population 65 years and older: Clearwater, Florida; Cape Coral, Florida; Honolulu, Hawaii; St. Petersburg, Florida; Hollywood, Florida; Warren, Michigan; Miami, Florida; Livonia, Michigan; Scottsdale, Arizona; and Hialeah, Florida.

Over 11 percent of New York City's population is 65 or older; in Philadelphia, that percentage is over 14 percent. More than 10 percent of the populations in Chicago, San Diego, San Antonio, Texas, and Detroit are 65 years or older.

Baby boomers, the generation of people born in the post–World War II period from 1946 through 1964, are a growing and valuable market. Those born during the early part of the baby boom, 1946 through 1950, showed the largest percentage growth of any five-year age group. The second fastest-growing group was 45- to 49-year-olds.

As a mortgage broker, you want to connect with this older population. For some, you may do deals as they buy new homes to downsize after their families are grown; for others, you might arrange financing for a vacation home now that they have more disposable income; and for others, now on a fixed income, you may help them tap into the equity of their homes with reverse mortgages.

Forward and Reverse: Two Mortgages, Two Purposes

A senior citizen on a fixed income may be sitting on a gold mine—his home. A *reverse mortgage* gives him a way of tapping into his home equity without having to sell it. It can provide the financial relief he needs while permitting him to remain in his own home.

Perhaps the best way to explain a reverse mortgage is to contrast it to the forward mortgage used to purchase a home. While both types of mortgages create debt and affect the owner's *home equity*, they do so in opposite ways.

With a forward mortgage:

 ◆ the purpose of the loan is to purchase a home

 ◆ there are income requirements in order to secure mortgage

 ◆ the homeowner borrows money that is repaid on a monthly basis

 ◆ the homeowner uses his income to repay his debt

 ◆ the homeowner reduces his debt with each payment

 ◆ the homeowner increases his home equity with each payment

 ◆ the homeowner is responsible for property taxes, homeowner's insurance, and necessary repairs

 ◆ if the mortgage is paid off, the homeowner's equity is equal to the value of the house

With a reverse mortgage:

 ◆ the purpose of the loan is to provide the homeowner with cash (as a lump sum, credit line, or combination)

 ◆ there are no income requirements to secure mortgage as there are no monthly payments

 ◆ the homeowner remains in the home he already owns

 ◆ the homeowner makes no monthly payments

 ◆ the homeowner is responsible for property taxes, homeowner's insurance, and necessary repairs

 ◆ the debt is due upon the homeowner's death or when he moves out of the house

 ◆ the debt increases on a monthly basis

def•i•ni•tion

A **reverse mortgage** is a loan against a home that does not have to be repaid for as long as the homeowner lives there. **Home equity** is what a home would sell for minus any debts against it.

- the owner's home equity decreases

- at the time of death, the homeowner's equity is dependent on how much debt he owes, but may be zero.

A reverse mortgage can be a lifesaver for a senior citizen. It can permit him to remain in his home when he would otherwise be forced to move because of financial con-

Did You Know? _____

In the next 25 years, the number of Americans over the age of 65 will almost double from 35 million to 60 million.

straints. But this is a difficult decision for many homeowners to make. Their home may be their largest financial asset and the only inheritance they can leave to their children or beneficiaries. You can help them make this decision by laying out the options and discussing the ramifications of each choice.

Suggest to the borrower that it might be wise to discuss this decision with their children/beneficiaries so they understand what is happening to their inheritance. Usually, offspring are happy that their parents have found a way to remain in their home and be more financially independent. But in any case, if the borrower doesn't want to talk over the decision with those in line to inherit, it would be wise to leave a copy of the loan agreement with the will.

You might also want to discuss whether a reverse mortgage is the best option to get additional cash.

- How much would the homeowner get if he sold his house?

- How much would it cost to buy a new, less expensive home? Would the cash difference be enough to meet his financial needs?

- If he sold his home, would the payout be enough if he rented, instead of bought, a new place to live or if he moved into an assisted-living facility?

You should also review with your client, before he takes a reverse mortgage, how long he envisions staying in his home. A reverse mortgage has significant start-up costs. It makes the most financial sense if the homeowner plans to stay in the house for a long time. If the homeowner plans to move within a few years, then he should consider other options. For example, if he qualifies for a low-cost home equity loan, and can meet the monthly payments, that might be a better choice.

It's not your job, as the mortgage broker, to make these decisions for the applicant. But by presenting all the options, you are helping him prioritize what he wants and needs. If he decides that he wants to remain in his own home if at all possible, then a reverse mortgage may be just the answer.

The Home Equity Conversion Mortgage (HECM)

The *home equity conversion mortgage (HECM)* is the only reverse mortgage insured by the Federal Housing Administration (FHA). HECM has specific eligibility requirements that a homeowner must meet, but once granted, provides homeowners with cash and the flexibility to use the money for any purpose.

Who Is Eligible for the HECM?

The HECM is available in all 50 states, the District of Columbia, and Puerto Rico. To be eligible:

- A homeowner must be at least 62 years old. If the home is jointly owned, both partners must be 62.

- The home must be the principal residence.

- The home must be a single-family dwelling or a two- to four-unit property. Townhouses, detached homes, and units in condominiums are eligible. Condominiums must be FHA approved.

- Some manufactured housing is eligible, but in general cooperatives and mobile homes are not.

- The home must be at least one year old.

- The home must meet HUD minimum property standards, but the HECM can be used to pay for required repairs.

- The borrower must discuss the loan with a HUD-approved counselor.

def•i•ni•tion

Home Equity Conversion Mortgage is a reverse mortgage insured by the federal government. It has specific eligibility requirements, but the homeowner may use the cash payout for any purpose.

How Much Can the Homeowner Borrow?

The amount of the loan is dependent on:

- The age of the owner. The older the homeowner is, the more cash he can borrow. If the home is jointly owned, it's based on the age of the younger borrower.

◆ Current interest rate. The lower the rate is at closing, the greater the loan amount.

◆ The value of the home. The greater the home's appraisal, the higher the loan can be.

◆ How the owner wants the loan to be paid: lump sum, credit line, monthly advance, or a combination of these options.

Federal Limits on Loans

HECM loan amounts are subject to limits that vary by county, as defined in Section 203b of the National Housing Act. You'll see references to "203b limits" or FHA Mortgage Limits in much of the literature on HECM loans. These limits are subject to change at least annually. HUD is studying whether to have a single national limit for HECM loans. Currently, the "203b limits" range from $172,632 in nonmetro areas to as much as $312,895 in urban areas. To check the limits in an area, go to https://entp.hud.gov/idapp/html/hicostlook.cfm.

If the appraised value of the house is greater than the "203b limit" for the area, the amount of the loan can still only be for the county limit. For example, if the home is valued at $450,000, but the county limit is $312,895, the loan will be issued as if the home's value were $312,895.

If the house is worth substantially more than the county limit, then you should discuss whether the owner would like to consider a "proprietary reverse mortgage" which has higher limits.

The Method of Payout Affects the Size of the Loan

The HECM can be paid out in different ways or a combination of them. The method of payout will affect the amount of cash the homeowner will have available. The homeowner can change his choices in the future (for a small fee).

◆ Lump sum: A lump sum gives the homeowner the total amount of the loan at one time. Once distributed, there is no more cash available from the reverse mortgage.

◆ Line of credit: A line of credit is available to the homeowner. He can decide when and how much to withdraw. Once the line of credit is exhausted, there is no more cash available from the reverse mortgage.

- Tenure: equal monthly cash payments for as long as at least one of the borrowers lives in the house and continues to use it as a principal residence.

- Term: equal monthly payments for a fixed period of months selected by the borrower.

- Modified tenure: a combination of a line of credit with monthly payments for as long as the borrower remains in the home.

- Modified term: a combination of a line of credit with monthly payments for a fixed period of months selected by the borrower.

For a $20 fee, the borrower can change his payment plan at any time.

The Line of Credit

The HECM line of credit has an advantage over normal lines of credit. The HECM line of credit continues to grow each month unless the borrower withdraws all remaining cash. The same total rate is charged to the loan balance. Here's how it works.

A homeowner takes out a HECM mortgage of $200,000, with an interest rate of 5 percent. He elects to have the full amount as a line of credit. In the first year, he uses $25,000 of the available cash, which would leave a balance of $175,000. However, with a HECM mortgage, the available credit line one year later, assuming no further withdrawals, would be $183,750 (5% × $175,000 = $8,750).

AARP has a calculator on their site which will estimate how much cash would remain in a HECM versus a nongrowing credit line. See www.rmaarp.org.

As a Source of Monthly Income

Some borrowers want to use their reverse mortgages to establish a monthly income. They can elect either a term or a tenure plan.

- A term plan gives the borrower a monthly income for a specific number of years that he designates. He doesn't have to repay it at the end of the term, but no further monthly payments will be made. Repayment is due when the borrower no longer lives in his home (through death or by selling the house).

- A tenure plan gives the borrower a monthly income for as long as he lives in his home.

Because the payments for a term plan are for a limited period, they are larger than a tenure plan provides. For example, if a 75-year-old borrower living in a $200,000 home takes a credit line of $45,000 and elects to have the remainder of the HECM as monthly checks for 10 years, he would receive $739. In contrast, if he elected a tenure plan, with payments to continue until he died or moved out of the home, the monthly payment would be $460.

Borrowers can elect to take monthly advances only, but depending on their financial situation, they may have no resources in case of emergency. By taking part of the money as monthly advances, and part as a credit line, the borrower has income plus a hedge against rising prices or emergencies.

Repayment Protocol

The advantage of the HECM, as well as other reverse mortgages, is that there is no repayment due until:

- the last surviving borrower dies

- all borrowers move to a new principal residence

- the last surviving borrower, due to physical or mental illness, fails to live in the home for 12 consecutive months

The loan can also be called if:

- the borrower allows the property to deteriorate, except for normal wear and tear, and doesn't make the necessary repairs

- the borrower fails to pay property taxes or hazard insurance

- the borrower declares bankruptcy

- the borrower donates or abandons the house

- the borrower perpetrates fraud or misrepresentation

- the local government invokes eminent domain or condemns the home

The lender may also invoke an acceleration clause to demand payment of the loan if:

- the borrower rents out part or all of the home

- the borrower adds a new owner to the title

- the borrower changes the zoning classification of the home

- the borrower takes out new debt on the house

Repayment is generally done through the sale of the house, either by the borrower or his heirs. If the value of the house has increased and is higher than the loan balance, the borrower or his heirs get the difference. If the debt is equal to the value of the home, there is no equity left. If the value of the home at sale is less than the debt, the lender accepts the amount and the debt is settled.

Financing Nitty-Gritty for HECM

Like most mortgages, almost all financing costs for a HECM can be paid from the proceeds of the loan. Point out to the borrower that while including financing costs does reduce the amount of the loan, it also reduces out-of-pocket expenses. The costs of the loan include:

- Origination fee: limited by HECM to 2 percent of the home's value or 2 percent of the county's 203-b limit, whichever is less. If the amount is less than $2,000, the lender may charge up to $2,000. For example, the origination fee on a $150,000 loan could be as much as $3,000. Since lenders have discretion, within the HECM regulations, on what they can charge for an origination fee, you will want to advise your clients if there is a lender who offers a lower fee or is willing to negotiate the fee.

- Third-party closing costs: this includes the appraisal, title search and insurance, surveys, inspections, recording fees, mortgage taxes, credit checks. The costs are generally the same in any given area, although they may vary based on the value of the home.

- *Mortgage insurance premium (MIP):* This is charged both at the closing and as an add-on to the interest rate. At closing, the MIP is charged as 2 percent of the home's value or 2 percent of the 203-b limit in the area, whichever is less. Plus, .5 percent is added to the interest rate charged on the loan balance.

- Servicing fee: While the servicing fee refers to the post-closing responsibilities (for example, sending account statements, changing payment preferences, paying property taxes, and so on), the fee can be financed with the loan. HECM regulations limit servicing fees to $30 per month if the loan has an annually adjustable interest rate, and to $35 if the rate is monthly adjustable.

It's a complicated maneuver to include the servicing fee in the loan. The lender must reserve the present value of the monthly fee from the time of closing until the borrower is age 100 (since most borrowers don't reach that age, the amount is clearly much more than needed). The lender deducts the amount from the available loan funds and then instead of adding it to the borrower's loan balance, the monthly fee is added to the loan balance each month.

Be sure to tell your client who will be servicing his loan.

def•i•ni•tion

Mortgage insurance premium (MIP) is an insurance policy on an HECM, paid as an up-front closing cost, as well as a .5 percent add-on to the interest rate charged on the loan balance. MIP insures that the borrower can live in his home regardless of what happens to the home's value and regardless of what happens to the lender who granted the loan. MIP guarantees the total debt can never be greater than the value of the home at the time the loan is repaid (when the home is sold).

Two Options for HECM Interest Rates

At this time, all lenders offer the same HECM rates. Borrowers can choose between an annually adjustable or a monthly adjustable rate. The rate is tied to the one-year Treasury Bill, with a margin set by Fannie Mae, the company that supplies the money for the HECM program.

For example, in January 2005, the annually adjustable rate was set at 3.1 percentage points higher than the T-rate. The monthly adjustable rate was set at 1.5 percentage points higher than the T-rate. Here's how it works.

In January 2005:

- ◆ the one-year T-rate was 2.77 percent
- ◆ the annually adjustable HECM rate was 5.87 percent (2.77 + 3.1 = 5.87)
- ◆ the monthly adjustable HECM rate was 4.27 percent (2.77 + 1.5 = 4.27 percent).

The adjustments to the rate, whether monthly or annual, are tied to the increases or decreases in the T-bill rate.

Here are the characteristics of each kind of loan so you can advise your clients.

For an annually adjustable rate …

- ◆ it is tied to current one-year T-bill, with a margin set by Fannie Mae.

◆ annual adjustments are subject to a cap of 2 percentage points per year and 5 total points over the lifetime of the loan.

◆ the rate changes once a year. A lower interest rate is charged to the loan balance whenever T-rate increases are greater than 3.6 points per year or 6.6 points over the life of the loan.

◆ if interest rates are rising, the borrower will not see the increase as quickly as one with a monthly adjustable loan.

◆ although the annually adjustable HECM has a higher interest rate, if rates are rising, the tighter annual rate caps may be a hedge against a fast-growing loan balance. The borrower might prefer to opt for the higher rate in order to have the tighter caps as protection against a rising loan balance which would eat into his home's equity at the end of the loan.

Did You Know?

Studying interest rates can be a lot like studying tea leaves. No guarantees for either prediction. But if you look at the history, according to the AARP, "during the 1990s, the difference between the lowest and highest one-year T-rate on a weekly basis was 5.48 points. But for the previous decade, that difference was 11.46 points." Understanding the overall economic climate and trends may help, but you can offer your client no guarantees.

For a monthly adjustable rate ...

◆ it is tied to current one-year T-bill with a margin set by Fannie Mae.

◆ loan advances are larger.

◆ if rates fall, the borrower sees the change more quickly than an annually adjustable loan. Of course, if the rates rise, the borrower sees that change more quickly, too.

◆ the rate for a monthly adjustable HECM will remain lower than an annually adjustable loan as long as the increases in the T-rate are less than 3.6 percentage points per year or 6.6 points over the life of the loan.

◆ the rate cap is 10 percentage points over the life of the loan.

◆ the increases or decreases in the rate monthly is the same amount as the increase or decrease in the T-rate.

♦ the rate can decrease by more than 2 points per year, and by more than 5 points over the life of the loan.

♦ borrowers may believe that the T-rate is unlikely to exceed the annual caps for any extended time or that even if the rising rates cost more, the larger cash advances are worth it.

Refinancing HECM Loans

A borrower may be interested in refinancing his HECM loan if:

♦ the value of his home increases significantly

♦ HUD increases its 203-b limits

♦ interest rates drop

You will want to review with the borrower whether refinancing makes sense. You need to lay out the cost of the refinance as compared to the increase in available funds that a refinancing would provide. The borrower needs to understand exactly how much more cash will be available once he pays the refinancing costs—and what the higher loan will do to the equity in his home.

Total Annual Loan Cost (TALC) of HECM

The lender is required to provide a *total annual loan cost (TALC)* to the borrower. However, reverse mortgages present problems in calculating the total costs. In addition to the specific costs charged on the loan, to be accurate, the TALC would factor in how long the borrower lives in the home and what happens to its value during that time. But of course, that's not possible to project precisely. TALC rates are highest when the borrower repays the loan within a few years (because the up-front costs are still a large part of the loan). TALC rates are lowest when the borrower stays in the home for a long time and the home's value grows little or even declines.

def•i•ni•tion

Total annual loan cost (TALC) is a good-faith projection of the total cost of the credit.

But there are two other limitations to the current calculation of TALC. According to an AARP report, the vast majority of reverse mortgage borrowers select a credit line as the means of payout. The true cost of the credit line is dependent on the size and timing of the cash advances during the life of the loan. However, TALC regulations require the lender to assume that the borrower will request one half of the credit line at the time of closing and none thereafter. Clearly not all borrowers follow that pattern. Furthermore, it doesn't reflect that HECM loans have a growing line of credit, unlike other reverse mortgages that have a nongrowing line of credit.

In addition, TALC regulations assume that the initial interest rate charged on the loan will never change. Obviously there is no guarantee that interest rates will not change, and if they rise significantly the loan costs will increase.

Other Options for Seniors

A home equity conversion mortgage is one option, but as discussed, it may not meet a homeowner's needs. For example, the HECM cost to value is reduced if the homeowner doesn't intend to stay in his home for a long period of time. Other homeowners have properties that are worth significantly more than the 203-b limits of HECM loans and want to tap into that higher value. Here are some other alternatives.

Proprietary Reverse Mortgage

These mortgages are open to any homeowner over the age of 62 and can be used for any purpose. If a home is worth more than the 203-b limits, this type of loan, while more expensive, can offer larger cash advances.

These loans are offered by banks, mortgage companies, and other private lenders. There are no income requirements. The underlying premise is the same as the HECM loans. The homeowner receives a cash advance, generally a nongrowing credit line, with repayment due when the owner moves out of the home.

Home Equity Loan

A home equity loan is another option for seniors who own their homes. While more expensive and requiring monthly payments, it may be worth considering, especially if the homeowner plans to move relatively soon. See Chapter 21 for more information on home equity loans.

A New Home

Rather than secure a reverse mortgage or even a home equity loan on their current home, another option is to sell and buy a less expensive property. If a home's value has increased significantly, selling it and taking the equity may provide the income the senior citizen needs. You can advise on mortgage options for the new home since for tax purposes, the owner may still want to carry a mortgage.

Seniors May Also Qualify for These Types of Loans

As a mortgage broker, you won't handle, nor should you act as an expert advisor on, these types of loans. This is to give you a broader understanding of the types of assistance for which seniors may qualify.

Property Tax Deferral (PTD)

Some state and local governments have programs that grant loans to senior citizens to pay their property taxes. Repayment is due only when the owner no longer lives in the house. Senior citizens should check with the government agency to which they pay their taxes to determine if they are eligible. Generally, a homeowner can't have a reverse mortgage and still be eligible for a PTD.

Deferred Payment Loan (DPL)

Homeowners may be eligible to combine a deferred payment loan with an HECM, as long as the DPL lender agrees to be repaid after the HECM is repaid. These low-interest loans are a one-time, lump-sum payment to be used for home repair or improvement. These loans have a variety of names and descriptions, and are administered by different agencies. Suggest that the senior citizen contact the city or county housing department, the office on aging, community action agency, or development agency. The state housing finance agency may also be helpful. Not all states or local governments offer these loans.

The Least You Need to Know

- ◆ Senior citizens are an important and growing market.
- ◆ Home equity conversion mortgages can provide senior citizens a steady source of income while they remain in their homes.
- ◆ Seniors must decide which kind of payout from a reverse mortgage meets their financial needs.
- ◆ Seniors should consider other options if their home's values are more than government limits for HECM loans.

Chapter 21

Home Equity Lines of Credit, Second Mortgages, and Refinancing Mania

In This Chapter

- ◆ Tapping home equity for additional cash
- ◆ Serial refinancing grows more popular
- ◆ The hidden costs of no-cost refinancing
- ◆ When a second mortgage makes sense

As housing prices rise, owners are looking to take advantage of the equity in their homes. Refinancing, once advised only if interest rates dropped a full two percent, now has become routine with much more minor rate reductions. A home equity line of credit (HELOC) is now used for many purposes. As we discussed in Chapter 15, a HELOC is sometimes utilized as a piggyback loan in order to increase a buyer's down payment and avoid private mortgage insurance. Other owners take out a HELOC to help pay for big-ticket items like home repairs or their offspring's college tuition bills. Second mortgages are a more traditional route of an owner getting additional funds.

And you, the mortgage broker, are at the core of all this financial rearranging. You will earn commissions on all of these deals. Your goal is to help the client find the one that meets his needs. And this chapter will help you understand these different types of financing options.

When to Refinance

Like much of life, the decision to *refinance* is often a mix of solid financial analysis and gut instinct. Sure there are clear calls. Mortgage rates were skyrocketing when the owner bought his home and have now returned to earth and are at least two percentage points lower. For sure, sign up to get a new mortgage.

def•i•ni•tion

Mortgage **refinancing** is the process of replacing the current loan with a new loan at a lower interest rate and/or better terms.

But there are less clear-cut cases. For example, what do you advise your client when the rates have gone down only one point? You know they need to factor in closing costs, and that the long-term savings aren't as significant. The decision may still be to refinance. For some clients, lower monthly payments are worth it, even if they are actually paying more in interest in the long run. For those who are in a cash flow crunch, it's worth it to sacrifice the long-term for the short-term improvement of a lower monthly payment.

Here are other circumstances when refinancing makes sense:

♦ The owner has built up the equity in his home and now wants to take some of it out.

♦ The owner has a subprime mortgage with a high interest rate (see Chapter 18). After a few years, he has established a good credit rating and is looking to refinance to get a lower rate with a traditional mortgage.

♦ The owner has an ARM, rates have gone down, and he wants to lock into a fixed rate mortgage.

♦ The owner wants to either reduce his monthly payments by lengthening the term of his mortgage, switching from a 15-year fixed rate to a 30-year fixed rate *or* wants to accelerate paying off his mortgage by switching from a longer- to a shorter-term mortgage.

The traditional rule of waiting for rates to drop precipitously was based on the expense of refinancing. You had to put so much money up front that the real savings from refinancing were much reduced. Even though the monthly payments were smaller, a more accurate analysis should have included an amortization of the closing costs. But now with the popularity of low-cost and no-cost refinancing loan products, owners are more inclined to take advantage of much smaller dips in the interest rate roller coaster.

> **Heads Up!**
> I have a quick trick to determine if refinancing makes sense. Ask your client to compare his current mortgage payment with a refinanced mortgage payment (that includes all closing costs). If the new payment is lower, he's saving money from day one and it's worth it.

But as I've said repeatedly, there is no free ride in the mortgage business. As we'll see in the section on low-cost and no-cost refinancing deals, the owner pays for the privilege of minimal closing costs with a higher interest rate. That may be worth it, but you need to be clear with the client about what the deal really costs.

Advise your clients that a decision to refinance should be based on several factors:

- How long he plans to remain in the home

- How much equity he has in the home

- How much lower the new payment will be and whether he has to pay points in order to get it

- The closing costs involved

- The actual savings if all costs are included

The tax implications of paying for points vary depending on whether it's an original mortgage, a refinance, or a second (or more) refinance of the same property. The points for the original mortgage can be deducted in full in the year the house is purchased; points paid to refinance are amortized over the life of the loan; when a property is refinanced a second (or more) time, the balance remaining on the points from the first refinance can be deducted in full, and the points paid for

> **Heads Up!**
> Here's another quick (simplified) rule of thumb for calculating if a refinance is worth it. Will the amount the borrower saves in his monthly payments equal the refinancing costs within 30 months?

the second refinance are then amortized. Advise clients to check with a tax professional. Depending on the borrower's tax bracket, the savings from the deductions may be seen as offsetting the refinancing costs.

The Closing Cost Challenge

Clients need to consider the settlement costs of refinancing when deciding if it makes sense financially to proceed. While low-cost and no-cost loan products are heavily promoted, we know that the charges have actually been rolled into the slightly higher interest rate that the borrower is willing to pay. And that may be worth it to your client in order to avoid having to pay any money up front to close the loan. For example, for a $200,000 refinance loan, aim to keep the increase to about a quarter percent in rate. You should get an even better rate for a bigger loan.

Remember: when the mortgage is inflated to pay closing costs, the borrower is, in effect, paying interest on those costs for the life of the loan. For example, if the borrower rolls the $8000 closing costs of a $200,000 mortgage into the loan, now making it a $208,000 loan, it will take him almost three years of payments to reduce the principal to $200,000. Plus, for the life of the loan, his yearly payments will remain $545 higher than if he had borrowed only $200,000, even though he has, in effect, paid off the "$8,000 closing costs."

Cutting Closing Costs

There are other ways that the client might be able to reduce his closing costs.

The lender of a refinance deal may be willing to reuse the last home appraisal, or have the appraisal or title re-certified (for a lower cost than getting a new one), if it's the same institution that holds the original mortgage.

Do Points Make Sense?

Points to reduce the interest rate generally make sense when the borrower first buys a house. For tax purposes, the points are totally deductible. Furthermore, if he stays in the house at least five years, the owner essentially pays off the cost of the points with the savings from a lower interest rate.

But that premise changes in a refinance scenario, especially one that is hard on the heels of first buying the house. The points in a refinance are not totally deductible, but must be amortized over the life of the loan. But even more troubling is that the points paid for the original mortgage become, in effect, a prepayment penalty. Other than the tax deduction, the savings from the lower interest rate hasn't yet been realized.

The Serial Refinancer

A new breed of borrower has emerged in the last five years: the serial refinancer. It's not unusual for homeowners to refinance three, four, five, or more times—and as a mortgage broker, you earn a commission every time a new deal is struck.

Make sure your clients understand all the ramifications and costs of refinancing in their states. For example, in Florida, state documentary stamps and intangibles tax add even more to the expense and may discourage serial refinancing. Costs vary widely from state to state. Some less than reputable brokers and lenders do not abide by the good faith estimates they are required by law to provide their clients. You are always better off being honest with your clients about the charges they will find at closing. Your reputation as a straight shooter is critical to your success as a mortgage broker.

> **Did You Know?**
>
> Serial refinancing may make sense for your client, but lenders won't pay you your full fee if you bring them the same client within a short period of time (4 to 12 months, depending on the lender). To collect your full fee, you should either shop the loan to another lender or collect your fee from the borrower.

Other points an owner should consider before refinancing:

Point 1. If the owner is refinancing every three years, he's paying a lot of interest and not much principal.

In the first three years of a mortgage, payments are 85 percent interest. The owner has a minimal amount of equity in the property.

By serially refinancing, the owner is constantly paying off interest without putting a dent in the principal or building up any real equity in the property.

Note: In a 30-year mortgage, it's not until year 20 that the amount going to repay principal exceeds the amount going to pay interest.

Point 2. Conversely, if the owner has been paying a mortgage for more than seven years, he has paid a chunk of change in interest and by refinancing, he is now about to start the process from square one. Even if interest rates have dropped and his monthly payments are less, the total amount of interest he will have paid on the same house, over the long run, is significantly higher. One way to mitigate that effect is to secure a mortgage for a shorter time frame, for example, 25 years instead of 30. (This is true even if the borrower buys a new house and takes out a new loan.)

Note: Lenders will customize mortgages in five-year increments (20- and 25-year loans are available if requested).

Did You Know? _____

The Federal Housing Administration, the VA, Fannie Mae, and Freddie Mac all have streamlined procedures to reduce settlement costs for a borrower who frefinances with the same lender. It also should reduce the hassle factor. However, these procedures are only applicable for a refinance that does not generate cashout for the owner at closing.

Cashing Out in a Refinance

Some clients will want to *cash out* when they do a refinance. That's when the owner borrows additional funds beyond the mortgage loan. For example, if a home is appraised at $100,000, and the owner's outstanding loan is $60,000, he could refinance at an 80 percent cash-out. His new mortgage would be $80,000, of which he will use $60,000 to pay off the original mortgage, and can use the remaining $20,000 to pay off other debts, make home improvements, pay for college tuition, and so on. His new mortgage is $80,000.

def•i•ni•tion _____

To **cash out** in a refinance is to take a larger mortgage than the outstanding debt in order to get funds that can be used for other purposes such as home improvement, reducing credit card debt, paying for big-ticket items, and the like.

A **no cash-out** mortgage means no additional funds are borrowed above the balance of the debt and nonrecurrent closing costs. A limited cash out means that the closing costs are refinanced in the loan amount based on the borrower's home equity and a limited amount of additional money can be taken out, up to 2 percent.

A *no cash-out* mortgage allows the borrower to pay off the mortgage and all nonrecurring closing costs such as attorney fees, survey, and appraisal; a limited cash out refers to a scenario in which closing costs are refinanced in the loan amount based on the borrower's home equity. The refinanced mortgage can include the balance of the loan, settlement costs, and 2 percent of the new loan amount or $2,000, whichever is less, on top of all that.

Let's take a different scenario. A homeowner has a first mortgage and a second mortgage on his home. The second mortgage was not used to buy the house, but taken out a few years later. He now wants to refinance and pay off the second mortgage as part of the deal. According to Fannie Mae regulations, any refinance that includes a refinance of a second mortgage not used to buy the property will be considered a cash-out mortgage. Fannie Mae will permit a limited cash-out refinance mortgage to pay off the outstanding principal balance of any second mortgage provided it was used in whole to buy the property. However, if it's a seasoned loan, one that's at least 12 months old, even if it was taken out after the home is bought, it can be paid off as part of a no cash-out deal.

A smart use of a cash out is to pay off higher-rate loans. For example, use the cash out from a 5.5 percent mortgage to get rid of a car loan that has a rate of 10 percent or credit card debt that charges 14 percent. But suggest to your clients that they apply their former monthly car or credit card payments to their home equity loan so they reduce that loan as quickly as possible. Otherwise, they'll be paying off a car over 30 years, instead of the original 5 years of the auto loan.

> **Heads Up!**
> A homeowner can refinance an FHA loan to obtain a lower interest rate, but only for the current loan balance. The only exception is if the owner has built up sufficient equity in the home, he may use that equity to finance the closing costs. If an owner wants to cash out, however, he must refinance with a conventional mortgage.

Home Equity Loans

Using a home as collateral to secure a loan to pay for big-ticket items or pay down debt has become a common method of personal finance. A homeowner can secure a *home equity line of credit (HELOC)* or a *standard home equity loan*, also known as a term loan, a closed-end loan, or a second mortgage. With either type, it's another lien on the property. You can help your clients determine which is the better option.

> **def•i•ni•tion**
> Home equity line of credit (HELOC) is a revolving credit line using the home as collateral. A standard home equity loan is for a specified amount of money, loaned in a lump sum, for a specified period of time, using the home as collateral.

Home Equity Line of Credit

In Chapter 15 we talked about piggyback loans as a way to up the down payment on a home by getting a line of credit at the time of purchase. As I pointed out, I advise my clients to get a home equity line of credit at that time whether they intend to use it or not since all the paperwork is already completed.

Heads Up!

Some banks will charge a penalty if the borrower pre-pays the line of credit before a set period of time, usually one to three years. Make sure you inform your clients.

A HELOC uses the home as collateral for the loan. So if the client is delinquent in payment, his house is at risk. The interest rates are variable and usually tied to the prime rate.

With the prime rate rising in the last year, lenders are seeing an increase in the number of borrowers who are refinancing their first-lien mortgages in order to cash out and pay down the home equity lines of credit whose rates are higher than the rates of 30-year fixed rate mortgages.

The Inner Workings of a HELOC

A home equity line of credit requires much of the same documentation as a first-lien mortgage—which is why I suggest to clients that they apply for one when buying a home.

The requirements of a HELOC include:

◆ property appraisal

◆ income and asset information

◆ copy of deed

◆ title search

◆ some HELOCs may have yearly membership or maintenance fees

◆ there may be a minimum draw

The HELOC is for a specific amount of credit, usually based on a percentage of the appraised value of the home minus the balance owed on the existing loan, also known as *loan-to-value, LTV*.

For example: the original mortgage is an $80,000 loan on a $100,000 house. That means it has an 80 percent LTV. If there is a $10,000 second mortgage on that same house, it has a *combined loan-to-value, CLTV,* of 90 percent.

For example, let's assume that a home is appraised at $100,000 and has mortgage debt of $35,000. If the lender sets the percentage at 75 percent, the potential credit line would be $40,000 ($100,000 × .75 = $75,000 − $35,000 = $40,000).

def•i•ni•tion

Loan-to-value, LTV, is the ratio of the fair market value of the house to the loan that will finance its purchase. **Combined loan-to-value, CLTV,** is the ratio of the fair market value of the house to all the loans on the property.

The line of credit is set for a fixed amount of time (usually 10 years), although some lenders allow the owner to renew the credit line, while others may call for full repayment of any outstanding balance. Others permit repayment over a fixed time. Review carefully the payoff requirements for the HELOC.

HELOCs vary in how the owner can draw the money.

◆ Some plans require the owner to borrow a minimum amount each time the line of credit is used. For example, the plan may require that each withdrawal be a minimum of $300.

◆ Some plans require a minimum amount outstanding.

◆ Some lenders require the borrower to take an initial draw when the HELOC is first established.

HELOC Rates

HELOC rates are tied to a publicly available index, such as the prime rate or a U.S. Treasury bill, plus a margin set by the lender. As the index changes, the HELOC rate changes. Some lenders will advertise a "loss leader," a temporarily discounted rate that is unusually low and lasts for a limited period.

HELOC rates have a cap on how high the rate can rise over the life of the plan. They may also have a payment cap to limit the increase in payments even as interest rates rise. However, many HELOCs permit the lender to freeze or reduce the credit line if the interest rate reaches the cap. Conversely, some plans have a limit on how low the interest rate may fall if the index drops.

Payback Time

Review with your clients the repayment requirements of their HELOC since the repayment schedules differ among plans.

- ◆ Some HELOCs set minimum payments that cover some principal plus accrued interest. However, unlike a typical installment loan, the amount of principal paid over the course of the loan is not enough to have repaid the debt at the end of the term.

- ◆ Some HELOCs allow interest-only payments during the term of the loan, with the full principal due when the plan ends.

- ◆ If there is a balloon payment at the end of the term, the borrower can refinance with the lender or with another lender.

Since the interest rate is variable, monthly payments may change. For example, say an owner borrows $10,000 of his HELOC under a plan that calls for interest-only payments. If the initial rate was 10 percent, he would pay $83 a month. But if the rate rose to 15 percent, his monthly payments would be $125.

> **Heads Up!**
>
> If your client intends to lease his home, make sure he checks the HELOC agreement. Some plans prohibit leasing the home.

Some HELOCs permit keeping payments level throughout the plan. But as with everything else, there's no free ride. When the loan is due, the lender will expect a full repayment of principal and any outstanding interest.

Second Mortgages

Instead of the now more common line of credit, some owners still prefer to borrow the more traditional home equity or second mortgage loan. Although the home is still used as collateral, the payment schedule calls for equal payments over the life of the loan, at the end of which the entire loan is paid off.

Owners may choose this type of loan if they need a specific amount of money for a specific purpose; for example, putting on an addition to their home.

The interest on second mortgages (and a HELOC) can be deductible as long as the total for the home loans and mortgages is for $1 million or less, and is not for more than two residences. Advise your clients to check with a tax professional.

Heads Up!

It's apples and oranges when comparing APR rates for a traditional mortgage loan and a home equity line of credit. The APR of the traditional mortgage includes the interest rate plus points and other finance charges. The APR of a home equity line is based solely on the period interest rate.

The Least You Need to Know

◆ A cash-out refinancing allows owners to tap into the equity of their homes.

◆ Fannie Mae, Freddie Mac, VA, and FHA loans prohibit cash-out refinancing, except for a small amount to cover closing costs if the owner has sufficient equity in the property.

◆ A home equity line of credit has a variable interest rate that is tied to an index, such as the prime rate.

◆ Advise clients to simultaneously apply for a HELOC when purchasing a home, even if they don't intend to draw on it at the time, since all the paperwork is already complete.

Part 6

Striking Out on Your Own

Now that you've become a successful mortgage broker, you may be ready to hang out your shingle and open your own company. In this part, I'll share what I've learned about the process of starting your own business. It's demanding, scary, and incredibly rewarding. There are loads of details required, but I'll explain how to develop a solid business plan that will help you get the financing you'll need, plus suggest the kinds of employees you should hire who will help make your firm successful. You'll find marketing tips from the best in the business, and finally suggestions for making sure that you keep a work-life balance.

Chapter 22

Make a Plan, Check It Twice

In This Chapter

- ◆ Are you ready to take the next step?
- ◆ Writing a business plan helps you focus
- ◆ Financial resources for your company
- ◆ The absolute essential you can't afford to cut

After a few years in the business, you may decide, as I did, to open your own mortgage broker company. I'd worked as a broker for six years before buying my company, Financial Access Corporation. What's the secret to an easy transition from employee to owner? Increasing my responsibilities in the office as I continued working with my clients. So over time, I formulated the company's marketing plan, expanded the referral network of realtors, developed the corporate operating budget, established new lender relationships, and finally, took responsibility for all the bookkeeping and payroll. By the time I signed the papers that officially transformed me into owner, I had a fair amount of experience of running a company under my belt.

In this chapter, we're going to look at what steps you need to take if you've decided that you want to add "owner" after your name. If you have the opportunity to get some on-the-job training in your current office, so much the better. If not, you'll find here a broad outline of how to develop a compelling business plan that will convince lenders they should help finance your company. We'll talk about some of the essentials that you need to consider before you open your doors for business.

Do You Have What It Takes to Be an Owner?

Working on commission is good training for being an owner. You already know what it's like to be dependent on your own efforts for your earnings. There are no salary guarantees for a company owner—just like there are no guarantees for a mortgage broker. Taking a calculated risk doesn't scare you. If you wanted safe and predictable, then you wouldn't have gone into this career. And that willingness to trust your ability to make it work is one of the important characteristics of successful business owners.

Answer these questions and see if you've got the goods to be a company owner:

1. Are you self-motivated?

   Do you need to someone else to develop projects, organize your time, follow up on details? Or can you be counted on to work hard without someone hounding you to produce?

2. Are you a people person?

   Sure you have to be comfortable connecting with strangers in order to be successful as a mortgage broker, but this is more. You will need to be able to accommodate the different personalities who will be working with you, as well as the vendors who make your company work. Can you put aside your ego to work with a temperamental employee who's a huge rainmaker for your company?

3. Can you make decisions?

   Yes, everyone has to make decisions, but this is more than that. Do you dither over minor issues, or can you make fast, smart decisions under pressure—and then move on? To quote Harry Truman, "the buck stops here." You're the one who has the ultimate say-so. Are you comfortable with that responsibility?

4. Do you have the stamina to run a business?

   This is hard work, emotionally and physically. Certainly in the beginning, the hours are long, and the financial payoff may be down the road. Being the company owner means hanging tough when the going gets rough.

5. Are you well organized? Do you plan ahead?

    The devil is in the details—and many of them are small, but critical. You've got to be well organized—or hire someone who is—to handle all the mechanics of running a business— payroll, personnel, schedules, computer systems, the list is endless.

Did You Know?

Check out the Small Business Administration, www.sba.gov. It's an excellent resource, offering advice and programs for new start-ups.

6. Are you burned out before you begin?

    You've got to want to do this. You can't be wishy-washy about whether or not you want to own a business. There are too many demands and too much money involved to do this half-heartedly. You need drive and ambition to succeed.

7. What's the personal toll if you open your own business?

    The first few years of a new business are especially demanding. You're on call 24/7, and every day away from the business is a deal that may be lost. In Chapter 25, we'll talk about finding a balance in your life. But you have to consider the toll on your family life if you decide you want to start your own company. The personal effect of being away from the family may be too hard. And financially, in the beginning, you may make less money than you did as an employee. You will need to plow much of your profits back into the business and you may find yourself unable to take on as many clients because of the demands of running the company.

If after answering these questions and carefully considering the implications you're still interested in opening your own business, the sections that follow describe what you need to do.

It Starts with a Plan

You need a business plan. It will help you focus your energies on the nitty-gritty details of creating a business, as well as give you a broad perspective of your short- and long-term goals. This same information can be used for a loan proposal when you approach lenders for funding.

While you may be someone who can keep a running list in your head, mentally checking off each item, that's not enough for this purpose. You need to do thorough research and then compile the information into a printed report.

There are five parts to a business plan, but each section has multiple questions that you need to answer. Expect to take several months getting the data you'll need. While you may veer somewhat from what you propose, the numbers and rationale need to make sense to a lender.

The sections are:

◆ Introduction

◆ Marketing

◆ Financial management

◆ Operations

◆ Concluding statement

Introduction

In this section, you begin the most important sales job you'll have. You will make the case for yourself as an entrepreneur, and the need for another mortgage broker firm in your community. There are other firms, both local and national franchises. You have to explain why your mortgage firm will be different—and more importantly, why it will succeed.

◆ Give a detailed description of the business and its goals. Will it be a full-service company or focus on a niche, like co-op apartments?

◆ Explain who will own the business and its legal structure. Is it going to be a sole proprietorship or will you have a partner? You will need to talk to a lawyer about the state regulations of corporations, as well as to an accountant about the tax implications of various organizational structures. You'll need an accountant to help you set up the payroll structure of your business, as well as prepare your company's tax returns.

◆ List the skills and experience you bring to the business.

◆ Make clear the advantages your company has over its competition.

Marketing

You need to make a convincing case that you can reach the clients, realtors, builders, and contractors, who will support your mortgage broker business.

◆ Identify the customer demand for your company. How many homes sold in your area; the average mortgage; the growth in the community.

◆ Cite national housing statistics, as well as the increasing use of mortgage brokers as loan originators (65 percent of all home loans are originated by mortgage brokers).

◆ Identify your market, its size, and location.

◆ Explain how you will market your company: print, radio, television, Internet, mailings, via realtors, contractors, builders.

◆ Explain your pricing strategy. Will you waive certain fees or offer additional services, like will you have an insurance company or appraisal unit as part of your one-stop shopping experience?

Financial Management

You're going to have to crunch some numbers. These can't be estimates. You need to develop a detailed monthly operating budget for the first year. That means researching how much you'll spend for rent, taxes, salaries, office materials, marketing, and so on.

◆ Explain your source of funding. Will you be seeking a commercial loan? How much of your own resources are you putting into the business? Is anyone else putting in money, and what is the plan to repay their initial investment?

◆ Develop an expected return on investment and monthly cash flow plan for a full year.

◆ Provide projected income statements and balance sheets for a two-year period.

◆ Explain your break-even point.

◆ Describe your own balance sheet and method of compensation. What will you live on during this period? If you project your income will be significantly reduced from previous years, explain how you will make up the difference.

◆ Explain who will maintain your accounting records. While previously you may have completed your own income tax forms, if you are starting a company, you should hire an accountant and a tax professional.

◆ Explain how you will handle any potential problems that might arise in the first year. For example, emergency repairs or replacement of office equipment, delays in settlements that could produce cash flow crises.

Operations

You will need to describe the specifics of the company operations.

◆ Explain the day-to-day management of the business: who will run the office, handle payroll, hire employees, and so on

◆ Discuss hiring and personnel procedures

◆ Review insurance, lease, and rental agreements

◆ Detail the office equipment you will buy or lease

Concluding Statement

Like the term papers you did in school, you now need to sum up your case.

◆ Outline your business goals and objectives. Be specific about how many deals you anticipate concluding in the first year and why you believe it's a realistic number. For example: I will do $35 million of loans in the first year of business. I have a contract with the builder of the new 60-home development now under construction in Smithtown to serve as the mortgage broker for the project. I anticipate revenues of $14 million from this project in the first year with the opening of two divisions. This is in addition to the steady stream of clients I already have, built on my network of contacts with local realtors, contractors, and builders.

◆ State plainly and clearly your determination to make the company a success.

Once you have completed your business plan, review it with owners of other established businesses for their input and advice. Or you can contact a counselor at the Service Corps of Retired Executives, www.score.org, or the Small Business Development Center for your state.

Financing Your Business

You need money to start a business. Even if you are confident that you will immediately have a steady stream of clients, it generally takes three months from application to closing and commissions aren't paid until the closing. There are a multitude of up-front costs. You'll need to lease space, furnish it, buy office equipment, pay legal and accounting fees, licenses fees, employee benefits (including your own), and much more.

You may be able to tap your own equity for start-up costs, but it's unlikely to be enough. You could also approach family and friends for loans, possibly offering a small stake in the company as collateral. Once you have developed a budget and projected your expenses and income over a year, it will be clear exactly how much you'll need.

> **Did You Know?**
>
> The SBA has a loan prequalification program to have loan applications for $250,000 or less analyzed and potentially sanctioned by the SBA before you take it to a lender for consideration. See the SBA website, www.sba.gov/financing/frprequal.html.

The Small Business Administration offers several loan programs to assist small businesses. In most cases, the SBA is primarily a guarantor of loans made by private banks and other institutions. You may be eligible for a Basic 7(a) Loan Guaranty, which is the SBA's primary business loan program to help qualified small businesses obtain financing when they might not be eligible for business loans through normal lending channels. Loan proceeds can be used for working capital, furniture, and fixtures, and the loan maturity is up to 10 years for working capital. It's delivered through commercial lending institutions. Check the Small Business Administration website, www. sba.gov/financing/fr7aloan.html.

Most small business owners borrow start-up money from a commercial bank, but it's a hard sell and you'll need to be prepared. You'll use your business plan as the basis for your loan proposal. Since there are different formats for loan proposals, contact the lender to see what they use.

> **Heads Up!**
>
> Don't assume that the lender understands the mortgage broker industry. Include industry-specific details and trends in your loan proposal.

In addition to the information in the business plan, you'll also need to provide …

◆ the resumé of each owner (if you have a partner).

def•i•ni•tion

A **guarantor** is a person who makes a legally binding promise to pay another person's debt if that person defaults.

Heads Up!

Lenders require at least two sources of repayment. The first is cash flow from company profits; the second is the collateral used to pledge the loan.

- personal financial statements of each owner and any *guarantors* (someone who guarantees to repay the loan in the event that you default). The financial statement(s) cannot be more than 90 days old and should include the most recent tax return(s).

- projections of future operations of the business. These should be for at least one year or until positive cash flow can be shown. Include your rationale for expenses and earnings. The projections should be in a profit and loss format. This section is critical to your loan approval. You must be able to support your projected figures with clear, documentable explanations.

- copies of your lease for office space (or proposed space), purchase agreement (if you are buying an established mortgage broker company), articles of incorporation, copies of licenses, letters of reference, contracts, and partnership agreement.

- a list of the real property and other assets to be held as collateral for the loan.

Will the Lender Say Yes?

Lenders typically consider the 5 Cs of credit when making a small business loan. Each element is important but may not have equal weight when the lender is making the final decision on your particular loan. For example, if the economy is in a downturn and the housing market has slowed significantly, they may be less interested in a loan to start a mortgage broker company, even if you have a stellar credit rating and proven record of success as a broker. The 5 Cs are:

- Capacity: your ability to repay the loan is probably the most critical element. Your existing credit history of repayment of loans will be used as a predictor of future payment performance. Lenders also want to know about your contingency plans for repayment in the event that the business doesn't generate enough cash.

- Capital: the money you personally plan to invest in the business. Lenders expect you to invest your own money and assets in the business, to assume a personal financial risk to establish the business. They believe that a borrower with a financial stake in the business will work harder to make it succeed.

◆ Collateral: this can be in the form of personal assets, but another alternative is to get someone to serve as a guarantor of the loan.

◆ Conditions: what will you use the money for? Is it working capital or for additional equipment? Conditions also refers to the local and national economic conditions that could affect your mortgage broker company.

◆ Character: this is all about you. The lender will judge whether you have proven, through your credit history, letters of reference, education, and business experience, that you are a good risk and will repay the loan.

Heads Up!

Lenders want to see that you are investing your money into the business, as well as theirs. There are no 100 percent loans to start a company. Most lenders want the total liabilities or debt of a business to be not more than 4 times the amount of equity. For example, if you have concluded that you need $100,000 to start your new mortgage broker company, most lenders will expect you to put in $20,000 as equity. The loan will be for $80,000. The debt to equity ratio is 4:1.

If the Bank Says No

If the bank says yes, then congratulations! But if the lender turns you down, don't take it personally. You can approach another lender with your proposal. But do take the time to ask the lender the reasoning behind the decision. It may help you strengthen your proposal for the next lender—or rethink your strategy for the business.

Heads Up!

Check the licensing requirements for your state (see Appendix B). As the owner of a mortgage broker company, you may be required to put your fingerprints on file. Your local police department may offer that service or check in the Yellow Pages under "fingerprinting." You may also be required to post a surety bond. It's an insurance policy that guarantees that you will perform the contract as mortgage broker in accordance with its terms. Check with your insurance agent.

Understanding Collateral

Your assets carry different values when used as collateral to secure a loan. The following table shows how lenders and the Small Business Administration value the collateral you pledge for a loan.

Collateral Type	Bank	SBA
HOUSE	Market Value × .75 – Mortgage balance	Market Value × .80 – Mortgage balance
CAR	nothing	nothing
TRUCK & HEAVY EQUIPMENT	Depreciated Value × .50	same
OFFICE EQUIPMENT	nothing	nothing
FURNITURE & FIXTURES	Depreciated Value × .50	same
INVENTORY (Perishables)	nothing	nothing
JEWELRY	nothing	nothing
OTHER	10%–50%	10%–50%
RECEIVABLES	Under 90 days × .75	Under 90 days × .50
STOCKS & BONDS	50%–90%	50%–90%
MUTUAL FUNDS	nothing	nothing
IRA	nothing	nothing
CD	100%	100%

The bank will calculate your collateral coverage ratio as part of the loan evaluation process. This is calculated as follows: total discounted collateral value/total loan request.

Should You Buy an Existing Mortgage Broker Company?

I bought the mortgage broker company where I'd worked for six years. It had been a family business, so obviously that made some difference. But a strong argument can be made that buying an existing company makes a lot of sense, especially if it's one that has a good reputation in the community.

The following are advantages of buying a business:

- drastic reduction in start-up costs

- big savings in the time and energy necessary to build a company from scratch

- pre-existing goodwill of customers, lenders, vendors, and network of contacts

- easier financing if company has good track record

The following are disadvantages of buying a business:

- initial cost may be high since owner is selling not only the business but the corporate reputation as well

- possible hidden problems with the business—insist on a full disclosure of all accounting

Heads Up!

Nearly half of all new small to medium businesses fail each year, according to Helen Chan, senior analyst, small and medium business strategies, at Yankee Group. The high failure rate is due primarily to: lack of experience, insufficient capital, and competition. With proper planning and effort on your part, you can beat the odds.

You'll need to compare the costs in terms of time, energy, and money, to see if you want to start from the beginning or buy an existing mortgage broker company. If you decide to start your own firm, can the area support yet another mortgage broker company?

Insurance Just in Case

When you were considering your first mortgage broker job, we talked about the need for health insurance. I said that if it wasn't being offered, it might be the deal breaker (unless you get coverage from another source). Especially when you're first starting out, paying the total costs for your own health insurance can be a huge chunk out of your limited income.

Now that you're starting your own business, you can't afford to let your coverage lapse. But you also have to have other insurance policies for yourself and your business.

- Liability: for you and your employees. Talk to an insurance professional about how much coverage you need.

◆ Property: talk to your insurance agent to determine how much coverage you need to insure for the continuation of your business and the amount you would need to replace it. Be sure to discuss the limitations and waivers.

◆ Business Interruption (also known as Business Income): property insurance may cover damaged equipment; this policy can provide funds to pay your fixed expenses during the time your business is not operational.

◆ "Key Man": this policy is used to provide continuity in operations during a period of ownership transition caused by the death or incapacitation of the "key man"—you.

◆ Automobile: if the company buys a company car, you will need to carry insurance for liability and replacement purposes. But if you use your own personal vehicle for company business, you also need "non-owned automobile coverage," which protects the business from liability for any damage which may result from such usage.

◆ Home Office: if you're establishing an office in your home, talk to your insurance agent to update your coverage to include office equipment. It's not automatically included in a standard homeowner's policy.

The Least You Need to Know

◆ Many of the characteristics that make you a successful mortgage broker will also make you a successful small business owner.

◆ Take the time to research and formulate your business plan.

◆ Most lenders demand a debt/equity ratio of 4:1 before they approve a small business loan.

◆ When planning to open your own company, you'll need a good lawyer, accountant, and insurance agent.

Chapter **23**

Hiring the Help You Need

In This Chapter

- How much help do you need?
- When rainmakers cause problems
- Outsourcing some tasks
- Payroll, taxes, benefits, and the real cost of hiring help

You're going to need help with your new mortgage broker company. This can't be a one-person office. There are too many details in this business—you need some backup. Plus, since you're already a successful mortgage broker, the only way to significantly increase your income is to begin to earn money on other brokers' deals.

In this chapter, we're going to review some key elements about hiring, firing (it happens), and most of all, retaining, the right employees for your company. It's about building a team that supports each other, communicates with each other, and understands that the success of one will only be for the benefit of all.

Who's the First Hire?

When you start your own mortgage broker company, you're cautious about spending any unnecessary money. Leasing a place, hiring a lawyer and accountant to handle all the legal and financial details, buying office equipment, paying for your own benefits, you're now responsible for everything, even the office coffee.

Hiring employees has a financial impact, but don't underestimate the psychological effect. All of a sudden you're responsible for someone else. If the business fails, not only are you out of work, but you now carry the burden of knowing that others are also out of a job. It's kind of like getting married. Now you can't just think of yourself.

But you do need help and you do want to grow. Who's the first person to hire?

I'd vote for spending good money on the best loan processor you can find (see Chapter 3 for a description of the job and responsibilities). You need someone experienced, who, ideally, already has good relationships with the lenders, appraisers, realtors, title companies, and the like, that you'll be dealing with on a daily basis. A loan processor isn't a *rainmaker*. She's not bringing in any clients (except perhaps her own friends and contacts). Nonetheless, an efficient loan processor frees you (and any other broker in your company) to do what you do best—make deals.

def·i·ni·tion

A **rainmaker** is a person who creates a significant amount of new business for the company.

Next in line: a general office manager. Since it's a small shop, you need an individual who can basically do it all, although you may decide to outsource some tasks, like payroll. You still need to supervise, especially in the beginning, and you need to sign every company check. But an office manager can generate the checks for signature, prepare invoices, reconcile bills, answer phones, send out mailings, call repair personnel as needed, and so on. While it would be ideal to hire someone who's worked in a mortgage broker company before, I'd opt for an experienced office manager and assume she can learn the details of the business.

Hiring Mortgage Originators

You know what characteristics are needed to be a success as a mortgage broker—you are one. So when you're ready to hire mortgage brokers for your firm, you know what to look for in the interview. But do you try to lure away an experienced broker from another firm or do you hire a promising entry-level individual?

For me, I always opt for an eager, smart, hungry beginner. He can take a course to learn the technical side of the business (see Chapter 5). I know I'll have to supervise an entry-level person closely, and steer business his way when he first starts. But there is an energy level, enthusiasm, and desire to succeed that is found in someone at the beginning of his career.

While an experienced broker may bring a customer base with him, he also brings baggage. He has his way of doing things, which aren't necessarily my way. Plus if he joins my firm, leaving behind deals in progress, he'll expect some form of compensation from me to make up for his losses. Especially when you're first starting out, you don't want to get that invested in someone.

The ideal candidate would be someone who's been in the business for about a year. He's learned the basics, started to make some connections, and may be ready to be a bigger fish in a smaller pond.

The Rainmaker Syndrome

Here's the dilemma. If the loan processor, office manager, or even an entry level mortgage broker screws up badly, you can fire them. With regret, perhaps, but if it's really not working out, then you give them severance and hang up the "help wanted" sign.

But it's not quite so easy when you're talking about a rainmaker in your firm. This is the brilliant, successful mortgage broker who is bringing in a significant amount of new business, but who's driving you or the other employees in your office crazy. What do you do then? Is the financial gain worth the aggravation?

As with many of life's decisions, the answer is "maybe" or "it depends." You've got some choices to make if the rainmaker is poisoning your company's environment. Certainly, you should try to talk to the individual about his behavior. If he's obnoxious to the loan processor, office manager, and fellow brokers, you can insist on a level of civility. I wish I could tell you that a simple talk would do the trick, but it's rarely that easy. I've known too many people who have essentially a split personality: charming, effective salesman to customers and bosses, and boorish, inconsiderate oaf to subordinates. You need to have the chat, but obnoxious is often their default personality.

But before you pull the plug on the rainmaker, are there any other methods of coping?

You might try to assign a separate loan processor, for just the rainmaker. That will probably create resentment among the other brokers, and does add to your costs, but may be worth it for the additional business.

But at some point the rainmaker becomes too expensive, no matter how much business he brings in. How long you tolerate the behavior will probably be a result of how much it impacts your staff on a daily basis. If you can help them see the value of having him around—because certainly he's improving the bottom line of the company, which is good for everyone who works there—if you can soften the blow of his personal interactions, you may be able to ride it out, at least for a while. But at some point, you need to start looking for other brokers who can replace the business you'll lose when you eventually have to replace the rainmaker. You need to build a solid team that meshes well and eliminate the ones who are undermining that effort.

Retaining the Best Employees

Once you have a great team assembled, the goal is to keep them together. Like a car's engine that runs more efficiently once it gets broken in, your team will gel as you work together. So what can you do to retain the best employees?

> **Did You Know?**
>
> A survey by Ernst & Young found that the cost of replacing a high-level employee may be as much as 150 percent of the departing employee's salary.

The first piece of advice is so simple, it almost sounds cheesy. It's exactly what your mother always told you, but honestly, it's one of the most effective ways of retaining loyalty: say thank you. Not for one second am I minimizing the need to share the profitability of the company with the folks who helped make it happen. But research has shown that nearly one in four workers are dissatisfied with their jobs. It's not just about money. The company's work environment—is it friendly or cutthroat? is it supportive or dismissive?—plays a huge role in an employee's decision to remain in a job. So tell them—and yes, show them—but tell each person who works for you when he does a good job, when she makes an extra effort, when he tries something new, exciting, or innovative and it works. Like with our kids, make your praise specific.

Now Let's Talk About Bonuses ...

When you created your business plan, you had to develop short- and long-term goals for your company. You had to map out how much you thought you would accomplish in the first year, and then project further down the line. You needed a plan—and the lender for your small business loan based his approval on the likelihood of you achieving those goals.

Each year I sit down individually with each of my brokers, loan processors, and office help, to talk about the forthcoming year. And here's the second tip for retaining employees. Bring them into the discussion about the future of their company. If they feel they have a stake in the company, and not even a financial one, but that their advice is valued, it reinforces the concept that this is the place to work.

For the brokers, we set specific goals—the number of loans they hope to close, as well as the anticipated level of those loans. Volume is important, but so is the quality of the loans. How big is the deal? How many points? Yield spread? We talk about the local housing market, but we also put it in the context of the national economy. These goals should be realistic. Remember, even if the housing market in your region is tanking, someone is still going to be buying and selling some houses. So the discussion should be how you're still going to capture your share or better of the loans being made.

For the loan processors, we talk about how they can improve their efficiency. This isn't just about their own efforts. It's also about what I and the brokers can do to make their jobs easier. Then we set goals for the number of loans they will be able to process each month.

For the office help, we review the procedures that make the place run. Again, we talk about how we can help them do their jobs better.

So by the end of the second week in January we all have specific goals for the forthcoming year. I make a point of setting goals for myself as company owner and as a mortgage broker.

When December rolls around, bonuses are based on achieving the goals set. If we all did our jobs, the company should be profitable and it's only fair for everyone to share in those profits. Of course, some of the profits must be plowed back into the business to build and expand it. But each broker receives a bonus relative to how much he has exceeded his goal.

Processors receive a bonus at the end of the year for exceeding their goals, but I also give bonuses to them during the year if they process more loans than expected during any given month. They shouldn't have to wait for a reward for extraordinary

Did You Know?

A recent survey revealed that six out of ten workers plan to leave their current employer for other pursuits within two years.

effort. (Brokers are on commission so they quickly get additional money when they make more and/or bigger deals. Loan processors are on straight salary so this is a way of rewarding their efforts.)

Office help also get bonuses at the end of the year to share in the company's profitability. It's an acknowledgment of their work to make the business run smoothly.

Other Incentives

Money is always in good taste, but there are other ways to show appreciation to your staff.

◆ Make the office a pleasant work environment. Provide air conditioning, good lighting, comfortable desk chairs, ergonomic workstations.

◆ Supply coffee and the like for your staff. You'll probably want it on hand for any customers, vendors, and reps, but give your employees the same courtesy. Bring in lunch for the staff occasionally—just because.

◆ Reimburse in a timely fashion. Don't ask your staff to wait to be paid back for office expenses. Reimbursements should be made within the same pay period.

◆ Pay, or at least share the cost, for any courses or continuing education programs that will help your employees do their job better.

◆ Show respect for the life of each employee. I work hard to keep my life and work in balance. I have a family I adore and a hobby that I enjoy. I make time for all that and work rigorously to make my company profitable. Recognize and respect that your employees have—and need—that balance, too.

A Tip That Costs Money, a Tip That Doesn't

Let's get to the tip that is good administration, doesn't cost money, and helps retain your employees. Don't micromanage your staff. If you've hired good workers, let them do their jobs and don't get in their way. There is a fine line between supervisor and buttinsky. You want to offer support and advice, but also trust. If you don't think they are capable of doing their jobs, then you shouldn't have hired them.

And the second tip may cost you bucks but makes sense in the long run. Hire help when you need it. If your employees are overworked, they can't be efficient and they certainly will become dissatisfied. If your company has grown, don't try to save money by eking it out with the staff you have. Invest in your company and expand when you are ready. Listen to what your staff is telling you about the workload.

When Outsourcing Makes Sense

There are some jobs that you may not have the expertise to do and some that take up too much of your valuable time to complete. So outsourcing some of the work may be a smart investment. You may want to hire an outside firm to handle security, janitorial, and grounds upkeep for your company.

You certainly want to consider hiring outside professionals to handle your payroll. While there are software programs that simplify the task, if your company is growing, an outside company ensures that you comply with all the legal filing requirements.

 Did You Know?

The two largest payroll service companies are Automatic Data Processing (ADP) and Ceridian. ADP provides paychecks to over 30 million workers.

Meeting the payroll is much more than writing out a salary check for your employees. Payroll taxes are due either semi-weekly or monthly depending on the size of your payroll. Payroll taxes include:

- ◆ Social Security and Medicare (FICA)

- ◆ Employment taxes—you are required to withhold federal income taxes, and most states and local governments require withholding as well

Employee paychecks may also have deductions for insurance and retirement funds.

And as a firm, you need to pay unemployment taxes, workers' compensation insurance, and your share of FICA, contributions to employee retirement funds, and so on.

An outside payroll service (or person) can fulfill the basic payroll-related responsibilities, but also deposit tax payments, prepare W-2s, and take care of insurance and retirement plans. You can't afford to take a chance, make a mistake, or be late about filing withholding taxes. The IRS penalties are significant.

 Did You Know?

Nearly 40 percent of small businesses have been penalized by the IRS for late or inaccurate tax filings.

The Least You Need to Know

◆ Carefully hire the help you need, and then trust their judgment to do their jobs.

◆ Share the profitability of your company with bonuses for your employees.

◆ Provide a corporate environment that encourages employee retention.

◆ Consider outsourcing your payroll to a professional firm in order to ensure that you are in compliance with federal, state, and local regulations.

Chapter 24

Marketing, Marketing, Marketing

In This Chapter

- Creating and delivering your message
- Internet strategies that carry a wallop
- The (search) engine that could
- Print, radio, and television ads that work

"If you build it, they will come." That might have worked when Kevin Costner was constructing his *Field of Dreams*, but you're going to need more than that when you open your mortgage broker business. Networking and word of mouth are key components, but you've also got to advertise to make your presence known in a community.

Spending big bucks isn't necessarily the answer. A good marketing campaign does cost money, and you need to include that in your company budget. But it's more important to target your efforts to make sure that you reach the audience you need with the message you want to deliver.

In this chapter, we're going to touch on a variety of marketing campaigns. Books have been written on each of these topics, so clearly this is just an overview. The purpose is to help you focus on what would work best to market your mortgage broker company. Take the time to think through an integrated campaign.

Planning Is Key

A marketing strategy is well conceived. You figure out who you want to reach, which should include not only customers, but the complementary businesses with which you'll work, like realtors, contractors, and builders.

You will need timely market information in order to best reach your target audience and develop the right type of message. You need a breakdown of the housing market in your company's area (if you've already been working in that region, this is easier). You need to know population shifts, legal developments, and the local economic situation.

Did You Know?

The Small Business Administration Development Center, www.sba.gov/sbdc, offers expertise on a wide range of issues facing small business owners, including marketing.

You also want to spend time analyzing your competitors. This is not only other mortgage broker companies, but also the lenders in the region—how effective is their outreach to the house-hunting community?

You want to coordinate the look and feel of all your marketing efforts. The online site should complement the off-line print, radio, and TV spots.

Whatever the method of distributing your message—print, radio, signage, television—repetition is the key element. You want the name of your mortgage broker company to become ingrained in the public's memory. It's the go-to place for financing. Roy H. Williams, a visionary entrepreneur and founder of Wizard Academy, www.wizardacademy.com, explains, "One of the most common mistakes made by small business owners today is trying to reach more people than they can reasonably afford to reach. Very few readers, listeners, or viewers will take action after just one or two exposures to your message. Would you rather reach 100 percent of the city and persuade them 10 percent of the way? Or 10 percent of the city and persuade them 100 percent of the way? The difference is repetition, but the cost is the same."

Listen to Feedback

In all your marketing efforts, there should be a space for customer feedback. Always make it easy for customers or visitors to make suggestions—and then read them. This isn't a pro forma exercise. You need to know what customers think of your outreach program.

On all loan applications, you should have a question about how the customer came to you: friend referral, realtor/builder/contractor referral, website, TV spot, newspaper ad, radio spot, Yellow Pages, and so on.

Refining Your Message

You're a mortgage broker company. That much is clear, but what that is may not be immediately apparent to potential customers. Does it mean you will lend them the money they need to buy a house? Reasonable question, even if the obvious answer is *no*. So getting the message out about who you are, what you do, and why you're better at it than the other three mortgage broker companies in your area is critical to your success. If you're the new kid on the block, it's important that you get the message out fast and clear. But projecting a strong message about your company is true whether you've been in business for three months or thirty years.

Traveling the Internet Highway in Search of Business

There aren't many hard-and-fast rules in running a company, but here's one: you have to have a website for your mortgage broker business. It needs to look sharp, professional, and cutting edge, yet accessible.

But Why Do I Need a Website?

Even if you don't intend to operate as an online mortgage brokerage, you still need to have a website. Why?

- People expect it. Nowadays, we assume that everything is available on the Internet—and if it's not there, we question why.

- It increases your visibility at a minimal cost. Start-up costs for design are an investment, but a website is the cheapest form of advertising you can buy. A radio or TV campaign of ten 30-second spots over three weeks can run between $5,000–$10,000, depending on your market. Literally hear it and it's gone. Print advertising is in the recycling bin by the end of the day or the length of the publication pull-date. In contrast, you can have a professional website designed and installed for less than $3,000, with annual maintenance costs of under $500. And it's a permanent form of advertising, accessible 24/7.

♦ Updates are easy, quick, and less expensive. You can announce new rate changes almost instantaneously, or quickly revise any company info. A company brochure is helpful, but once it's in print, you're stuck with the information.

♦ Customers can interact with your company on their terms. Research has shown that customers expect to do the heavy lifting on a website—and they prefer it. Potential clients can help themselves quickly, anonymously if they prefer, and whenever it's convenient for them. Your website needs to be interactive. Mine allows a visitor to run a variety of calculators so they can check how much a loan will cost them, contact me via e-mail, forward my site to their friends with a personalized message, look up mortgage broker terms, find links to sites of interest, even participate in a monthly sweepstakes. When we finally do talk, they've already got some of their questions answered.

♦ Tracking customer data is simpler. You can learn a lot from the traffic to your website. You can analyze (or have a professional interpret the stats for you) a host of data, for example, which pages are used most frequently (which can tell you what their biggest concerns may be) and where the visitors came from to arrive at your site. You can also provide a space for visitors to leave comments and opinions.

Make sure to keep your website easy to navigate. Make sure that a customer doesn't need to return to the homepage to get to another section of the site. Don't get carried away with fancy graphics and animation. Customers want to load pages quickly and those extra gizmos slow things down.

Did You Know? _____

Visitors to my website have the opportunity to enter a contest to win one month's mortgage payment, up to $5,000! The winner is selected on the last day of the month and visitors are limited to entering only once per month. I pay an annual fee to be part of this national contest so I'm not financially responsible for a winner each month. But I do get the valuable data of name, postal and e-mail address, why they visited my site (looking for a loan to buy a house, to refinance, consolidate debts, home equity loan, or other), as well as the current mortgage information of each person who enters the contest. It's an inexpensive, but effective, way to build a customer database.

What's in a Name?

Don't let ego or whimsy be the motivating factor in choosing your business's name. The name choice will affect your marketing campaign, especially any online efforts.

Search engines look for the title tag in a website. Those are the words that appear in the link users click on the search engine results page. And that's what makes the title tag one of the most important factors in achieving high search engine rankings. You want to focus on what your customers are looking for when they type in keywords for a search.

Make sure that the name of your company includes what you do: for example, Smithtown Mortgage Broker Company. Place it prominently on the title page and in the body text. That makes it easier for search engines to pick it up.

 Did You Know?

On average, 75 percent of search queries are for what a business does, not for a specific company.

Keep It Fresh and Updated

If any part of your website looks dated—even if it's just the notice of an open house that was held two weeks earlier—you've turned off the customer. It tells them that you don't pay attention to details. Keep in mind: the content of your site must be pertinent, current, and always user-friendly.

Update your site on an as-needed basis, but certainly review the evergreen material once a year.

Heads Up!

Post testimonials (with permission) from satisfied customers, realtors, builders, contractors, and so on. It adds credibility to your site.

When your site is originally designed, invest in a content management system (CMS) which simplifies updates.

Search Engine Marketing

Search engines are the most efficient way to find products on the Internet. They've also become one of the best ways to find and acquire customers. While there are several products on the market to help you design a website and coordinate search engine placement, I'd advise you to focus your energies elsewhere and hire a pro.

My designer has developed sites for other mortgage broker companies—although not in my area. I wanted someone who understands the business and already knows the keywords that will drive visitors to my site. I could probably figure it out, but I've got better uses for my time. Ask realtors in your area for recommendations of website designers.

But here are some tips about the process so that when you hire a designer you can judge his credentials.

Did You Know?

The online search industry is expected to reach nearly $7 billion in worldwide revenues by 2007.

Spend time developing the list of keywords for your site. Check out www.wordtracker.com, Yahoo!'s term suggestions, or Yahoo!'s "View Bids" tools under their Search Marketing advertiser center. The obvious ones are your company name, your own name, your location, mortgage, mortgage broker, loans, homeowners, interest rates, mortgage calculator, loan originator, refinance, fixed rates, and ARMs. These are the terms that you will input into search engines, and your company's name should appear.

The problem, of course, is that there are thousands of mortgage brokers in this country, and even in your own region, you're probably not a lone practitioner. You want to be on the first or second page of search results, so keywords may not be enough. You may want to optimize the search engine process by paying to influence the outcome.

There are two methods to do this:

♦ Pay-Per-Click or Cost-Per-Click. If you look at the top of a search page, when you type in the words "mortgage broker," you'll see sponsor results. These companies have paid for the privilege of being among the first businesses you see when you type in a description of your business. It's a bidding system, and the highest positions go to the top bidders. To get at the top of the list for a generic topic like "mortgage broker," you'd have to be willing to pay quite a lot for each click, especially if you are working with either Yahoo! Search Marketing or Google AdWords. They reach a huge audience, but you pay for the privilege, and when you are first starting out you need to consider if it's a worthwhile investment. One way to limit your investment is to sign up for the Local Sponsored Search option so that you only pay for clicks from customers in your area.

♦ Relevant Paid Search or Content-Targeted Advertising. This moves your sponsored link to a page with related content. For example, if a user was checking contractors in your area, he might also see your listing for a mortgage broker.

Keep Track of Your Website

It's almost a waste of money if you go to the trouble of setting up a website, and then don't bother to analyze the information that it can provide. Watching the traffic pattern on your website permits you to change what isn't working and beef up what is. There are a variety of tracking tools that can provide you with raw data on your site. Here is the important information you need to know:

- Tracking tools can tell you which search engines are sending you the most visitors. You want to know if the search engine ads and keyword buys are working.

- Tracking tools will show you if most of your traffic is coming from search engines or if you have on-ramps from other websites. Perhaps complementary businesses, like realtors and builders, are linked to you. If so, are they providing you with a significant number of visitors? This might tell you that you should be working even more closely with that company.

- Tracking tools will show you which are your most requested pages and from which most people exit. This tells you what's working and what's turning off visitors. You can make the appropriate changes.

- Tracking tools will tell you what kind of operating systems and what browsers your visitors are using. You want to be sure all visitors have equal experiences. Tracking tools can also tell you if there are any defects in the design of the site. It will alert you if a visitor is getting a nonexistent page when they attempt a link—an instant turnoff.

Cable Television and Local Radio

Let's assume that your company isn't ready for promoting on the Super Bowl. But that doesn't mean that local television and radio might not be a reasonable avenue for marketing. You can work with the cable company and radio station reps to develop small, focused ads.

Most cable companies can segment their broadcast area into smaller sections to better fit your budget. But remember, repetition is the key. Better to run three ads at the same time and days of the week, month after month, than to scattershot your ads. You are reaching the same people over and over again—and that's exactly what you want. When they buy a house, it's your company's name they remember. Yes, that's not the entire house-buying population, but the goal is to get the vast majority of a small, targeted segment of the public remembering you, rather than to get virtually none of a larger population. Similarly, radio ads should be in the same time slot on a daily basis.

Don't expect instant results from either avenue. Marketing campaigns are a long-haul proposition. You're building brand awareness, not advertising knives at the unbelievable price of $9.99 and the viewer needs to call "right now."

Signage and Print Advertising

Billboards and transit signs are low-tech, but effective. Roy H. Williams advises maximizing your signage as much as the city sign code allows, as this medium is "often the cheapest advertising your money can buy."

You reach not only the buying public, but also those who influence them: realtors, builders, contractors, lenders, community leaders. It's a permanent reminder of your company that can't be turned off, zapped, or ignored.

Don't forget newspapers and the Yellow Pages. These media don't build brand awareness, but should capture the attention of the person who is in an active search for a mortgage broker.

Roy H. Williams recommends small business owners should "buy mass media—radio from 6 A.M. to 7 P.M. and/or cable from 7 P.M. to midnight—to reach the baby boomers. And use dirt-cheap, pay-per-click Internet ads tied to specific keyword strings to reach the Gen X customer who's using the Internet like a phonebook."

Heads Up!

"The goal of advertising is to create a clear awareness of your company and its unique selling proposition. Unfortunately, most advertisers evaluate their ads by the comments they hear from the people around them. The slickest, cleverest, funniest, most creative, and distinctive ads are the ones most likely to generate these comments. See the problem? When we confuse response with results, we create attention-getting ads that say absolutely nothing."

—Roy H. Williams

Direct Mail

Whether it's a postcard, a letter, or even an e-mail, to promote your mortgage broker company, direct mail can be an effective way of reaching new customers, assuming that you're using an accurate database. And that's the key. Otherwise it's postage down the drain.

You need to work with a firm that will customize the data for you. One of the largest customer data companies is infoUSA, www.infoUSA.com. It's teamed with Microsoft Small Business Center and can provide lists of qualified sales leads from data from 2 billion leads. The basic cost gives you the prospect's name, address, and type of residence. For an additional fee, you get the phone number, marital status, age, size of the household, household income, homeowner or renter, average home value, whether the household includes children and/or pets, whether it has Internet users, even hobbies and interests, if available.

infoUSA recommends a direct mailing, followed up by a phone call a month later. This is a huge commitment of time and effort and might be a good project for an entry-level mortgage broker, or you could outsource it.

E-mail marketing is growing, but is being watched carefully by the Federal Trade Commission and state governments. You want to avoid being grouped with the spam of fake medical cures that flood inboxes. Some small mortgage broker companies find it more effective to advertise in the e-mail newsletters of related companies like realtors.

If you do send e-mail direct marketing, include links to your site for more information or to receive a special offer. For example, if you're a participant, tell them about your mortgage payment sweepstakes, but also offer to give them a free analysis of their current mortgage and how you can probably save them 10 percent or more in monthly payments. Use e-mail to invite prospective home buyers to a seminar you give on mortgage financing.

Heads Up!

Always ask any prospective customers to include both their postal address and their e-mail address in the information they give you. You can develop your own direct mail contact database.

The Least You Need to Know

◆ Include a marketing budget in your start-up costs for your mortgage broker company.

◆ Repetition is the key element in getting your company's name recognized.

◆ You want your marketing campaign to reach both potential customers and those who influence their decisions, such as realtors, builders, and contractors.

◆ A high-quality database is essential to the success of a direct marketing campaign.

25

Striking a Balance in Life

In This Chapter

◆ Defining work-life balance

◆ Does racing make me a better mortgage broker?

◆ Ten tips to achieve work life balance

◆ The bottom line in business and in life

On my resumé I list two awards I've won. I have other plaques on my wall, but these two, I think, are worth noting—plus they're ones of which I'm exceptionally proud.

I won the Top Producer honor my first year out of college. I worked hard, pulled out all the stops, and by closing the most deals in the company, earned that mark of distinction.

The second award I list is the 2001 North Atlantic Road Racing Championship-Sports Club Car of America. I'm enormously proud of that prize. It was a team effort; something I shared with my dad.

I can list the characteristics of a top producing mortgage broker and compare it to the list of qualities that make a winning race car driver. Many of the attributes would overlap: quick-thinking, confident, enjoys a challenge, takes pleasure in working alone while being part of a team, smart, fast, detail-oriented. But I can simplify the lesson: I'm a better mortgage broker and smarter business owner because I've got a hobby that gets my juices flowing and a family that I adore.

Achieving balance in your work and life is critical to your career success. That's what we're going to talk about in this chapter.

Defining Work-Life Balance

Jim Bird, CEO of WorkLifeBalance.com, a management training company with clients that include Coca-Cola, Sun Trust, and Hewlett-Packard, defines the premise clearly:

> "Work-Life Balance does not mean an equal balance. Trying to schedule an equal number of hours for each of your various work and personal activities is usually unrewarding and unrealistic. Life is and should be more fluid than that …. However, at the core of an effective work-life balance definition are two key everyday concepts that are relevant to each of us. They are daily achievement and enjoyment, ideas almost deceptive in their simplicity.

> Life will deliver the value and balance we desire when we are achieving and enjoying something every single day in all the important areas that make up our lives. As a result, a good working definition of Work-Life Balance is: Meaningful daily achievement and enjoyment in each of my four life quadrants: Work, Family, Friends, and Self."

Did You Know?

According to a study of executives by the Families and Work Institute, Catalyst, and Boston College Center for Work and Family, more than 20 percent of male execs have downsized their career aspirations. Number-one reason why: family and personal life demands.

The demands of work and family, including an adorable two-year-old, mean that I don't race every day, not even every week. But when I'm filling in my work calendar, I include my races and practice schedule as well. And more importantly, I encourage my staff to make time for their families and hobbies.

Work in the twenty-first century has radically changed from even just 25 years ago. According to a 2004 study by the Families and Work Institute, "The fast-paced, global 24/7 economy, the pressures of competition, and technology have blurred the traditional boundaries between work life and home life. Furthermore, this new economy calls for new skills—skills like responding quickly to competing demands and jumping from task to task."

This is a perfect description of your life as a mortgage broker—and compounded if you've now opened your own mortgage broker company. It's easy to be on call 24/7. The nature of the mortgage broker business is a juggling act by definition. And the struggles of any small business owner are legendary.

This same study found that cell phones, computers, e-mail, and the like—all the technology we discussed in Chapter 11 as necessary for you to do your job—blur the line between work and nonwork times. One in three employees, according to the group surveyed, was in contact with work once a week or more outside normal work hours. But if that were a survey just of mortgage brokers, I'd bet the answer would be 100 percent of brokers are in contact with work outside normal work hours—if you can even define what normal work hours are for a mortgage broker.

The issue of work-life balance is complicated for this industry and maybe even more important.

Work-Life Balance Makes Financial Sense

As we discussed in Chapter 23, finding the right staff is a key factor to the success of your mortgage broker company. Keeping that staff is critical. According to Susan R. Meisinger, president and CEO of the Society for Human Resources Management (SHRM), "For organizations to be successful at competing for new talent and retaining employees, they have to know what workers want, what keeps them happy, and what makes them stay. Addressing the essentials, including fair compensation, valuable benefits, and the ability to balance work and life are critical components of an organization's overall retention strategy."

In an extensive survey of human resources professionals and employees, SHRM found an interesting generational schism. Women and workers younger than 35 report that work-life balance is the most important component to their overall job satisfaction. Men rank work-life balance as fourth in their list, and workers 56 years or older don't list it all in their top five components of job satisfaction.

As you hire new staff, you will have an advantage in the competition for the best and the brightest if you develop a corporate culture that addresses the needs and demands of your workforce.

> **Did You Know?**
>
> According to the Families and Work Institute, "employees who have jobs that provide them more opportunities to learn, whose supervisors support them in succeeding on the job, who have the flexibility they need to manage their job and their personal and family life, and who have input into management decision-making are less likely to be overworked. This is true even when they work long hours and have very demanding jobs."

What Happens if You Don't Address the Work-Life Issue?

Making sure that you find a work-life balance—and encouraging your staff to find one, too—isn't just a feel-good topic. According to a study by the Families and Work Institute, overworked employees are:

◆ more likely to make mistakes at work

◆ more likely to feel angry at their employers for expecting them to do so much

◆ more likely to resent co-workers who don't work as hard as they do

◆ more likely to have higher levels of stress

◆ show more symptoms of clinical depression

◆ more likely to report that their health is poorer

◆ more likely to neglect caring for themselves

This is an issue that can't be ignored.

What Can You Do About It?

The truth is that starting a business takes time (it takes money, too, and finding that money takes time). So how can you achieve that work-life balance for yourself—and for your staff?

The Families and Work Institute study found that "employees who are dual- or family-centric versus work-centric are healthiest and most successful at work and at home. Having a life outside of work doesn't detract from work success—rather it appears to enhance it. Employers need to reframe how they think about employees and value and encourage, rather than disparage, dual-centric (in other words, putting an equally high priority on family and work) or family-centric employees."

Here are three tips to help you develop a work-life balance for you and your company:

1. Don't micromanage. As the owner, you have to let go of some of the reins and trust your staff. It's a round robin, but you need good staff to succeed *and* you need to provide a work environment that makes good staff want to stay. It's not an either/or proposition. You don't have to stop working and play 24/7. Nor does your staff. But making time for family and yourself is essential.

2. Focus on what you do best. Identify those issues that have high impact on your company, and focus on those. Marketing, building relationships with realtors, lenders, builders, and contractors, staying current on economic and housing trends, projecting their impact, and adjusting your corporate strategy as needed—these are key to your success as a company owner. Don't get hung up on small tasks that take time away from what you do best. For the brokers in your company, provide them with the environment and tools that let them do their jobs effectively.

3. Make personal life a priority. Schedule your personal commitments on the same calendar as those for your business. They have equal importance. Don't be embarrassed to admit that work and family carry equal weight in your life. That's not to say that customers have to adjust to meet your family's dinner time. You need to be available when customers are free. But it does mean that you carve out time for your family, just like you find the time for your continuing education classes.

I enjoy my career as a mortgage broker, even more now that I own the company. As I said in the opening chapter, this is an exciting, challenging, creative, fulfilling, and lucrative career. I'm glad I could share what I've learned from my years in the business. If you've now decided to become a mortgage broker—welcome!

The Least You Need to Know

◆ The new global economy and modern technology have blurred the lines between work life and home life.

◆ Overworked workers are more likely to make mistakes, feel angry and resentful, and have higher levels of stress.

◆ Younger workers put a premium on a work-life balance. To retain your best employees, you need to find a way to provide them with that balance.

◆ Focusing on what you do best and delegating the rest—and providing an environment and the tools for your employees to do their best—helps to create the necessary balance in work and life.

Appendix

Glossary

adjustable rate mortgage (ARM)   Mortgage with an interest rate that may change, usually in response to changes in the Treasury Bill rate or the prime rate.

adjustment period   Period during the life of an ARM between one rate change and the next.

amortization   Gradual elimination of a debt, like a mortgage, with regular fixed payments over a specified period of time.

annual percentage rate (APR)   Cost of the loan as an annual rate. It includes points paid to secure the loan, mortgage insurance, and other fees.

appraisal   Third-party estimate of the value of the property at a specific point in time

asset   Item of value.

back end ratio   Applicant's total housing expense plus all other monthly debt divided by total monthly pretax income.

basis points (BPs)   Each basis point is one hundredth of a percent. They are used in measuring the yield differences among bonds, but in the mortgage industry, BPs describe the percentage of commission a mortgage broker receives.

cash out   To take a larger mortgage, in a refinance, than the outstanding debt in order to get funds that can be used for other purposes such as home improvement, reducing credit card debt, paying for big-ticket items, and so on.

clouds   Defects or problems with the title of a property that must be resolved prior to closing.

combined loan-to-value (CLTV)   Ratio of the fair market value of the house to all the loans on the property.

commission   Fee or percentage paid to a mortgage broker for services rendered.

condominium   Building where each apartment or residence is individually owned and the common grounds are owned jointly by all the owners of the premises.

condotel   Condominium that is serviced as if it were a hotel. These kinds of units are becoming popular as vacation homes.

conforming loan   A loan that meets the requirements necessary to be eligible for purchase by Fannie Mae and Freddie Mac.

consumer price index   Measures the change in the cost of basic goods and services in comparison with a fixed base period.

cooperative (co-op)   Multi-unit housing complex in which owners have shares in the cooperative corporation that owns the property. Each shareholder has the right to occupy a specific unit or apartment.

depository institutions   Commercial banks, savings and loans, and credit unions.

discount interest rate   Set by the Federal Reserve, it is the rate at which commercial banks can borrow money from the Federal Reserve.

Fannie Mae (Federal National Mortgage Association)   Private corporation, chartered by Congress, that acts as a secondary mortgage market investor. Like Freddie Mac, it sets many of the guidelines for conventional mortgage loans.

fixed rate mortgage   Loan with an interest rate that does not change during the entire term of the loan.

flip tax   Fee levied by co-op if a shareholder re-sells the unit within a set period of time, usually three to four years.

float down   One-time opportunity to secure a lower rate, provided by lenders to borrowers who have locked in and interest rates have then fallen.

Freddie Mac (Federal Home Loan Mortgage Corporation)   Quasi-governmental, federally sponsored company that acts as a secondary mortgage market investor to buy and sell loans. Like Fannie Mae, Freddie Mac sets many of the guidelines for conforming loans.

front end ratio   Total monthly housing expenses (principal, interest, taxes, and insurance) divided by the applicant's total monthly pretax income.

Ginnie Mae (Government National Mortgage Association)   Government-owned corporation that securitizes pools of FHA, VA, Rural Housing Service, and Public and Indian Housing loans.

guarantor   Person who makes a legally binding promise to pay another person's debt if that person defaults.

hard prepayment   Clause in loan agreement that requires borrower to pay a penalty for paying off a loan before it's due.

home equity   Current market value of a home minus any debts against it.

home equity conversion mortgage (HECM)   A reverse mortgage insured by the federal government.

home equity line of credit (HELOC)   Revolving credit line using the home as collateral.

hybrid mortgage   Mortgage that is a combination of a fixed loan and an ARM. It begins as a fixed rate loan, but later becomes an ARM.

installment account   An account, like a mortgage, in which the amount of the payment and the number of payments is prefixed.

lender rebate   Also known as *yield spread premium*, it is the payment from a lender to a mortgage broker for originating a loan at an "above par" rate.

liability   Recurrent payment that an applicant owes, including monthly obligations such as rent and utilities, credit card debt, student loans, car loans, and child support.

lifetime cap   Also known as *rate ceiling*, it limits the amount of interest that can be charged over the life of an adjustable rate mortgage.

limited cash out   In a refinancing, closing costs are included in the loan amount, based on the borrower's home equity, plus a limited amount of additional money can be taken out, up to 2 percent.

liquid asset   Item of value that can be converted to cash.

loan originator   Serves as an intermediary between the lender and the borrower, also called a mortgage broker.

loan processor   Person who handles the paperwork to support the loan application. He works under the supervision of a mortgage broker.

loan-to-value (LTV)   Ratio of the fair market value of the house to the loan that will finance its purchase.

locking in   Legal commitment between the lender and the borrower that guarantees a specific interest rate for the loan.

mandatory rental pool   Requirement of owners of condotels to make their units available for rental, at least part of the time, when not in residence

margin   Number of percentage points a lender adds to the index to determine the ARM interest rate.

mortgage banker   A lending institution. Mortgage brokers deal with multiple lenders.

mortgage broker   Person who serves as an intermediary between the lender and the borrower, originating loans, sometimes called a loan originator.

mortgage insurance premium (MIP)   Insurance policy on a home equity conversion mortgage. It is charged both at the closing and as an add-on to the interest rate. At closing, the MIP is charged as 2 percent of the home's value or 2 percent of the 203-b limit in the area, whichever is less. Plus, .5 percent is added to the interest rate charged on the loan balance.

multi-family housing   Properties that contain more than one unit.

negative amortization   Occurs when the monthly payments are insufficient to cover the interest accruing on the balance. The difference is added to the remaining principal due.

negative points   Cash rebates offered by lenders to consumers as part of a higher-interest-rate loan. The rebate may only be used to defray settlement costs.

no cash-out mortgage   No additional funds are borrowed above the balance of the debt and nonrecurrent closing costs.

open house   House for sale is open to public viewing. Also realtors hold open houses for other agents prior to listing houses for sale.

option ARM   Adjustable rate mortgage that gives borrower a choice of monthly payment alternatives, including some which do not cover the interest due. This can result in negative amortization.

par rate   Lowest interest rate at which a lender will make a loan without charging discount points.

payment cap   Limits the monthly dollar increase at the time of each adjustment, usually expressed as a percentage of the previous payment. Only monthly ARMs have payment caps.

periodic cap   Limits the interest rate increase from one adjustment period to the next.

PITI   Acronym for components of a mortgage payment: principal, interest, taxes, and insurance.

points   Up-front charges, levied by the lender, to obtain a certain mortgage. Each point costs 1 percent of the loan.

pre-approved   Preliminary written, binding approval by a lender of the maximum amount a buyer can borrow for a mortgage.

pre-qualified   Process of giving an informal, nonbinding estimate, based on income and debt load, of the amount of money a buyer can spend on a house.

primary mortgage market   Lenders who make loans to home buyers. Primarily consists of mortgage originators like commercial banks, savings and loans, credit unions, and so on.

private mortgage insurance (PMI)   Insurance that protects the lender from loss in case of default by the borrower. Generally required for loans with less than 20 percent down payment.

producer price index   Measures wholesale price levels in the economy.

quitclaim   Legal document that transfers all interests a person, for example a former spouse, has in a property.

rainmaker   Person who creates a significant amount of new business for a company.

rate ceiling   Also known as *lifetime cap*, it limits the amount of interest that can be charged over the life of an adjustable rate mortgage.

refinancing   Process of replacing the current loan with a new loan at a lower interest rate and/or better terms.

reverse mortgage   Loan against a home that does not have to be repaid for as long as the homeowner lives there. Limited to owners who are 62 or older.

revolving account   An account, like a credit card, that requires at least a specified minimum payment each month plus a service charge on the balance.

sales transfer fee   Fee imposed by co-op on the shareholder when he sells his unit.

seasoned loan   Loan that is at least 12 months old.

secondary mortgage market   Institutions that buy and sell first mortgage trust deeds for investment from primary mortgage lenders through conduits like Freddie Mac, Fannie Mae, and Ginnie Mae, as well as private investment banks.

securitization   Creation of a security by pooling mortgage loans purchased from originators. These securities are sold as bonds and their value is derived from the original mortgages from which they are created.

soft prepayment   Clause in loan agreement that permits the borrower to repay the loan before it's due without penalty.

split   How the mortgage broker company divides the fees of a transaction.

sponsor   Individual or company that builds the co-op or was responsible for its conversion from a rental to co-op building.

standard home equity loan   Specified amount of money, loaned in a lump sum, for a specified period of time, using the home as collateral.

subprime market   Mortgages that are high-risk, high-interest loans.

title search   Thorough examination of all public records that involve title of a specific property. It is to guarantee that there are no outstanding claims against the property except for the liens that will be cleared at the closing.

total annual loan cost (TALC)   Good-faith projection of the total cost of the credit.

Truth in Lending Act (TIL)   Requires lenders to provide loan applicants a statement containing "good faith estimates" of the true cost of a loan. It will include the total finance charges and the annual percentage rate.

yield spread premium   Payment from lender to a mortgage broker for originating a loan at an "above par" rate. Also known as a *lender rebate*.

State-by-State Mortgage Broker Licensing Requirements

Alabama

$100 investigation fee
$500 license fee

Alabama State Banking Department
Center for Commerce, Suite 680
401 Adams Ave.
Montgomery, AL 36130-1201

Phone: (334) 242-3452
Fax: (334) 242-3500
Bureau of Loans Fax: (334) 353-5961

www.bank.state.al.us

Requirements: Resumé, evidence of completion of 12 hrs. of continued education, financial statement, 3 letters of reference from community, 3 letters of reference from lenders, certified copy of articles of incorporation and by-laws, copy of applicant's customer-broker agreement

Alaska

Alaska Division of Banking
Securities and Corporations

Juneau Mailing Address:
P.O. Box 110807
Juneau, AK 99811-0807

Physical Address:
150 Third Street, Suite 217
Juneau, AK 99801

Phone: (907) 465-2521
Fax: (907) 465-2549

www.dced.state.ak.us/bsc/mortgagelender.htm

Requirements: Alaska does not regulate the activities of first mortgage brokers; however, Alaska does recommend getting an Alaska business license

Arkansas

$750 fee

Arkansas Securities Department
Heritage West Bldg.
Suite 300, 201 E. Markham
Little Rock, AR 72201

Phone: (501) 324-9260

www.state.ar.us/arsec

Requirements: Surety bond

Arizona

$800 fee

Arizona Banking Dept.
2910 N. 44th Street, Suite 310
Phoenix, AZ 85018

Phone: (602) 255-4421
Toll-Free: (800) 544-0708
Fax: (602) 381-1225

http://azbanking.gov

Requirements: Fingerprints, written exam, surety bond, physical office required

California

$300 fee

Dept. of Corporations
320 West 4th Street, Suite 750
Los Angeles, CA 90013-1105

Phone: (213) 576-7500

www.corp.ca.gov

Surety bond, physical office, written exam

Colorado

Requirements: No license required

Connecticut

Dept. of Banking
Consumer Credit Division
260 Constitution Plaza
Hartford, CT 06103-1800

Phone: (860) 240-8200
Fax: (860) 240-8178

www.state.ct.us/dob

Delaware

$250 fee

Office of State Banking Commissioner
555 E. Loockerman St., Suite 210
Dover, DE 19901

Phone: (302) 739-4235
Fax: (302) 739-3609

www.state.de.us/bank/services/applicense/applyfor.shtml

Requirements: A minimum of three letters of reference from businesses currently doing business with the applicant company

District of Columbia

$1,100 fee

Department of Banking and
Financial Institutions
Safety and Soundness
Non-Depository Division
1400 L Street, NW, Suite 400
Washington, DC 20005

Phone: (202) 727-1563
Fax: (202) 727-1290

dbfi.dc.gov/dbfi/cwp/view%2Ca%2C3%2Cq%2C519186.asp

Requirements: Surety bond, background check

Florida

$350 filing fee
$15 fingerprint processing fee

Dept. of Securities and Finance
200 E. Gaines Street
Tallahassee, FL 32399-0372

Phone: (850) 410-9805
Fax: (850) 410-9748 Regulatory
Fax: (850) 410-9914 Licensing

www.fldfs.com/OFR/licensing

Requirements: Complete 24-hour classroom educational course, pass state examination, fingerprints, no financial net worth or security bond requirement

Georgia

$30 fingerprint card fee, $250 investigation fee, $500 annual license fee

Department of Banking and Finance
Mortgage Division
2990 Brandywine Road, Suite 200
Atlanta, GA 30341-5565

Phone: (770) 986-1633
Toll-Free: (888) 986-1633
Fax: (770) 986-1654

www.ganet.org/dbf/mortgage_forms.html

Requirements: Surety bond, background check, applicants must demonstrate successful completion of 40 course hours of education from an approved provider of mortgage education courses, minimum of 4 hours of education must be in a course or courses covering the Georgia Residential Mortgage Act and rules and regulations of the department, applicants must demonstrate a minimum of 2 years, full-time, prior experience/employment in the mortgage industry directly originating mortgage loans. Applicants for a broker's license relying on experience, whose principal place of business is not in Georgia, must still complete the 4 hours of education covering the Georgia Residential Mortgage Act.

Hawaii

$25 filing fee

Licensing Branch
Professional and Vocational Licensing Division
Dept. of Commerce and Consumer Affairs
P.O. Box 3469

335 Merchant St., Room 301
Honolulu, HI 96813

Phone: (808) 586-3000

www.hawaii.gov/dcca/areas/real/real_ed/gen_info

Requirements: Exam, surety bond, financial statement, 3–5 yrs. experience with professional broker in Hawaii, complete 80 hr. Hawaii pre-licensing course, have place of business in Hawaii that complies with government zoning codes

Idaho

$350 filing fee

Dept. of Finance
700 West State Street, 2nd Floor
Boise, ID 83702

P.O. Box 83720
Boise, ID 83720-0031

Phone: (208) 332-8000
Mortgage Licensing: (208) 332-8002
Toll-Free (within Idaho Only): (888) 346-3378

http://finance.idaho.gov/MortgageForm.aspx

Requirements: Surety bond, licensees not required to maintain a physical location in Idaho

Illinois

$1,200 annual license fee
$1,500 investigation fee (per yr.)

Illinois Department of Financial and Professional Regulation
Division of Banks and Real Estate - Community Relations

CHICAGO OFFICE
310 South Michigan, Suite 2130
Chicago, IL 60604-4278

Phone: (877) 793-3470
Fax: (312) 793-3977

SPRINGFIELD OFFICE
500 East Monroe Street
Springfield, IL 62701-1509

Phone: (217) 785-2903
Fax: (217) 782-6170

www.bre.state.il.us/RESFIN/Forms/rfformsb.htm

Requirements: Surety bond, fidelity bond for out-of-state applicants, physical office required unless broker can meet lender requirements, 3 yrs. of experience, or 30 hr. educational course, written exam

Indiana

$200 filing fee

Securities Division
302 W. Washington St., Rm E-111
Indianapolis, IN 46204

Phone: (317) 232-6681
Fax: (317) 233-3675

www.in.gov/sos/securities/index.html

Requirements: Surety bond, 24 hr. educational course

Iowa

$500 fee

Iowa Division of Banking
200 East Grand Ave, Suite 300
Des Moines, IA 50309-1827

Phone: (515) 281-4014
Fax: (515) 281-4862

www.idob.state.ia.us

Requirements: Surety bond

Kansas

$600 filing fee

Division of Consumer and Mortgage Lending
700 S.W. Jackson Street, Suite 300
Topeka, KS 66603-3796

Phone: (785) 296-2266
Fax: (785) 296-6037

www.osbckansas.org/DOCML/docmlapplications.html

Requirements: 8 hrs. of educational course, surety bond

Kentucky

$300 investigation fee

The Kentucky Department of Financial Institutions
1025 Capital Center Drive, Suite 200
Frankfort, KY 40601

Phone: (502) 573-3390

Toll-Free: (800) 223-2579
Fax: (502) 573-8787

http://dfi.ky.gov

Requirements: 30 hr. educational course, physical office in Kentucky, loan officers must be individually licensed and take a 12 hr. educational course, surety bond

Louisiana

$400 filing fee

The Office of Financial Institutions
8660 United Plaza Blvd.
Second Floor
Baton Rouge, LA 70809-7024

Phone: (225) 925-4660
Fax: (225) 925-4548

www.ofi.state.la.us

Requirements: 10 hrs. of educational course, exam, surety bond

Maine

Dept. of Professional and Financial Regulation
Bureau of Consumer Credit Protection
35 State House Station
Augusta, ME 04333-0035

Phone: (207) 624-8527
Fax: (207) 582-7699

www.state.me.us/pfr/ccp/applicat.htm

Requirements: There is no Maine mortgage broker license, but there is a supervised lender license: $500 Original Office filing fee, surety bond.

Maryland

Department of Labor, Licensing and Regulation
Commissioner of Financial Regulation
500 North Calvert Street, Suite 402
Baltimore, MD 21202

Phone: (410) 230-6100
Fax: (410) 333-3866 or (410) 333-0475

www.dllr.state.md.us/finance

Requirements: There is no mortgage broker license in Maryland, but there is a mortgage lending license: $100 investigation fee, $1,000 original office filing fee, surety bond depending on loan activity over the past 3 yrs.

Massachusetts

$115 investigation fee

Massachusetts Division of Banks
Consumer Compliance Unit
One South Station, 3rd Floor
Boston, MA 02110

Phone: (617) 956-1500 ext. 540
Fax: (617) 956-1599

www.mass.gov/dob

Requirements: Surety bond, audited financial statement, 3 letters of professional reference, including at least one from a bank

Michigan

$450 filing fee, $450 investigation fee

Licensing Division
611 W. Ottawa
Lansing, MI 48909
P.O. Box 30018

Phone: (517) 241-9288
Fax: (517) 241-9280

www.michigan.gov/cis/0%2C1607%2C7-154-10555_13044_13188---%2C00.html

Requirements: Surety bond, financial statement, letter of credit

Minnesota

$1,000 filing fee

Dept. of Commerce
Division of Financial Examinations
85 7th Place East, Suite 500
St. Paul, MN 55101-2198

Phone: (651) 282-9855
Fax: (651) 284-410

www.state.mn.us/cgi-bin/portal/mn/jsp/
content.do?id=-536881352&agency=Commerce

Requirements: Surety bond

Mississippi

$750 filing fee

Mississippi Dept. of Banking and Consumer Finance
Mortgage Division
501 N. West Street
901 Woolfolk Bldg., Suite A
Jackson, MS 39201

Phone: (601) 359-1031
Fax: (601) 359-3557

www.dbcf.state.ms.us/mortgage_lending.htm

Requirements: Fingerprint cards, maintain at least one office within Mississippi

Missouri

$300 investigation fee
$300 filing fee

Missouri Division of Finance
Harry S Truman State Office Building
Room 630
P.O. Box 716
Jefferson City, MO 65102

Phone: (573) 751-3242
Fax: (573) 751-9192

www.missouri-finance.org

Requirements: Surety bond, financial statement, maintain at least one full-service office within Missouri

Montana

$300 for mortgage brokers

Montana Department of Administration,
Banking and Financial Institutions Division
301 South Park, Suite 316
Helena, MT 59620

Phone: (406) 841-2920
Fax: (406) 841-2930

www.discoveringmontana.com/doa/banking

Requirements: An individual applying for a license as a mortgage broker must have a minimum of 3 years of experience working as a loan originator or in a related field, examination

Nebraska

$300 fee

Nebraska Department of Banking and Finance
P.O. Box 95006
Lincoln, NE 68509-5006
Financial Institutions Division

Phone: (402) 471-2171

www.ndbf.org/mb/mblicense.shtml

Requirements: Surety bond

Nevada

$1500 fee

Mortgage Lending Division (all applications to Carson City office)
Carson City, NV 89703

Phone: (775) 684-7060

www.mld.nv.gov

Requirements: Financial statement dated within 3 months of application and the two most recent fiscal year end financial statements, business plan, fingerprints

New Hampshire

$250 fee

State of New Hampshire Banking Department
64B Old Suncook Road
Concord, NH 03301

Phone: (603) 271-3561

www.state.nh.us/banking

Requirements: Surety bond

New Jersey

$300 fee

New Jersey Department of Banking and Insurance
P.O. Box 325
Trenton, NJ 08625-0325

Phone: (609) 292-5340

www.state.nj.us/dobi/index.shtml

Requirements: Surety bond, written exam, physical location in New Jersey

New Mexico

$400 fee

New Mexico Regulation and Licensing Department Financial Institutions Division
2550 Cerrillos Road, 3rd Floor
Santa Fe, NM 87505

Phone: (505) 476-4885
Fax: (505) 476-4670
Email: RLDFID@state.nm.us

www.rld.state.nm.us/fid/index.htm

Requirements: Surety bond

New York

$500 fee

State of New York Banking Department
New York State Banking Department
One State Street
New York, NY 10004-1417

Toll-Free: (877) 226-5697

www.banking.state.ny.us/iamb.htm

Requirements: Fingerprints, surety bond, credit report, professional references

North Carolina

$1,000 for broker

North Carolina Commissioner of Banks
316 W. Edenton Street
Raleigh, NC 27603

Mailing Address:
4309 Mail Service Center
Raleigh, NC 27699-4309

Phone: (919) 733-3016

www.nccob.org/NCCOB/Mortgage/Default.htm

Requirements: Credit report, criminal history check

North Dakota

$300 fee

North Dakota Department of Financial Institutions
2000 Schafer Street, Suite G
Bismarck, ND 58501-1204

Phone: (701) 328-9933

www.state.nd.us/dfi

Requirements: License is called a money broker

Ohio

$100 fee

The Ohio Department of Commerce
Division of Financial Institutions
77 South High Street, 21st Floor
Columbus, OH 43215-6120

Phone: (614) 728-8400

www.com.state.oh.us/dfi

Requirements: Criminal background check, fingerprints

Oklahoma

$750 application fee
$150 test fee

Oklahoma Department of Consumer Credit
4545 North Lincoln Boulevard, Suite 104
Oklahoma City, OK 73105-3408

Phone: (405) 521-3653
Fax: (405) 521-6740

In-state Consumer Hotline: (800) 448-4904

www.okdocc.state.ok.us

Requirements: Must have physical office in Oklahoma, pass written exam, the broker must have proof of 3 years' continuous experience within the last five years in the residential mortgage loan industry, real estate sales of lending industry. Also, they must have a trust account in a federally insured bank in Oklahoma.

Oregon

$500 fee

Division of Finance & Corporate Securities
P.O. Box 14480
Salem, OR 97309-0405

Phone: (503) 378-4140
Toll-Free: (866) 814-9710

www.cbs.state.or.us/external/dfcs

Requirements: Pass written exam, criminal record check

Pennsylvania

$500 fee

Licensing Division
Bureau of Licensing and Consumer Compliance

Department of Banking
333 Market Street, 16th Fl.
Harrisburg, PA 17101-2290

Phone: (717) 787-3717
Fax: (717) 787-8773

www.banking.state.pa.us/banking/site

Requirements: Criminal record check

Rhode Island

$550 fee

Department of Business Regulation
233 Richmond Street
Providence, RI 02903

Phone: (401) 222-2405
Fax: (401) 222-5628

www.dbr.state.ri.us

Requirements: Criminal background check

South Carolina

$750 fee

Department of Consumer Affairs
3600 Forest Drive, 3rd Floor
P.O. Box 5757
Columbia, SC 29250-5757

Phone: (803) 734-4200
Toll-Free: (800) 922-1594
Fax: (803) 734-4286

www.scconsumer.gov

Requirements: Surety bond

South Dakota

$365 fee

South Dakota Revenue and Regulation, Division of Banking
217½ West Missouri
Pierre, SD 57501-4590

Phone: (605) 773-3421
Fax: (605) 773-5367

www.state.sd.us/drr2/reg/bank/BANK-HOM.htm

Tennessee

$100 fee

Department of Financial Institutions
Nashville City Center
511 Union Street, Suite 400
Nashville, TN 37219

Phone: (615) 741-2236
Fax: (615) 741-2883

www.state.tn.us/financialinst

Texas

$375 fee

Texas Savings and Loan Department
2601 North Lamar, Suite 201
Austin, TX 78705

Phone: (512) 475-1350
Fax: (512) 475-1360

www.tsld.state.tx.us

Requirements: Written exam, criminal background check

Utah

$200 fee

Division of Real Estate
P.O. Box 146711
Salt Lake City, UT 84114-6711

Phone: (801) 530-6747
Fax: (801) 530-6749

www.commerce.utah.gov/dre/mortlicensing.html

Requirements: Written exam, continuing education requirements, fingerprints, surety bond

Vermont

License fee $250, application and investigation fee $250

Department of Banking, Insurance, Securities, and Health Care Administration
89 Main Street, Drawer 20
Montpelier, VT 05620

Phone: (802) 828-3307

www.bishca.state.vt.us/BankingDiv/lenderapplic/applicindex.html

Requirements: Surety bond

Virginia

$500 fee

Bureau of Financial Institutions
1300 E. Main Street, Suite 800
P.O. Box 640
Richmond, VA 23218-0640

Phone: (804) 371-9690
Fax: (804) 371-9416

www.scc.virginia.gov/division/banking

Requirements: Surety bond

Washington

$371.60 fee

Washington State Department of Financial Institutions
P.O. Box 41200
Olympia, WA 98504

Phone: (360) 902-8700
Fax: (360) 586-5068

www.dfi.wa.gov/#Industry%20Info

Requirements: Surety Bond, fingerprints

West Virginia

$350 fee

West Virginia Division of Banking
1900 Kanawha Boulevard, East Building #3, Room 311
Charleston, WV 25305-0240

Phone: (304) 558-2294
Fax: (304) 558-0442

www.wvdob.org/professionals/n_mortgage.htm

Requirements: Surety bond, fingerprints, background check

Wisconsin

$750 fee

Department of Financial Institutions
345 W. Washington Avenue
Madison, WI 53703

Phone: (608) 261-9555
Fax: (608) 261-7200

www.wdfi.org

Requirements: Surety bond

Wyoming

$500 fee

Department of Audit – Division of Banking
Herschler Building
3rd Floor East
122 W. 25th Street
Cheyenne, WY 82002

Phone: (307) 777-7797
Fax: (307) 777-3555

http://audit.state.wy.us/banking

Requirements: Surety bond

Sample Forms

In the following pages you will find samples of the forms and documents you will be using in your work as a mortgage broker. Take a few moments to review and become familiar with the language and requirements of each form. You will not have to generate any of these forms, as they are part of the mortgage broker software packages.

This form is completed by the borrower and details his employment history, income, debts, assets, and liabilities.

Uniform Residential Loan Application

This application is designed to be completed by the applicant(s) with the Lender's assistance. Applicants should complete this form as "Borrower" or "Co-Borrower", as applicable. Co-Borrower information must also be provided (and the appropriate box checked) when ☐ the income or assets of a person other than the "Borrower" (including the Borrower's spouse) will be used as a basis for loan qualification or ☐ the income or assets of the Borrower's spouse will not be used as a basis for loan qualification, but his or her liabilities must be considered because the Borrower resides in a community property state, the security property is located in a community property state, or the Borrower is relying on other property located in a community property state as a basis for repayment of the loan.

I. TYPE OF MORTGAGE AND TERMS OF LOAN

Mortgage Applied for:	☐ VA ☐ FHA	☑ Conventional ☐ USDA/Rural Housing Service	☐ Other (explain):	Agency Case Number	Lender Case Number

Amount $	Interest Rate %	No. of Months	Amortization Type:	☑ Fixed Rate ☐ GPM	☐ Other (explain): ☐ ARM (type):

II. PROPERTY INFORMATION AND PURPOSE OF LOAN

Subject Property Address (street, city, state, ZIP)	No. of Units

Legal Description of Subject Property (attach description if necessary)	Year Built

Purpose of Loan ☑ Purchase ☐ Construction ☐ Other (explain): ☐ Refinance ☐ Construction-Permanent	Property will be: ☑ Primary Residence ☐ Secondary Residence ☐ Investment

Complete this line if construction or construction-permanent loan.

Year Lot Acquired	Original Cost $	Amount Existing Liens $	(a) Present Value of Lot $	(b) Cost of Improvements $	Total (a+b) $

Complete this line if this is a refinance loan.

Year Acquired	Original Cost $	Amount Existing Liens $	Purpose of Refinance	Describe Improvements ☐ made ☐ to be made Cost: $

Title will be held in what Name(s)	Manner in which Title will be held	Estate will be held in: ☑ Fee Simple ☐ Leasehold (show expiration date)

Source of Down Payment, Settlement Charges and/or Subordinate Financing (explain)

III. BORROWER INFORMATION

Borrower	Co-Borrower
Borrower's Name (include Jr. or Sr. if applicable)	Co-Borrower's Name (include Jr. or Sr. if applicable)
Social Security Number / Home Phone (incl. area code) / DOB (MM/DD/YYYY) / Yrs. School	Social Security Number / Home Phone (incl. area code) / DOB (MM/DD/YYYY) / Yrs. School
☐ Married ☐ Separated ☐ Unmarried (include single, divorced, widowed) / Dependents (not listed by Co-Borrower) no. / ages	☐ Married ☐ Seperated ☐ Unmarried (include single, divorced, widowed) / Dependents (not listed by Borrower) no. / ages
Present Address (street, city, state, ZIP) ☐ Own ☐ Rent ___ No. Yrs.	Present Address (street, city, state, ZIP) ☐ Own ☐ Rent ___ No. Yrs.
Mailing Address, if different from Present Address	Mailing Address, if different from Present Address

If residing at present address for less than two years, complete the following:

Former Address (street, city, state, ZIP) ☐ Own ☐ Rent ___ No. Yrs.	Former Address (street, city, state, ZIP) ☐ Own ☐ Rent ___ No. Yrs.

IV. EMPLOYMENT INFORMATION

Borrower	Co-Borrower
Name & Address of Employer ☐ Self Employed / Yrs. on this job	Name & Address of Employer ☐ Self Employed / Yrs. on this job
	Yrs. employed in this line of work/profession		Yrs. employed in this line of work/profession
Position/Title/Type of Business / Business Phone (incl. area code)	Position/Title/Type of Business / Business Phone (incl. area code)

If employed in current position for less than two years or if currently employed in more than one position, complete the following:

Name & Address of Employer ☐ Self Employed / Dates (from-to)	Name & Address of Employer ☐ Self Employed / Dates (from-to)
	Monthly Income $		Monthly Income $
Position/Title/Type of Business / Business Phone (incl. area code)	Position/Title/Type of Business / Business Phone (incl. area code)
Name & Address of Employer ☐ Self Employed / Dates (from-to)	Name & Address of Employer ☐ Self Employed / Dates (from-to)
	Monthly Income $		Monthly Income $
Position/Title/Type of Business / Business Phone (incl. area code)	Position/Title/Type of Business / Business Phone (incl. area code)

Freddie Mac Form 65   01/04
Calyx Form 1003 Loanapp1.frm 01/04

Page 1 of 4

Borrower _____
Co-Borrower _____

Fannie Mae Form 1003   01/04

V. MONTHLY INCOME AND COMBINED HOUSING EXPENSE INFORMATION

Gross Monthly Income	Borrower	Co-Borrower	Total	Combined Monthly Housing Expense	Present	Proposed
Base Empl. Income*	$	$	$	Rent	$	
Overtime				First Mortgage (P&I)		$
Bonuses				Other Financing (P&I)		
Commissions				Hazard Insurance		
Dividends/Interest				Real Estate Taxes		
Net Rental Income				Mortgage Insurance		
Other (before completing, see the notice in "describe other income." below)				Homeowner Assn. Dues		
				Other:		
Total	$	$	$	Total	$	$

* Self Employed Borrower(s) may be required to provide additional documentation such as tax returns and financial statements.

Describe Other Income *Notice:* Alimony, child support, or separate maintenance income need not be revealed if the Borrower (B) or Co-Borrower (C) does not choose to have it considered for repaying this loan.

B/C		Monthly Amount
		$

VI. ASSETS AND LIABILITIES

This Statement and any applicable supporting schedules may be completed jointly by both married and unmarried Co-borrowers if their assets and liabilities are sufficiently joined so that the Statement can be meaningfully and fairly presented on a combined basis; otherwise, separate Statements and Schedules are required. If the Co-Borrower section was completed about a spouse, this Statement and supporting schedules must be completed about that spouse also.

Completed ☑ Jointly ☐ Not Jointly

ASSETS Description	Cash or Market Value	Liabilities and Pledged Assets. List the creditor's name, address and account number for all outstanding debts, including automobile loans, revolving charge accounts, real estate loans, alimony, child support, stock pledges, etc. Use continuation sheet, if necessary. Indicate by (*) those liabilities which will be satisfied upon sale of real estate owned or upon refinancing of the subject property.		
Cash deposit toward purchase held by:	$			
		LIABILITIES	Monthly Payment & Months Left to Pay	Unpaid Balance
List checking and savings accounts below		Name and address of Company	$ Payment/Months	$
Name and address of Bank, S&L, or Credit Union				
		Acct. no.		
Acct. no.	$	Name and address of Company	$ Payment/Months	$
Name and address of Bank, S&L, or Credit Union				
		Acct. no.		
Acct. no.	$	Name and address of Company	$ Payment/Months	$
Name and address of Bank, S&L, or Credit Union				
		Acct. no.		
Acct. no.	$	Name and address of Company	$ Payment/Months	$
Name and address of Bank, S&L, or Credit Union				
		Acct. no.		
Acct. no.	$	Name and address of Company	$ Payment/Months	$
Stocks & Bonds (Company name/ number & description)	$			
		Acct. no.		
		Name and address of Company	$ Payment/Months	$
Life Insurance net cash value	$			
Face amount: $				
Subtotal Liquid Assets	$			
Real estate owned (enter market value from schedule of real estate owned)	$	Acct. no.		
		Name and address of Company	$ Payment/Months	$
Vested interest in retirement fund	$			
Net worth of business(es) owned (attach financial statement)	$			
Automobiles owned (make and year)	$	Acct. no.		
		Alimony/Child Support/Separate Maintenance Payments Owed to:	$	
Other Assets (itemize)	$			
		Job Related Expense (child care, union dues, etc.)	$	
		Total Monthly Payments	$	
Total Assets a.	$	Net Worth (a minus b) =>	$	Total Liabilities b. $

Freddie Mac Form 65   01/04
Calyx Form 1003 Loanapp2.frm 01/04

Page 2 of 4

Borrower _____
Co-Borrower _____

Fannie Mae Form 1003   01/04

VI. ASSETS AND LIABILITIES (cont.)

Schedule of Real Estate Owned (if additional properties are owned, use continuation sheet)

Property Address (enter S if sold, PS if pending sale or R if rental being held for income)	Type of Property	Present Market Value	Amount of Mortgages & Liens	Gross Rental Income	Mortgage Payments	Insurance, Maintenance, Taxes & Misc.	Net Rental Income
		$	$	$	$	$	$
Totals		$	$	$	$	$	$

List any additional names under which credit has previously been received and indicate appropriate creditor name(s) and account number(s):

Alternate Name	Creditor Name	Account Number

VII. DETAILS OF TRANSACTION

a. Purchase price	$
b. Alterations, improvements, repairs	
c. Land (if acquired separately)	
d. Refinance (incl. debts to be paid off)	
e. Estimated prepaid items	
f. Estimated closing costs	
g. PMI, MIP, Funding Fee	
h. Discount (if Borrower will pay)	
i. Total costs (add items a through h)	
j. Subordinate financing	
k. Borrower's closing costs paid by Seller	
l. Other Credits(explain)	
m. Loan amount (exclude PMI, MIP, Funding Fee financed)	
n. PMI, MIP, Funding Fee financed	
o. Loan amount (add m & n)	
p. Cash from/to Borrower (subtract j, k, l & o from i)	

VIII. DECLARATIONS

If you answer "yes" to any questions a through i, please use continuation sheet for explanation.

Borrower Yes No / Co-Borrower Yes No

a. Are there any outstanding judgments against you?
b. Have you been declared bankrupt within the past 7 years?
c. Have you had property foreclosed upon or given title or deed in lieu thereof in the last 7 years?
d. Are you a party to a lawsuit?
e. Have you directly or indirectly been obligated on any loan which resulted in foreclosure, transfer of title in lieu of foreclosure, or judgment? (This would include such loans as home mortgage loans, SBA loans, home improvement loans, educational loans, manufactured (mobile) home loans, any mortgage, financial obligation, bond, or loan guarantee. If "Yes," provide details, including date, name and address of Lender, FHA or VA case number, if any, and reasons for the action.)
f. Are you presently delinquent or in default on any Federal debt or any other loan, mortgage, financial obligation, bond, or loan guarantee? If "Yes," give details as described in the preceding question.
g. Are you obligated to pay alimony, child support, or separate maintenance?
h. Is any part of the down payment borrowed?
i. Are you a co-maker or endorser on a note?
j. Are you a U. S. citizen?
k. Are you a permanent resident alien?
l. Do you intend to occupy the property as your primary residence? If "Yes," complete question m below.
m. Have you had an ownership interest in a property in the last three years?
(1) What type of property did you own-principal residence (PR), second home (SH), or investment property (IP)?
(2) How did you hold title to the home-solely by yourself (S), jointly with your spouse (SP), or jointly with another person (O)?

IX. ACKNOWLEDGMENT AND AGREEMENT

Each of the undersigned specifically represents to Lender and to Lender's actual or potential agents, brokers, processors, attorneys, insurers, servicers, successors and assigns and agrees and acknowledges that: (1) the information provided in this application is true and correct as of the date set forth opposite my signature and that any intentional or negligent misrepresentation of this information contained in this application may result in civil liability, including monetary damages, to any person who may suffer any loss due to reliance upon any misrepresentation that I have made on this application, and/or in criminal penalties including, but not limited to, fine or imprisonment or both under the provisions of Title 18, United States Code, Sec. 1001, et seq.; (2) the loan requested pursuant to this application (the "Loan") will be secured by a mortgage or deed of trust on the property described herein; (3) the property will not be used for any illegal or prohibited purpose or use; (4) all statements made in this application are made for the purpose of obtaining a residential mortgage loan; (5) the property will be occupied as indicated herein; (6) any owner or servicer of the Loan may verify or reverify any information contained in the application from any source named in this application, and Lender, its successors or assigns may retain the original and/or an electronic record of this application, even if the Loan is not approved; (7) the Lender and its agents, brokers, insurers, servicers, successors and assigns may continuously rely on the information contained in the application, and I am obligated to amend and/or supplement the information provided in this application if any of the material facts that I have represented herein should change prior to closing of the Loan; (8) in the event that my payments on the Loan become delinquent, the owner or servicer of the Loan may, in addition to any other rights and remedies that it may have relating to such delinquency, report my name and account information to one or more consumer credit reporting agencies; (9) ownership of the Loan and/or administration of the Loan account may be transferred with such notice as may be required by law; (10) neither Lender nor its agents, brokers, insurers, servicers, successors or assigns has made any representation or warranty, express or implied, to me regarding the property or the condition or value of the property; and (11) my transmission of this application as an "electronic record" containing my "electronic signature," as those terms are defined in applicable federal and/or state laws (excluding audio and video recordings), or my facsimile transmission of this application containing a facsimile of my signature, shall be as effective, enforceable and valid as if a paper version of this application were delivered containing my original written signature.

Borrower's Signature: X   Date: Co-Borrower's Signature: X   Date:

X. INFORMATION FOR GOVERNMENT MONITORING PURPOSES

The following information is requested by the Federal Government for certain types of loans related to a dwelling in order to monitor the lender's compliance with equal credit opportunity, fair housing and home mortgage disclosure laws. You are not required to furnish this information, but are encouraged to do so. The law provides that a Lender may discriminate neither on the basis of this information, nor on whether you choose to furnish it. If you furnish the information, please provide both ethnicity and race. For race, you may check more than one designation. If you do not furnish ethnicity, race, or sex, under Federal regulations, this lender is required to note the information on the basis of visual observation or surname. If you do not wish to furnish the information, please check the box below. (Lender must review the above material to assure that the disclosures satisfy all requirements to which the lender is subject under applicable state law for the particular type of loan applied for.)

BORROWER ☐ I do not wish to furnish this information   **CO-BORROWER** ☐ I do not wish to furnish this information

	BORROWER		CO-BORROWER	
Ethnicity:	☐ Hispanic or Latino	☐ Not Hispanic or Latino	☐ Hispanic or Latino	☐ Not Hispanic or Latino
Race:	☐ American Indian or Alaska Native ☐ Asian ☐ Black or African American ☐ Native Hawaiian or Other Pacific Islander ☐ White		☐ American Indian or Alaska Native ☐ Asian ☐ Black or African American ☐ Native Hawaiian or Other Pacific Islander ☐ White	
Sex:	☐ Female ☐ Male		☐ Female ☐ Male	

To be Completed by Interviewer This application was taken by:	Interviewer's Name (print or type)	Name and Address of Interviewer's Employer
☐ Face-to-face interview ☐ Mail ☐ Telephone ☐ Internet	Interviewer's Signature Date Interviewer's Phone Number (incl. area code)	**Financial Access Corporation** 100 Stony Brook Court Newburgh, NY 12550 (P) 845-562-5000 (F) 845-562-2096

Freddie Mac Form 65   01/04
Calyx Form 1003 Loanapp3.frm   01/04   Page 3 of 4   Fannie Mae Form 1003   01/04

Continuation Sheet/Residential Loan Application

Use this continuation sheet if you need more space to complete the Residential Loan Application. Mark B for Borrower or C for Co-Borrower.	Borrower:	Agency Case Number:
	Co-Borrower:	Lender Case Number:

Borrower	III. BORROWER INFORMATION	Co-Borrower
Former Address (street, city, state, ZIP) ☐ Own ☐ Rent _____ No. Yrs.		Former Address (street, city, state, ZIP) ☐ Own ☐ Rent _____ No. Yrs.

I/We fully understand that it is a Federal crime punishable by fine or imprisonment, or both, to knowingly make any false statements concerning any of the above facts as applicable under the provisions of Title 18, United States Code, Section 1001, et seq.

Borrower's Signature:	Date	Co-Borrower's Signature:	Date
X		**X**	

Freddie Mac Form 65   01/04
Calyx Form 1003 Lnap4add.frm 01/04

Page 4 of 4

Fannie Mae Form 1003   01/04

The mortgage broker provides the borrower with an estimate of the charges he will likely incur at the loan settlement.

GOOD FAITH ESTIMATE

Applicants:
Property Addr:
Prepared By: Financial Access Corporation Ph. 845-562-5000
100 Stony Brook Court, Newburgh, NY 12550

Application No:
Date Prepared:
Loan Program:

The information provided below reflects estimates of the charges which you are likely to incur at the settlement of your loan. The fees listed are estimates-actual charges may be more or less. Your transaction may not involve a fee for every item listed. The numbers listed beside the estimates generally correspond to the numbered lines contained in the HUD-1 settlement statement which you will be receiving at settlement. The HUD-1 settlement statement will show you the actual cost for items paid at settlement.

Total Loan Amount $ Interest Rate: %   Term: mths

800	ITEMS PAYABLE IN CONNECTION WITH LOAN:		PFC S F POC
801	Loan Origination Fee	$	
802	Loan Discount		
803	Appraisal Fee		
804	Credit Report		
805	Lender's Inspection Fee		
808	Mortgage Broker Fee		
809	Tax Related Service Fee		
810	Processing Fee		
811	Underwriting Fee		
812	Wire Transfer Fee		

1100	TITLE CHARGES:		PFC S F POC
1101	Closing or Escrow Fee:	$	
1105	Document Preparation Fee		
1106	Notary Fees		
1107	Attorney Fees		
1108	Title Insurance:		

1200	GOVERNMENT RECORDING & TRANSFER CHARGES:		PFC S F POC
1201	Recording Fees:	$	
1202	City/County Tax/Stamps:		
1203	State Tax/Stamps:		

1300	ADDITIONAL SETTLEMENT CHARGES:		PFC S F POC
1302	Pest Inspection	$	

Estimated Closing Costs

900	ITEMS REQUIRED BY LENDER TO BE PAID IN ADVANCE:			PFC S F POC
901	Interest for days @ $	per day	$	
902	Mortgage Insurance Premium			
903	Hazard Insurance Premium			
904				
905	VA Funding Fee			

1000	RESERVES DEPOSITED WITH LENDER:			PFC S F POC
1001	Hazard Insurance Premium	months @ $	per month	$
1002	Mortgage Ins. Premium Reserves	months @ $	per month	
1003	School Tax	months @ $	per month	
1004	Taxes and Assessment Reserves	months @ $	per month	
1005	Flood Insurance Reserves	months @ $	per month	
		months @ $	per month	
		months @ $	per month	

Estimated Prepaid Items/Reserves

TOTAL ESTIMATED SETTLEMENT CHARGES
COMPENSATION TO BROKER (Not Paid Out of Loan Proceeds): $

TOTAL ESTIMATED FUNDS NEEDED TO CLOSE:			TOTAL ESTIMATED MONTHLY PAYMENT:
Purchase Price/Payoff (+)		New First Mortgage(-)	Principal & Interest
Loan Amount (-)	0.00	Sub Financing(-)	Other Financing (P & I)
Est. Closing Costs (+)	0.00	New 2nd Mtg Closing Costs(+)	Hazard Insurance
Est. Prepaid Items/Reserves (+)	0.00		Real Estate Taxes
Amount Paid by Seller (-)			Mortgage Insurance
			Homeowner Assn. Dues
			Other

Total Est. Funds needed to close   0.00   Total Monthly Payment

☐ This Good Faith Estimate is being provided by _____ , a mortgage broker, and no lender has been obtained. These estimates are provided pursuant to the Real Estate Settlement Procedures Act of 1974, as amended (RESPA). Additional information can be found in the HUD Special Information Booklet, which is to be provided to you by your mortgage broker or lender, if your application is to purchase residential real property and the lender will take a first lien on the property. The undersigned acknowledges receipt of the booklet "Settlement Costs," and if applicable the Consumer Handbook on ARM Mortgages.

Applicant _____ Date ____   Applicant _____ Date ____

Calyx Form gfe.frm 11/01

Uniform Underwriting and Transmittal Summary

This form, with applicant information and property description, is submitted to the underwriter of the lending institution.

I. Borrower and Property Information

Borrower Name _____ SSN _____

Co-Borrower Name _____ SSN _____

Property Address _____

Property Type	Project Classification	Occupancy Status	Additional Property Information
☐ 1 unit	☐ A/III Condo ☐ E PUD ☐ 1 Co-op	☑ Primary Residence	Number of Units _____
☐ 2-4 units	☐ B/II Condo ☐ F PUD ☐ 2 Co-op	☐ Second Home	Sales Price $_____
☐ Condominium	☐ C/I Condo	☐ Investment Property	Appraised Value $_____
☐ PUD ☐ Co-op	Project Name _____		**Property Rights**
☐ Manufactured Housing			☑ Fee Simple
☐ Single Wide ☐ Multiwide			☐ Leasehold

II. Mortgage Information

Loan Type	Amortization Type	Loan Purpose	Lien Position
☑ Conventional	☑ Fixed-Rate—Monthly Payments	☑ Purchase	☑ First Mortgage
☐ FHA	☐ Fixed-Rate—Biweekly Payments	☐ Cash-Out Refinance	Amount of Subordinate Financing
☐ VA	☐ Balloon	☐ Limited Cash-Out Refinance (Fannie)	$_____
☐ USDA/RHS	☐ ARM (type) _____	☐ No Cash-Out Refinance (Freddie)	(If HELOC, include balance and credit limit)
	☐ Other (specify) _____	☐ Home Improvement	☐ Second Mortgage
		☐ Construction to Permanent	

Note Information

Original Loan Amount $_____

Initial P&I Payment $_____

Initial Note Rate _____%

Loan Term (in months) _____

Mortgage Originator

☐ Seller

☐ Broker

☐ Correspondent

Broker/Correspondent Name and Company Name:

Buydown

☐ Yes

☑ No

Terms _____

If Second Mortgage

Owner of First Mortgage

☐ Fannie Mae ☐ Freddie Mac

☐ Seller/Other

Original Loan Amount of First Mortgage

$_____

III. Underwriting Information

Underwriter's Name _____ Appraiser's Name/License # _____ Appraisal Company Name _____

Stable Monthly Income

	Borrower	Co-Borrower	Total
Base Income	$_____	$_____	$_____
Other Income	$_____	$_____	$_____
Positive Cash Flow (subject property)	$_____	$_____	$_____
Total Income	$_____	$_____	$_____

Qualifying Ratios

Primary Housing Expense/Income _____%

Total Obligations/Income _____%

Debt-to-Housing Gap Ratio (Freddie) _____%

Loan-to-Value Ratios

LTV _____%

CLTV/TLTV _____%

HCLTV/HTLTV _____%

Qualifying Rate

☐ Note Rate _____%

☐ _____% Above Note Rate _____%

☐ _____% Below Note Rate _____%

☐ Bought-Down Rate _____%

☐ Other _____%

Level of Property Review

☐ Exterior/Interior

☐ Exterior Only

☐ No Appraisal

Form Number: _____

Risk Assessment

☐ Manual Underwriting

☐ AUS

　☐ DU ☐ LP ☐ Other _____

　AUS Recommendation _____

　DU Case ID/LP AUS Key# _____

　LP Doc Class (Freddie) _____

Representative Credit/Indicator Score _____

Escrow (T&I)

☑ Yes ☐ No

Source of Funds _____

No. of Months Reserves _____

Interested Party Contributions _____%

Community Lending/Affordable Housing Initiative ☐ Yes ☑ No

Home Buyers/Homeownership Education Certificate in file ☐ Yes ☑ No

Present Housing Payment: $_____

Proposed Monthly Payments

Borrower's Primary Residence

First Mortgage P&I	$_____
Second Mortgage P&I	$_____
Hazard Insurance	$_____
Taxes	$_____
Mortgage Insurance	$_____
HOA Fees	$_____
Leasehold/Ground Rent	$_____
Other	$_____
Total Primary Housing Expense	$_____
Other Obligations	
Negative Cash Flow (subject property)	$_____
All Other Monthly Payments	$_____
Total All Monthly Payments	$_____

Borrower Funds to Close

Required $_____

Verified Assets $_____

Underwriter Comments _____

IV. Seller, Contract, and Contact Information

Seller Name _____

Seller Address _____

Seller No. _____ Investor Loan No. _____

Seller Loan No. _____

Master Commitment No. _____

Contract No. _____

Contact Name _____

Contact Title _____

Contact Phone Number _____ ext. _____

Contact Signature _____

Date _____

Freddie Mac Form 1077 01/04

Calyx Form Transum_2004.frm 01/04

Page 1 of 1

Fannie Mae Form 1008 01/04

Signed by the borrower, this form gives the mortgage broker authorization to verify the information the borrower submitted in support of his loan application and also authorizes a consumer credit report.

Borrower Signature Authorization

Privacy Act Notice: This information is to be used by the agency collecting it or its assignees in determining whether you qualify as a prospective mortgagor under its program. It will not be disclosed outside the agency except as required and permitted by law. You do not have to provide this information, but if you do not your application for approval as a prospective mortgagor or borrower may be delayed or rejected. The information requested in this form is authorized by Title 38, USC, Chapter 37 (if VA); by 12 USC, Section 1701 et. seq. (if HUD/FHA); by 42 USC, Section 1452b (if HUD/CPD); and Title 42 USC, 1471 et. seq., or 7 USC, 1921 et. seq. (if USDA/FmHA).

Part I - General Information

1. Borrower	2. Name and address of Lender/Broker
	Financial Access Corporation
	100 Stony Brook Court
	Newburgh, NY 12550
	TEL: 845-562-5000 FAX: 845-562-2096

3. Date	4. Loan Number	

Part II - Borrower Authorization

I hereby authorize the Lender/Broker to verify my past and present employment earnings records, bank accounts, stock holdings, and any other asset balances that are needed to process my mortgage loan application. I further authorize the Lender/Broker to order a consumer credit report and verify other credit information, including past and present mortgage and landlord references. It is understood that a copy of this form will also serve as authorization.

The information the Lender/Broker obtains is only to be used in the processing of my application for a mortgage loan.

_____   _____

Borrower   Date

Calyx Form - cbsa.hp (10/96)

Borrowers' Certification and Authorization

CERTIFICATION

The Undersigned certify the following:

1. I/We have applied for a mortgage loan from **Financial Access Corporation** _____. In applying for the loan, I/We completed a loan application containing various information on the purpose of the loan, the amount and source of the downpayment, employment and income information, and the assets and liabilities. I/We certify that all of the information is true and complete. I/We made no misrepresentations in the loan application or other documents, nor did I/We omit any pertinent information.

2. I/We understand and agree that **Financial Access Corporation** _____ reserves the right to change the mortgage loan review processes to a full documentation program. This may include verifying the information provided on the application with the employer and/or the financial institution.

3. I/We fully understand that it is a Federal crime punishable by fine or imprisonment, or both, to knowingly make any false statements when applying for this mortgage, as applicable under the provisions of Title 18, United States Code, Section 1014.

AUTHORIZATION TO RELEASE INFORMATION

To Whom It May Concern:

1. I/We have applied for a mortgage loan from **Financial Access Corporation** _____. As part of the application process, **Financial Access Corporation** _____ and the mortgage guaranty insurer (if any), may verify information contained in my/our loan application and in other documents required in connection with the loan, either before the loan is closed or as part of its quality control program.

2. I/We authorize you to provide to **Financial Access Corporation** _____ and to any investor to whom **Financial Access Corporation** _____ may sell my mortgage, any and all information and documentation that they request. Such information includes, but is not limited to, employment history and income; bank, money market and similar account balances; credit history; and copies of income tax returns.

3. **Financial Access Corporation** _____ or any investor that purchases the mortgage may address this authorization to any party named in the loan application.

4. A copy of this authorization may be accepted as an original.

Borrower Signature _____

Co-Borrower Signature _____

SSN: _____ Date: _____

SSN: _____ Date: _____

BORCERA.frm-calyx-9/98

Signed by the borrower certifying that the information provided in support of the loan application is true and complete, and authorizes release of information.

Form submitted to the Internal Revenue Service to request tax return information.

Form **4506-T** (January 2004) Department of the Treasury Internal Revenue Service	**Request for Transcript of Tax Return** Do not sign this form unless all applicable parts have been completed. Read the instructions on page 2. Request may be rejected if the form is incomplete, illegible, or any required part was blank at the time of signature.	OMB No. 1545-1872

TIP: Use new Form 4506-T to order a transcript or other return information free of charge. See the product list below. You can also call 1-800-829-1040 to order a transcript. If you need a copy of your return, use **Form 4506**, Request for Copy of Tax Return. There is a fee to get a copy of your return.

1a Name shown on tax return. If a joint return, enter the name shown first.

1b First social security number on tax return or employer identification number (see instructions)

2a If a joint return, enter spouse's name shown on tax return.

2b Second social security number if joint tax return

3 Current name, address (including apt., room, or suite no.), city, state, and ZIP code

4 Address, (including apt., room, or suite no.), city, state, and ZIP code shown on the last return filed if different from line 3

5 If the transcript or tax information is to be mailed to a third party (such as a mortgage company), enter the third party's name, address, and telephone number. The IRS has no control over what the third party does with the tax information.

CAUTION: Lines 6 and 7 must be completed if the third party requires you to complete Form 4506-T. *Do not* sign Form 4506-T if the third party requests that you sign Form 4506-T and lines 6 and 7 are blank.

6 **Product requested.** Most requests will be processed within 10 business days. If the product requested relates to information from a return filed more than 4 years ago, it may take up to 30 days. Enter the return number here and check the box below.

a **Return Transcript,** which includes most of the line items of a tax return as filed with the IRS. Transcripts are generally available for the following returns: Form 1040 series, Form 1065, Form 1120, Form 1120A, Form 1120H, Form 1120L, and Form 1120S. Return transcripts are available for the current year and returns processed during the prior 3 processing years. . . . . ☐

b **Account Transcript,** which contains information on the financial status of the account, such as payments made on the account, penalty assessments, and adjustments made by you or the IRS after the return was filed. Return information is limited to items such as tax liability and estimated tax payments. Account transcripts are available for most returns. . . . . ☐

c **Record of Account,** which is a combination of line item information and later adjustments to the account. Available for current year and 3 prior tax years. . . . . ☐

d **Verification of Nonfiling,** which is proof from the IRS that you did not file a return for the year. . . . . ☐

e **Form W-2, Form 1099 series, Form 1098 series, or Form 5498 series transcript.** The IRS can provide a transcript that includes data from these information returns. State or local information is not included with the Form W-2 information. The IRS may be able to provide this transcript information for up to 10 years. Information for the current year is generally not available until the year after it is filed with the IRS. For example, W-2 information for 2003, filed in 2004, will not be available from the IRS until 2005. If you need W-2 information for retirement purposes, you should contact the Social Security Administration at 1-800-772-1213 . . . . ☐

CAUTION: If you need a copy of Form W-2 or Form 1099, you should first contact the payer. To get a copy of the Form W-2 or Form 1099 filed with your return, you must use Form 4506 and request a copy of your return, which includes all attachments.

7 **Year or period requested.** Enter the ending date of the year or period, using the mm/dd/yyyy format. If you are requesting more than four years or periods, you must attach another Form 4506-T.

/ /   / /   / /   / /

Signature of taxpayer(s). I declare that I am either the taxpayer whose name is shown on line 1a or 2a, or a person authorized to obtain the tax information requested. If the request applies to a joint return, **either** husband or wife must sign. If signed by a corporate officer, partner, guardian, tax matters partner, executor, receiver, administrator, trustee, or party other than the taxpayer, I certify that I have the authority to execute Form 4506-T on behalf of the taxpayer.

Telephone number of taxpayer on line 1a or 2a ( )

Sign Here

Signature (see instructions)   Date

Title (if line 1a above is a corporation, partnership, estate, or trust)

Spouse's signature   Date

For Privacy Act and Paperwork Reduction Act Notice, see page 2.   Cat. No. 37667N   Form **4506-T** (1-2004)

Calyx Form tax4506t1.frm (04/04)

Form 4506-T (1-2004) Page 2

A Change To Note

• **New Form 4506-T,** Request for Transcript of Tax Return, is used to request tax return transcripts, tax account transcripts, W-2 information, 1099 information, verification of non-filing, and a record of account. **Form 4506,** Request for Copy of Tax Return, is now used only to request copies of tax returns.

Instructions

Purpose of form. Use Form 4506-T to request tax return information. You can also designate a third party to receive the information. See line 5.

Where to file. Mail or fax Form 4506-T to the address below for the state you lived in when that return was filed. There are two address charts: one for individual transcripts (Form 1040 series) and one for all other transcripts.

Note: *If you are requesting more than one transcript or other product and the chart below shows two different service centers, mail your request to the service center based on the address of your most recent return.*

Chart for individual transcripts (Form 1040 series)

If you lived in and filed an individual return:	Mail or fax to the Internal Revenue Service at:
Maine, Massachusetts, New Hampshire, New York, Vermont	RAIVS Team 310 Lowell St. Stop 679 Andover, MA 01810 978-691-6859
Alabama, Florida, Georgia, Mississippi, North Carolina, South Carolina, West Virginia, Rhode Island	RAIVS Team 4800 Buford Hwy. Stop 91 Chamblee, GA 30341 678-530-5326
Arkansas, Colorado, Kentucky, Louisiana, New Mexico, Oklahoma, Tennessee, Texas	RAIVS Team 3651 South Interregional Hwy. Stop 6716 Austin, TX 78741 512-460-2272
Alaska, Arizona, California, Hawaii, Idaho, Montana, Nevada, Oregon, Utah, Washington, Wyoming	RAIVS Team Stop 38101 Fresno, CA 93888 559-253-4992
Delaware, Illinois, Indiana, Iowa, Kansas, Michigan, Minnesota, Missouri, Nebraska, North Dakota, South Dakota, Wisconsin	RAIVS Team Stop B41-6700 Kansas City, MO 64999 816-823-7667
Ohio, Virginia	RAIVS Team 5333 Getwell Rd. Stop 2826 Memphis, TN 38118 901-546-4175

Connecticut, District of Columbia, Maryland, New Jersey, Pennsylvania, a foreign country, or A.P.O. or F.P.O. address	RAIVS Team DP SE 135 Philadelphia, PA 19255-0695 215-516-2931

Chart for all other transcripts

If you lived in:	Mail to the Internal Revenue Service at:
Alabama, Alaska, Arizona, Arkansas, California, Colorado, Florida, Georgia, Hawaii, Idaho, Iowa, Kansas, Louisiana, Minnesota, Mississippi, Missouri, Montana, Nebraska, Nevada, New Mexico, North Dakota, Oklahoma, Oregon, South Dakota, Tennessee, Texas, Utah, Washington, Wyoming	RAIVS Team Mail Stop 6734 Ogden, UT 84201 801-620-6922
Connecticut, Delaware, District of Columbia, Illinois, Indiana, Kentucky, Maine, Maryland, Massachusetts, Michigan, New Hampshire, New Jersey, New York, North Carolina, Ohio, Pennsylvania, Rhode Island, South Carolina, Vermont, Virginia, West Virginia, Wisconsin	RAIVS Team P.O. Box 145500 Stop 2800F Cincinnati, OH 45250 859-669-3592

Line 1b. Enter your employer identification number if your request relates to a business return. Otherwise, enter the first social security number (SSN) shown on the return. For example, if you are requesting Form 1040 that includes Schedule C (Form 1040), enter your SSN.

Signature and date. Form 4506-T must be signed and dated by the taxpayer listed on line 1a or 2a. If you completed line 5 requesting the information be sent to a third party, the IRS must receive Form 4506-T within 60 days of the date signed by the taxpayer or it will be rejected.

Individuals. Transcripts of jointly filed tax returns may be furnished to either spouse. Only one signature is required. Sign Form 4506-T exactly as your name appeared on the original return. If you changed your name, also sign your current name.

Corporations. Generally, Form 4506-T can be signed by: (1) an officer having legal authority to bind the corporation, (2) any person designated by the board of directors or other governing body, or (3) any officer or employee on written request by any principal officer and attested to by the secretary or other officer.

Partnerships. Generally, Form 4506-T can be signed by any person who was a member of the partnership during any part of the tax period requested on line 7.

All others. See section 6103(e) if the taxpayer has died, is insolvent, is a dissolved corporation, or if a trustee, guardian, executor, receiver, or administrator is acting for the taxpayer.

Documentation. For entities other than individuals, you must attach the authorization document. For example, this could be the letter from the principal officer authorizing an employee of the corporation or the Letters Testamentary authorizing an individual to act for an estate.

Privacy Act and Paperwork Reduction Act Notice. We ask for the information on this form to establish your right to gain access to the requested tax information under the Internal Revenue Code. We need this information to properly identify the tax information and respond to your request. Sections 6103 and 6109 require you to provide this information, including your SSN or EIN. If you do not provide this information, we may not be able to process your request. Providing false or fraudulent information may subject you to penalties.

Routine uses of this information include giving it to the Department of Justice for civil and criminal litigation, and cities, states, and the District of Columbia for use in administering their tax laws. We may also disclose this information to Federal and state agencies to enforce Federal nontax criminal laws and to combat terrorism.

You are not required to provide the information requested on a form that is subject to the Paperwork Reduction Act unless the form displays a valid OMB control number. Books or records relating to a form or its instructions must be retained as long as their contents may become material in the administration of any Internal Revenue law. Generally, tax returns and return information are confidential, as required by section 6103.

The time needed to complete and file Form 4506-T will vary depending on individual circumstances. The estimated average time is: **Learning about the law or the form,** 10 min.; **Preparing the form,** 11 min.; and **Copying, assembling, and sending the form to the IRS,** 20 min.

If you have comments concerning the accuracy of these time estimates or suggestions for making Form 4506-T simpler, we would be happy to hear from you. You can write to the Tax Products Coordinating Committee, Western Area Distribution Center, Rancho Cordova, CA 95743-0001. **Do not** send the form to this address. Instead, see **Where to file** on this page.

Calyx Form tax4506t2.frm (04/04)

A pre-application form that is full disclosure of the application process and fees.

PRE-APPLICATION DISCLOSURE AND FEE AGREEMENT

Company Name :   Financial Access Corporation
Company Address :   100 Stony Brook Court
  Newburgh, NY 12550
Telephone :   845-562-5000
Fax :   845-562-2096

Registered Mortgage Broker, NYS Banking Department, Loans Arranged with 3rd Party Lenders

---

In the following disclosure, I=applicant; you=mortgage broker.

You have advised me that you are authorized and prepared to assist me in securing financing. I understand that your services may include, but are not limited to the following:

. Counseling on available mortgage products;
. Counseling on general mortgage qualification procedures and requirements;
. Counseling on my financial capabilities;
. Assistance in obtaining information required to complete the mortgage application.
. Asssistance in processing the loan application, and in meeting conditions of the loan commitment, such as

I hereby agree to engage you for the purpose of advising me about financing and to provide the services described above. This agreement will continue until the earlier of the declination of my loan request(s), the closing of my loan or my termination of your services.

I acknowledge that prior to paying any fees or completing any application(s), I was advised of the following:

. Your services are advisory and administrative in nature;
. You are not authorized to make mortgage loans or commitments;
. You cannot guarantee acceptance into any particular loan program or specific loan terms or conditions;
. You may be eligible to receive a lender-paid bonus (cash or non-cash) if my loan is placed with a particular lender, and you will notify me if this occurs.

.

.

Initial _____   Initial _____

CALYX Form BROFEE1.FRM 07/00

1

PRE-APPLICATION DISCLOSURE AND FEE AGREEMENT

Company Name :   Financial Access Corporation
Company Address : 100 Stony Brook Court
                      Newburgh, NY 12550
Telephone :   845-562-5000
Fax :   845-562-2096

BROKER FEE:

I understand that, as compensation for your services, you will be paid as checked below:

_____   The lender will pay you a fee of _____ % of the loan amount or $_____. The compensation you will receive from the lender for your services is included in the rate, points, fees and terms of the loan as quoted by the lender in its commitment. The maximum points paid, including premium pricing payable by the lender to you, shall not exceed _____ points.

_____   The fee the lender will pay you is not known at this time but will be disclosed to me at the time of lock-in or when the rate is set. The maximum points paid, including premium pricing payable by the lender to you, shall not exceed _____ points.

_____   I will pay you, from the loan proceeds, a fee of _____ % of the loan amount or $_____. I authorize the lenders attorney to collect this fee from me at closing.

_____   I will pay you, directly, upon my signed acceptance of a commitment, _____ or at closing _____ , a fee of _____ % of the loan amount or $_____

MORTGAGE BROKER FEE ACKNOWLEDGEMENT:

I acknowledge that this mortgage broker fee will be paid to you. I further acknowledge that there is no other mortgage broker fee agreement between us.

I understand that I am required to pay the following fees at application:

.   Application fee $ _____
.   Property appraisal fee * $ _____
.   Credit report fee * $ _____

* The property appraisal fee and the credit report fee are estimates of the actual cost of the services. Should the actual costs exceed the estimate, I understand that I will be billed and will pay the shortfall at or prior to closing.

Initial _____   Initial _____

CALYX Form BROFEE2.FRM 07/00
                                        2

PRE-APPLICATION DISCLOSURE AND FEE AGREEMENT

Company Name :   Financial Access Corporation
Company Address :   100 Stony Brook Court
                      Newburgh, NY 12550
Telephone :   845-562-5000
Fax :   845-562-2096

.   The application fee is refundable if

.   The credit report and appraisal fees are non-refundable except that amounts collected in excess of the actual cost will be refunded. If the credit report and appraisal have not been done, the fees will be refunded in full.

.

.

PROCESSING FEE:

     Processing Fee $ _____

PREPAYMENT PENALTIES:

     I understand that certain mortgage products impose a prepayment penalty on the borrower. You will disclose the amount of, or the formula for calculating, the prepayment penalty, and the terms of the prepayment penalty, if any, as soon as you know them.

APPLICATION QUESTIONS:

I understand that I may address question or comments about my application to
_____ at _____ .

If I live more than 50 miles from the office at which my file is being processed, I may call you at 1-_____ or if unavailable, I may call you collect.

** Applicant _____   Date_____

** Applicant _____   Date_____

** Do not sign this form if spaces are left blank.

CALYX Form BROFEE3.FRM 07/00   3

PRE-APPLICATION DISCLOSURE AND FEE AGREEMENT

Company Name :   Financial Access Corporation

Company Address :   100 Stony Brook Court

Newburgh, NY 12550

Telephone :   845-562-5000

Fax :   845-562-2096

DESIGNATED LENDERS:

I understand that you place loans primarily with three or fewer lenders as designated below:

1.

2.

3.

PRIVATE LENDERS:

This loan will be placed with a private lender that is neither an exempt organization nor licensed pursuant Article 12-D of the Banking Law. Therefore, certain consumer protections and lender disclosures required by New York Law and Regulations do not apply to the loan. A balloon mortgage placed with a private lender need not have a term of at least three (3) years.

DIVISION OF FEES:

The fees received by you are being divided between you and
_____. You shall receive a fee of $_____ or a good faith estimate of $_____ and _____ shall receive a fee of $_____ or a good faith estimate of $_____ .

By signing below, I acknowledge receipt of a copy of this pre-application disclosure and fee agreement.

** Applicant _____   Date _____

** Applicant _____   Date _____

** Do not sign this form if spaces are left blank.   4   CALYX Form BROFEE4.FRM 07/00

Index

Numbers

A

B